WHY CAN'T CHURCH
BE MORE LIKE AN AA MEETING?

Why Can't Church Be More Like an AA Meeting?

And Other Questions Christians Ask about Recovery

Stephen R. Haynes

WILLIAM B. EERDMANS PUBLISHING COMPANY
GRAND RAPIDS, MICHIGAN

Wm. B. Eerdmans Publishing Co.
4035 Park East Court SE, Grand Rapids, Michigan 49546
www.eerdmans.com

Published 2021
Printed in the United States of America

27 26 25 24 23 22 21   1 2 3 4 5 6 7

ISBN 978-0-8028-7885-4

Library of Congress Cataloging-in-Publication Data

Names: Haynes, Stephen R., author.
Title: Why can't church be more like an AA meeting? : and other questions
    Christians ask about recovery / Stephen R. Haynes.
Description: Grand Rapids, Michigan : William B. Eerdmans Publishing Com-
    pany, [2021] | Includes bibliographical references and index. | Summary: "An
    appeal to American Christians to consider the ways Twelve-Step recovery
    can be a model for churches seeking to become communities of authenticity
    and healing"—Provided by publisher.
Identifiers: LCCN 2021015726 | ISBN 9780802878854 (paperback)
Subjects: LCSH: Recovery movement—Religious aspects—Christianity. | Alco-
    holics Anonymous. | Twelve-step programs—Religious aspects—Christian-
    ity. | Church work with recovering addicts. | Christianity—United States.
Classification: LCC BT732.45 .H39 2021 | DDC 248.8/629—dc23
LC record available at https://lccn.loc.gov/2021015726

To the Together in Hope meeting of Recovering Couples Anonymous—
"beyond our wildest dreams"

Contents

Acknowledgments

Among those who have helped make this book possible are my wife and children, friends, colleagues at Rhodes College, members at Idlewild Presbyterian Church, and fellow travelers in recovery. You all know who you are. I must also acknowledge the strangers I have met in recovery meetings, retreats, workshops, and worship services across the country. For their help in imagining a recovering church I am deeply indebted.

But more than anyone, I want to acknowledge the help and support of my good friend Oscar Carr IV. Since this project began to take shape in my mind six years ago, Oscar and I have engaged in dozens of conversations about the church, therapy, addiction, and recovery, each of which has shaped this book in some way. For his thoughtful questions and wise advice I am forever indebted.

Why Can't Sunday Be More Like Saturday?

(it's not what you think)

Without doubt, we live in an age of addiction. Despite a bewildering variety of counseling and treatment options, addiction numbers continue to trend upward. For instance, a 2017 study noted that between 2012 and 2013 harmful levels of alcohol consumption increased in almost all US demographic groups, with the largest rises among women, older people, and ethnic minorities. During this period, high-risk drinking rose sharply, and the number of people receiving a diagnosis of alcoholism rose by 49 percent to about one in eight Americans. Whether we measure the cost of alcohol abuse in dollars (expenses associated with lost productivity, crime, incarceration, and health care are at least $250 billion per year) or human lives (American deaths related to alcohol more than doubled between 1999 and 2017), the societal toll is staggering.[1]

These statistics, of course, only hint at the impact of addiction to substances other than alcohol. After briefly dipping in 2018, in 2019 American drug overdose deaths reached an all-time high of seventy-two thousand—a number that exceeded the highest yearly death totals ever recorded for car accidents, gun violence, or AIDS—and estimates for 2020 suggest the problem may be getting worse. More difficult to quantify is the impact of easily available internet pornography, although problematic pornography use (PPU, which the World Health Organization classifies as a compulsive sexual behavior disorder) appears to be growing exponentially. This trend is provoking concern among public health experts, who have identified links between pornography use and intimate partner violence, risky sexual behavior, and deviance toward children.[2]

A significant uptick in pornography use during 2020 is just one indication of the way the COVID-19 pandemic has made those who struggle with addictive behavior more susceptible to relapse. In fact, several features of "the new normal"—loss of human connection, reduced access to therapeutic care and treatment, increased anxiety, depression and loneliness, work uncertainty, and difficulty finding face-to-face recovery meetings—have prompted experts to warn of a "collision of epidemics" that is likely to exacerbate addiction and heighten the mortality rates associated with alcohol, drugs, and suicide in so-called deaths of despair.[3]

Yet even as the development of new vaccines brings the end of the COVID crisis into view, it is becoming apparent that there is no inoculation against the pandemic of "revenge addiction" that has infected our political culture. As Yale psychiatrist James Kimmel Jr. notes, because harboring a grievance activates the same neural reward circuitry involved in narcotics addiction, "your brain on grievance" looks a lot like "your brain on drugs." Similar to addicts in need of a fix, those who develop a dependency on grievance seek pleasure and relief by retaliating, violently or otherwise, against perceived enemies. The contagion of revenge is then transmitted to others via grievance-based messages that activate their brains' reward and habit circuits. In another sign of our times, treatment professionals are beginning to describe and offer support for "conspiracy theory addiction."[4]

Yet our age is stamped not only with the scourge of addiction but with the promise of recovery as well. As of 2018, twenty-two million Americans identified as being "in recovery" from alcohol or drug addictions. While it is difficult to estimate how many more are recovering from behavioral or "process" addictions to food, sex, gambling, and gaming (not to mention from codependency or being "adult children" of addictive or dysfunctional families), it seems safe to assume that the numbers are also in the millions. And if the prevalence of those with substance-use disorders who remain untreated is any indication, the people in recovery from process and relationship addictions represent a small fraction of the number who need to be.[5]

Although there is no universally agreed upon definition of recovery, there is a broad consensus that, in addition to abstinence, it involves improved functioning and an increase in general welfare. Drawing on previous attempts to define the concept, in 2020 a group of researchers suggested that recovery be understood as "a dynamic process of change characterized by improvements in health and social functioning, as well as increases in well-being and purpose in life." This holistic vision of recovery reflects the influence of Alcoholics Anonymous (AA), whose goal is not only to encourage abstinence but to help alcoholics discover a way of life that does not involve alcohol. Generally speaking, people "in recovery" from any addiction value being honest with themselves, handling negative feelings without mind-numbing substances, and engaging in a lifelong process of growth and development.[6]

Although there is a long tradition of recovering people jealously guarding their anonymity, public advocacy groups like Faces and Voices of Recovery are working to destigmatize recovery by portraying addiction as a treatable condition compatible with happiness and fulfillment. Meanwhile, print and visual media have done much to normalize addiction and recovery as natural features of our cultural landscape. Recovery memoirs, studies of addiction as a "brain disease," and self-help books that tout an array of Twelve-Step and therapeutic principles have found a permanent (and profitable) place in the world of print media. For their part, the television and motion picture industries have mainstreamed addiction and recovery in ways that both reflect and influence the larger culture. In addition to dozens of recovery-themed films, a number of popular television shows feature characters in recovery. These include *Elementary*, a primetime network drama about a recovering drug addict who freelances as a police detective and is assisted by his "sober companion" (a term that, along with "sober coach" and "sober curious," has recently entered our cultural lexicon).[7]

Also helping to normalize addiction and recovery is the demographic reality that since the 1970s, tens of millions of people have spent time in one or more "rehab" facilities or participated in outpatient treatment programs. If they are not currently "in" recovery, these veterans of addiction treatment are at least familiar with its language and culture. Finally, meetings of AA and other Twelve-Step fellowships have become ubiquitous, particularly in urban areas. If you are somewhere within the United States as you read this, there is very likely an AA meeting underway within a short drive of your location. You would be less likely to find an in-person meeting of one of the dozens of Twelve-Step fellowships adapted from AA—which include groups for adult children of alcoholics, codependents, clutterers, debtors, gamblers, gamers, food addicts, smokers, sex addicts, workaholics, and survivors of incest—but you would have plenty of online options.[8]

Only in passing will I mention non- and post-Twelve-Step fellowships, professional entities (counselors, clinics, and centers) associated with "therapeutic recovery culture," and applications of the Twelve Steps to social issues such as white privilege. Such phenomena have led scholars to describe a "generalized 12-Step consciousness" that pervades American culture. And if you doubt whether this consciousness has penetrated the walls of religious communities, consider that the most popular church programming movement of the past thirty years is Celebrate Recovery (CR), a Christian adaptation of Alcoholics Anonymous that boasts thirty-five thousand groups worldwide.[9]

My Recovery Story

My own education in addiction and recovery began in 2008, when my wife sought inpatient treatment for the effects of long-ignored trauma. Doing so not only saved her life but bequeathed an unexpected gift to me as well, as her "family week" challenged me to confront my own addictive behaviors and the ways they had triggered her trauma and complicated our relationship. As a result of that experience I began to explore the wounded parts of myself that had caused me to wound someone I love. When my wife returned from treatment, we both joined Twelve-Step fellowships and started to see professional counselors who specialize in the treatment of addiction and trauma.

My wife and I remained active in our church community, in which we both occupy leadership positions; but we did not reveal much about our struggles, even to our closest church friends. We wanted to avoid the stigma of marital struggle and, as we were in uncharted emotional territory, we had a great deal of fear about the future. Our therapists suggested that, instead of jumping back into our home life, we begin a "therapeutic separation" of indefinite length, and we agreed this was probably the best way forward. I stayed in our home, she moved into an apartment nearby, and our four-year-old son split time between the two residences.

We saw this as a temporary arrangement, but intensive couples therapy revealed that our issues were deeper and of longer standing than either of us had understood; over time, in fact, it became increasingly uncertain whether our marriage would survive. This realization was particularly painful for me, as I knew firsthand what divorce would do to our son. Ten years earlier, I had watched my five- and eight-year-old children endure the dissolution of my first marriage, and, despite my best efforts to shield them from the chaos that ensued, the fracturing of their family had taken an enormous emotional toll. I was determined not to put another child through that hell, but it was becoming clear that the work of repairing my second marriage would be neither quick nor easy. Without intending to, my wife and I had done real harm to one other and had dredged up long-suppressed issues that could not be reburied.

What to do? Our therapist insisted there was hope for us, and we felt we had no choice but to trust him. He strongly suggested that we begin attending a Twelve-Step fellowship called Recovering Couples Anonymous (RCA), a group based on the principles of AA. We were not opposed to the idea. But since we were about to travel overseas for most of the summer, attending Twelve-Step meetings in person was not an option. So we spent the months abroad coping the best we could, pretending for the students and colleagues we lived and worked among that all was as it appeared to be. Desperate to begin the work of rebuilding our relationship, after returning home we attended our first in-person RCA meeting.

I had been dismayed to learn that the group met on Saturdays at five o'clock in the afternoon, which because it was the start of college football season seemed like an inconvenient time for any gathering that did not involve flat-screen televisions and hot wings. My wife had her own reasons for hesitation, but we were united by a reluctance to reveal our marital struggles in a group of perfect strangers. Fortunately, our hesitancy was outweighed by what people in recovery refer to as "the gift of desperation." When we heard the words "many of us were headed for separation or divorce," we concluded that perhaps we were in the right place. We also heard that the only requirement for group membership was "the desire to remain committed to each other and to develop new intimacy." We qualified on that count, and the very existence of the fellowship represented hope for the healing we craved. The words "rarely have we seen a couple fail who has thoroughly followed our path" boosted our confidence in the program, which was further stoked by "The Promises" recited at the conclusion of RCA meetings:

> No matter how close to brokenness we have come, we will see how our experiences can benefit others. That feeling of uselessness, shame, and self-pity will disappear. We will lose interest in selfish things and gain interest in our partners, families, and others. Self-seeking will slip away. Our whole attitude and outlook on life will change. Fear of people and of economic insecurity will leave us. We will intuitively know how to handle situations which used to baffle us. We will be better parents, workers, helpers, and friends. We will suddenly realize that God is doing for us what we could not do for ourselves.[10]

Was it too much to hope that these promises would materialize in our complicated and damaged marriage? We both wanted to believe they could; so, desperate and lacking options, we committed to attending Saturday RCA meetings whenever we were in town.

Becoming comfortable in RCA was a slow process, in part because we saw ourselves—and wanted to be seen by others—as decent people who had simply hit a speedbump in our marital journey. Each of us had a great deal invested in this image. My wife was the daughter of a well-respected local minister. I was a college professor who served on the staff of a prominent church. What would people think if they knew we were attending recovery meetings? To make matters worse, in RCA people introduce themselves as couples, and for us to pose as a couple at this point in our relationship seemed to perpetuate a lie. We occasionally joined in postmeeting meals but remained on the group's margins. We hoped to get close enough to glimpse others' "experience, strength, and hope" but stay distant enough to avoid being seen ourselves.

Eventually the program began to do its work, in part through the disarming effect of other couples' authenticity. Even for someone like myself who prefers honesty to politeness, the level of candid sharing in RCA meetings was unnerving. Week after week we heard gripping narratives of the ways addiction, betrayal, and vow violations of one sort or another had fractured trust in relationships, the kind of stories people keep to themselves or recite as requiems to failed marriages. Yet I was struck by how little blame was present in these tales of betrayal and alienation. While couples typically enter RCA with the roles of identified perpetrator and identified victim clearly delineated, over time these labels fade and are eventually forgotten. As each member acknowledges his or her part in the relationship's troubles and engages in his or her own "work," the blame/shame dynamic is replaced by common pursuit of a healthy coupleship.

For us these insights were slow in coming because we had a lot of what RCA literature calls "coupleship shame," which in our case was multilayered. For starters, we were ashamed of being separated. Most people assume that the words "we're separated" are a polite way of saying "we are in the early stages of divorce," and we suspected that in our case they were probably right. We were also ashamed of the wounds we had inflicted on one another, the details of which we were reluctant to discuss with anyone outside our therapist's office. Personally, I felt shame at being fifty years old and facing the loss of a second marriage. But the real kicker was that, as an ordained clergyman, I had over the years provided premarital counseling to many couples, solemnly imparting the secrets of a strong partnership. What a hypocrite I felt like now, attending RCA meetings on the campus of a church in my own denomination.

After several months of sitting quietly, shifting in our metal chairs, and marinating in shared humiliation, we finally worked up the courage to speak at a meeting. Once that ice was broken, real healing could begin. The pace of change quickened as we realized how unshocked others appeared to be as we shared larger and larger pieces of our story. In fact, we noticed that our feelings of safety and belonging increased with our level of self-disclosure: the more we revealed about our hurts and failures, the more authentic we felt, and the more others trusted us with their own stories. Eventually we became regular participants in postmeeting dinners and developed a bond with other couples that is difficult to describe. They knew more about us than our own families, let alone the couples with whom we typically socialized; yet our shameful secrets appeared to be safe with them.

It soon became clear that the key to long-term recovery in RCA—as in every Twelve-Step fellowship—is working the Steps under the guidance of a sponsor. In RCA, sponsorship takes place in pairs, so we searched for a sponsor couple willing to help us navigate the challenge of rebuilding our marriage. Eventually we approached a couple who, like us, was managing a blended family. When we learned that we had been married on the same day in 2002, the choice seemed providential. They gave us assignments and deadlines and checked up on us to ensure we were making progress. More importantly, they sat with us (in person or by phone) as we argued, made accusations, took each other's inventories, and went silent. Many nights they accepted our calls when we were struggling with something that couldn't wait until our next counseling session. No matter how frustrated and impatient we were at the pace of our healing, they assured us we were right where we needed to be.

Regardless of whether that was ever true, we desperately needed to hear it. For it gave us the confidence to continue working through the Steps, the first three of which we shared at group meetings. While it was scary to unpack our personal and family secrets in a room full of other couples, doing so strengthened our bond and our willingness to stay with the program. Eventually, another couple asked us to sponsor *them*, explaining that they saw something in our relationship they wanted for themselves. Was this really possible? we wondered. If so, how had this miracle taken place? As a scholar of religion, I use the term *miracle* advisedly; but one hears it again and again in RCA and other Twelve-Step meetings when oldtimers are relating their stories. And it certainly felt like something miraculous had happened to us.

Upon reflection, I have become convinced that these and other Twelve-Step meetings are routinely visited by the Holy Spirit. This is not language most people in our RCA group would use, many of whom are alienated from organized religion. But how else does one explain the fact that every Saturday evening—in a cramped, stuffy, wood-paneled, linoleum-floored Sunday school room in an otherwise empty suburban church—ten to fifteen couples of a variety of ages and backgrounds gather to encourage one another with stories of suffering and redemption, stories that testify to the truth that God "could and would [restore our relationship] if He were sought," stories that suggest the promises of recovery will "materialize if we work for them"?

Watching these promises come to fruition—"sometimes quickly, sometimes slowly"—brought me a sense of spiritual fulfillment unrivaled by anything I would experience in a typical week. In fact, after a Saturday evening in the presence of recovering couples expecting God to do for them what they could not do for themselves, Sunday morning services at our church were often a letdown. Usually, when someone speaks of the tension between Saturday night and Sunday morning, they are referring to the proverbial conflict between churchgoing and partying. But my Saturday night–Sunday morning problem was a mirror image of that one, reflecting the disconnect I felt between the informal genuineness and transparency of Saturday evenings and the fine clothes, polished smiles, and careful choreography of Sunday mornings.

Don't get me wrong; I love my church. It has been an ideal place for our kids to grow up, for my wife to recover from the effects of being raised as a preacher's kid, and for me to engage in pastoral work without the expectations that come with being part of the paid staff. It is a beautiful church full of beautiful, generous people. But the longer my wife and I attended RCA on Saturday evenings, the less fulfilling Sunday mornings became for me. Something needed to change, but what? My church affiliation? My level of involvement? My expectations?

Recovering Church: A Personal Quest

In exploring the church's relationship to Twelve-Step recovery, I have learned that over the years, many Christians have found themselves facing a dilemma similar to mine. Compared with their recovery communities, their churches feel like real-world versions of Facebook—screens on which people project idealized versions of themselves in unspoken competition with others who are doing the same thing, all of them curating and consuming images designed to show that they are fine, even great. Why, these Christians who have experienced the authentic human connection of Twelve-Step recovery wonder, can't my church be more like an AA meeting?

Convinced that it cannot, some end up withdrawing from their congregations or building an impossible barrier between their recovery and their faith. Others, aware how much of Twelve-Step recovery is based in what AA adopted from an early twentieth-century Protestant revival movement known as the Oxford Group, have become engaged in a project I call "recovering church," which involves reclaiming the gifts Christians bequeathed to AA at its birth. For me, the desire to recover church is part of a long search that began around 1970 when I first experienced what it was like to be part of a vibrant spiritual community.

Through the ministry of a local congregation, at age thirteen I made a personal commitment to Christ and was introduced to the institutions, ideas, and habits of the American evangelical subculture. With other church members I attended Explo '72, a week-long rally in Dallas the *New York Times* called a "religious Woodstock." I practiced personal evangelism using the four spiritual laws, sported a "One Way" T-shirt, wore a wooden *ichthys* fish around my neck, read *The Late Great Planet Earth*, and looked for signs of the impending rapture. In an affluent American suburb during a time of declining religiosity, growing cultural malaise, and prodigious drug use, I forged a countercultural identity that was life-changing, outreach-minded, and miracle-expecting.

Although I eventually left the evangelical fold, I held onto the conviction that faith should be vital, that is, deeply felt and evident in every aspect of one's life. Increasingly, however, I found this sort of vital faith difficult to sustain. While there were glimpses of God in prayer and meditation, music and worship, parenthood and friendship, I often longed for a sense of the divine presence that had seemed so accessible in my adolescent years. Then, in my fifties, recovery unexpectedly became a source of the intimacy with God and other people that had been so formative for me as a young man, and that I had tried so long to recapture.

Recovery has not offered the sort of ecstatic experiences I remember as a teenager; but it has made me confident that the Spirit will show up when people come together in humility and brokenness. Discovering other Christians who have a similar confidence in the power of recovery has been transformative for me. In fact, when I first encountered a "tribe" of people committed to integrating faith and recovery in ways church makes difficult, I released tears of joy and relief. In such moments, the hope and authentic connection to others I have found to be synonymous with recovery mediate an experience of God's presence that bypasses my protective ego and resonates in my body at a cellular level.

I wrote this book because I want church to be a place where such experiences are more frequent and more widely accessible. In other words, I want to recover church, that is, make it more like AA by reclaiming what the fellowship borrowed from American Christianity nearly a century ago.

What Can the Church Learn from AA?

(quite a bit)

What is a clergyman and lifelong churchgoer to make of the fact that the spiritual highlight of his week more often than not is a secular recovery meeting? As I've puzzled over this question, it has been oddly reassuring to learn that I'm far from the first to entertain it. For decades, in fact, the spiritual vitality of Twelve-Step fellowships has led Christians to ask what the church might learn from them. The first to do so may have been Robert K. Nace, who in a 1949 article in the *Journal of Clinical and Pastoral Work* asked whether there was "anything which the Church can learn from A.A.?" Answering his own question, Nace pointed to AA's view that salvation begins with a recognition of one's sin, its emphasis on "the weak helping the weak," and its understanding of Twelfth-Step (service) work as integral to one's salvation.[1]

Nace was writing to inform pastors how they might cooperate with AA in a professional capacity. But in the mid-1950s the question "what can the church learn from AA?" took on a critical edge, particularly when it was being explored by writers who had experience in both environments. Among the first to claim that Twelve-Step communities evince a spirituality often lacking in the church was Jerome Ellison. After years of psychotherapy that do nothing to curb his destructive drinking, Ellison decides he is an alcoholic and joins AA, embracing the fellowship as the mechanism God will use to free him from his desire to drink. Curious, Ellison attends church to determine whether the Spirit he has experienced in AA can be found there as well. While he does encounter the "Holy Spirit, waiting, welcoming, expectant," Ellison finds a congregation that is "going on with their automatic motions and habitual sounds and trivial talk, as if He weren't there." He concludes that if American Christians have become immune to the church's message, it is because "the relief of being accepted can never be known by one who never thought himself unacceptable." "The last place where one can be candid about one's faults is in church," he writes sardonically. "In a bar, yes, in a church, no. I know; I've tried both places."[2]

If Ellison laments the church's estrangement from the Spirit that animates AA meetings, in "What the Church Has to Learn from Alcoholics Anonymous" Episcopal priest Samuel Shoemaker offers Christians a formula for retrieving it. As rector of Calvary Episcopal Church in New York City in the 1930s when AA cofounder Bill Wilson had "found his initial spiritual answer," Shoemaker is aware of the roles played by the church and the Oxford Group in "the unfolding" of Alcoholics Anonymous. Speaking at an AA convention in 1955, Shoemaker reasons that since the fellowship had derived much of its inspiration from Christianity, the time had come for the church itself to be "re-awakened and re-vitalized" by AA's insights and practices.

Shoemaker identifies four things the contemporary church can learn from AA, the first being the necessity of acknowledging a "clearly defined need." As Shoemaker observes, people do not come to AA "to get made a little better" or because "the best people are doing it," but out of desperation and in search of healing. Second, Shoemaker says, the church needs to be reminded that people find redemption only in "a life-changing fellowship" where people become bound to one another. He relates hearing a member of AA say he could skip a Veterans' gathering or church service without anyone noticing, but if he missed his AA meeting "his telephone would begin to ring the next day!" How many times would we have to be absent from church before concerned friends started calling us? Shoemaker asks. A third thing the church can learn from AA, according to Shoemaker, is the necessity of "definite personal dealing with people," something that is rare in churches where Christians are "so official, so polite, so ready to accept ourselves and each other at face value." Finally, the church can learn from AA the necessity of "true conversion," which Shoemaker sees modeled in AA's self-presentation as "a society of the 'before and after.'"[3]

With the emergence of recovery as a cultural phenomenon in the 1980s, what the church might learn from AA becomes a question frequently raised by Christian writers. Frederick Buechner addresses the issue in *Whistling in the Dark: A Doubter's Dictionary* (1988), in which he describes AA as a fellowship without hierarchy, dues, budget, or buildings, a place where no one lectures or is lectured to, where people take special responsibility for one another, where "healing happens" and "miracles are made." Buechner then reflects wistfully:

> You can't help thinking that something like this is what the Church is meant
> to be and maybe once was before it got to be Big Business. Sinners Anony-
> mous. "I can will what is right but I cannot do it," is the way Saint Paul put

it, speaking for all of us. "For I do not do the good I want, but the evil I do not want is what I do" (Romans 7:19).

"I am me. I am a sinner."

"Hi, you."

Hi, every Sadie and Sal, Hi, every Tom, Dick and Harry. It is the forgiveness of sins, of course. It is what the Church is all about.

Buechner notes that AA members can attend meetings anywhere in the world, confident in finding "strangers who are not strangers to help and to heal, to listen to the truth and to tell it." Although he believes this is exactly "what the Body of Christ is all about," Buechner wonders how many Christians would expect to find this sort of welcome in a church away from home.[4]

Over time, Christian treatments of this topic have produced some very personal laments. In *Tree of Renewed Life* (1992), Terry Webb relates that, upon her return from inpatient addiction treatment, she was "abandoned by the very group of Christians I needed and wanted to be with." After discovering in a group of recovering addicts the "warm personal relationships that I never thought were possible—with them, with God, and, after many months, with myself," Webb stops attending church altogether. Yet she stresses that what she has found in recovery is not a new brand of Christianity, just "the old original brand" under a different name. Similarly, in *Walking with God through the Twelve Steps* (1996), Frances Jay writes of finding in AA a sense of "shared weakness" desperately lacking among the church people in whom she tries to confide. Unlike her congregation, which does not seem to contain any "sinners," Jay discovers in AA "a sanctuary where people [can] . . . admit there [is] a problem and do something about it—together."[5]

Seminary professor Linda Mercadante began visiting Twelve-Step meetings while researching her 1996 book *Victims and Sinners: The Spiritual Roots of Addiction and Recovery*. Although skeptical of what she calls "the addiction-recovery paradigm," Mercadante must concede that these meetings offer "a degree of compassion, tolerance and mutual aid" that often surpasses anything one finds in churches. She even relates that some of the students whom she requires to attend Twelve-Step meetings claim to have encountered there the "true church." Edward T. Welch is another Christian writer who is a grudging admirer of Twelve-Step recovery. In *Addictions: A Banquet in the Grave* (2001), he wonders why, if addictions are the "spiritual diseases" Twelve-Step fellowships claim, Christians so often seek healing outside the church. Welch suggests the answer lies in what AA is *not*: a place where one does *not* have to explain oneself; where one does *not* receive counsel that is "thoughtless, naïve or judgmental"; where one does *not* hear sermon-length orations; where people do *not* hesitate to call you on your "stuff."[6]

In the twenty-first century, Christian authors have increasingly come to regard Twelve-Step recovery as a spiritual resource for a church alienated from its own message. In *Breathing under Water: Spirituality and the Twelve Steps* (2011), Franciscan friar and spiritual activist Richard Rohr argues that the Twelve Steps of AA offer useful correctives to the church's (mis)reading of Jesus and the Bible. Specifically, he claims, the Twelve-Step program "parallels, mirrors and makes practical" Jesus's message without spiritualizing it or pushing it into a future realm of existence. "When the churches forget their own Gospel message," Rohr argues, "the Holy Spirit sneaks in through the ducts and the air vents," AA meetings providing "very good ductwork." What aspects of Jesus's message can Twelve-Step spirituality assist the church in recovering? Honesty, for one. According to Rohr:

> A.A. is the only group I know that is willing and honest enough to just tell people up front, "You are damn selfish!" Or, "Until you get beyond your massive narcissism you are never going to grow up." They are just like Jesus who told us without any hesitation that we had to "renounce ourselves" (Mark 8:34) to go on the path. Most of us still do not believe that, much less like it.[7]

Confession is another mechanism through which Twelve-Step practice can help reconnect the church with its message, argues Rohr. For instance, he sees AA's Step 5—"we admitted to God, ourselves, and another person the exact nature of our wrongs"—as both a remedy for the church's institutionalization of confession through an "uninvolved third party" and a recipe for returning "the mystery of forgiveness" to the sort of peer-to-peer confession Jesus had in mind. Finally, Rohr says, AA reminds Christians that since "grace is not grace unless it is totally free," the starting point for healing must be a recognition of one's unworthiness.[8]

In *Grace in Addiction: The Good News of Alcoholics Anonymous for Everybody* (2012) Protestant pastor John Z. offers his own list of lessons the church can learn from AA, which he claims offers a better example of Christian community than can be found in most churches. How is this possible? he asks. "It is almost as if God cut out a substantial portion of His heart in the late

1930s and hid it in the church basements and community centers across the country and the world." Z. explains that as a hidden conduit of the Spirit AA is able to reflect back to its parent underappreciated elements of its own legacy, including a "theology of the cross" that contemporary Christians have largely abandoned in favor of a "theology of glory." Z. believes that because it embodies the Lutheran *theologia crucis* that understands the cross as a primary source of knowledge about God and redemption, AA reminds the church that beneath their "fine" exterior, churchgoers are the sort of respectable sinners Jesus referred to as "whitewashed tombs." In a fellowship shaped by a theology of the cross, Z. writes, spiritual growth is conceived not as inevitable upward movement but as "a perpetual cycle of confession and absolution."[9]

According to Z., another theological correction AA provides the church can be found in its "rigorous . . . honesty about human limitations," a message in which he hears echoes of the Reformation emphasis on justification by faith. Z. explains that as the sober alcoholic continues to struggle with the same powerlessness that afflicted her in the midst of her drinking, she becomes aware that she is *both* alcoholic and sober (or not), *both* fallen and redeemed, and that staying sober requires keeping this paradoxical identity in mind. In this sense, AA embodies the classical Protestant notion of *simul iustus et peccator*, which teaches us that the redeemed are "simultaneously justified and fallen." Forgetting the truth that its own members are always *both* good and bad, Z. writes, leads to a distortion of the church's message by the common misconception that Christianity is "about good people getting better, not bad people coping with their failure to be good."[10]

The Question That Won't Go Away

Over the past decade or so, what the church might learn from AA has become an increasingly common theme in Christian contributions to online forums. In fact, in 2019 a casual Google search of the phrase "what AA can teach the church" revealed over a dozen recent treatments of the topic by pastors, theologians, church consultants, and lay Christians.

In "15 Things AA Can Teach the Church," consultant Rebekah Simon-Peter suggests that since AA's success has resulted partly from its emulation of the early church, it is time for Christians to reclaim their own history through emulating AA—by learning to stick to a single purpose such as disciple-making, by focusing on evangelism (in the spirit of the AA adage "you can't keep it unless you give it away"), by emphasizing spirituality and deemphasizing celebrity, by refusing to shoot its wounded (Simon-Peter notes that in AA "relapsers are welcomed back with open arms"), by focusing on newcomers, and by letting the hierarchy serve the local group rather than the other way around.[11]

In "Sinners Anonymous," blogger R. Brad White calls AA a place of "healing, support, encouragement, and accountability" and asks why this description does not apply to more churches. Perhaps if we renamed our congregations "Sinners Anonymous" or "First Church of Sinners," he writes, this would assist us in making them feel more like AA. Lee Wolfe Blum asks readers of her blog whether they have ever walked into church on Sunday morning with "your pants crisply ironed, your hair done just right and a pleasant smile on your face . . . when only an hour ago [you] were fighting in the car and you were ready to disappear to a desert island. Or a spa." Admitting that all of these apply to her, Blum asks readers to imagine a church without a dress code, where strangers hug each other and make you feel "as if you are home," where acknowledgment of your deepest struggles is met with "yes, we understand" and "we *are all in this together.*" Blum herself longs for just this sort of congregation, a place where members can admit that "we are all bleeding. We all struggle."[12]

Blogger Scot McKnight sees an important lesson for the church in the shepherding role played by Twelve-Step sponsors, as well as in the sheer immersion AA offers its participants, as evidenced by the practice of encouraging newcomers to attend ninety meetings in their first ninety days. McKnight also believes the church can learn from the prominence of storytelling in Twelve-Step fellowships, which can have the effect of changing what a newcomer believes is possible. James Tower brings an evangelical Quaker perspective to the question of what Christians stand to learn from AA, finding inspiration in the fellowship's Twelve Traditions. He draws particular attention to Tradition 10 ("Alcoholics Anonymous has no opinion on outside issues; hence the A.A. name ought never be drawn into public controversy"), which challenges Christians to identify with what they stand for rather than what they stand against, and Tradition 12 ("anonymity is the spiritual foundation of all our traditions, ever reminding us to place principles before personalities"), which reminds believers that they are shaped by Christ, not "[their] really cool pastor, or Christian author [they] are reading."[13]

Reflecting on his own brief experience attending AA meetings, Michael Patton is struck by the "realness" of these gatherings, particularly compared to church environments in which lives are "built around the idea that I am not what I am, I am what other people think I am." Patton longs for a community that values transparency, a place where people are willing to take the sort of "fearless moral inventory" that exposes the false self. "I have searched in churches all over and never found this kind of community," he laments, since even the best require "a veneer of protection, a mask, if you will, that we are handed at the door." The deeper he gets into AA, Patton writes, the more he is impressed with the fellowship and the more jealous he is for the church.[14]

In "The Church Gathering Should Be Like a Good AA Meeting," church planting consultant David Fitch opines that AA has become the "single best expression and most alive form of church in N[orth] America." To flesh out this claim, he describes a conversation with a recovering alcoholic that leaves him struck by how much a good AA meeting resembles the ideal church gathering: people engaging in a ritual of "being present" with one another in their sin, admitting powerlessness, receiving a sermonic challenge from the AA Big Book, committing to a practice of reconciliation, and gaining the spiritual sustenance to live faithfully for another day.[15]

Writing on the Roman Catholic site Crux, Kathleen Hirsch claims that if she had a dollar for every time she has heard the question "why can't church be more like AA?" she would be dining out every night. On why it is *not* more like AA, Hirsch explains that the Twelve Steps address those who have suffered spiritual injuries in ways the church cannot, since in Twelve-Step meetings there is no "dressing up," physically or emotionally. "The ethos is authenticity," she writes, as opposed to acting out a "socially sanctioned script." In Twelve-Step fellowships, Hirsch notes, "struggle is the common ground, and honesty the *lingua franca*"; people are heard because there is no intermediary, no "expert."[16]

Women's ministry specialist Nicole Unice describes herself as a "distant admirer" of AA who begins attending meetings to fulfill a course requirement. In the process, she becomes surprised by how much she can glean about leadership "in those church basements," including lessons on presenting oneself authentically, resisting the urge to "have it all together," and being willing to examine one's own failings. Unice writes that as she attempts to create a similar ethos in her own community by sharing her "true heart" with mentors and teammates, she is shocked by the grace and compassion she experiences in return. She concludes by encouraging readers to visit an AA meeting, where they will "experience an environment of humility, confession, and devotion that can inspire you to make some much-needed changes."[17]

"I . . . have friends who are recovering alcoholics and who often speak of their AA experiences in the most intriguing ways. So I decided to see for myself what they were talking about." So begins an article in *Christianity Today*'s

Leadership Journal by Grant McDowell, chancellor of Denver Seminary. When McDowell's friends learn of his plan to begin attending AA meetings, they are understandably concerned: What if you meet someone you know? What if you're spotted coming out of the building? Aren't you worried about rumors that you're drinking? Undeterred, McDowell discovers much in AA meetings that appeals to him, including the warm welcome offered to newcomers. At his first meeting, in fact, four men share their cell numbers with him, along with the words "call me anytime, and I'll come and meet you if you need a friend." By the end of his sojourn in AA, McDowell is leaving meetings deeply moved, sometimes in tears. He is particularly struck that there is "not an ounce of judgment . . . just small groups of men and women present to each other, persuading each other to stay sober." Surprised at the number of people he encounters who are church members wishing their congregations offered what they experience at AA meetings, McDowell suggests church leaders begin asking AA folk, what is God "doing among you that we need to allow him to do among us?"[18]

Biola University professor Kent Dunnington sounds many of these themes in a piece for *Christianity Today* titled "Small Groups Anonymous," in which he argues that the small groups which are a common feature of evangelical culture would be more spiritually vital if they emulated AA. Like Mercandante, Dunnington reports that many of the students he sends to visit AA groups find them to be the most spiritually "real" communities they've witnessed. Speculating about the reasons for this, Dunnington suggests that AA possesses "a clear theory of personal transformation" codified in easily accessible practices and traditions. How might church small groups become more like AA meetings? Dunnington asks. While it is not practical to duplicate their desperation and anonymity, less emphasis on comfort and communal dining might help. The "drab simplicity" of AA gatherings is not accidental, he writes, but "an aesthetic complement to the meeting's purpose," which is welcoming the downtrodden and confessing failure, pain, and humiliation. "When comfort and decorum are at a premium," Dunnington concludes, "sincerity and honesty tend to be in short supply."[19]

What, Exactly, Should the Church Learn from AA?

Whether their comments are offered as observations, laments, or strategies for ecclesial renewal, over the past seventy years American Christians have repeatedly drawn attention to AA's lessons for the church. Significantly, authors in this tradition of AA envy do not imagine that there is something unique about people who attend Twelve-Step fellowships; rather, they point to something distinctive in the way these people are encouraged to negotiate their flawed humanity. While these authors highlight specific Twelve-Step *practices* (such as prayer, meditation, reading, Step work, storytelling, and confession) and *convictions* (for instance, that service is a natural outgrowth of one's own healing), their focus is on what might be called the "recovery ethos."

A feature of this ethos highlighted in many Christian assessments of AA is the expectation that *people present themselves in their brokenness.* In fact, writers marvel at the way human struggle becomes the basis for establishing common ground in AA, the way acknowledgment of failure becomes the fare of entry, or, as *Twelve Steps and Twelve Traditions* puts it, the way pain is "the price of admission into a new life." This openness to the entirety of human experience elicits admiration from Christians who find in Twelve-Step fellowships spaces in which to feel fully authentic. As one Christian blogger writes after attending about thirty AA meetings, "I have entered into a group that is real . . . I mean really, real . . . more so than I have ever seen in a church setting."[20]

A second aspect of the recovery ethos that is celebrated in Christian assessments of AA is one Sam Shoemaker noted in the 1950s: because people in AA are *desperate* and *in search of transformation*, it is in reality the sort of "life-changing fellowship" the church purports to be in theory, a community of "re-made people" in search of "true conversion." More recent authors have echoed Shoemaker in noting that if change and healing occur with regularity in AA, it is because the group aims at nothing less than personal transformation. In the words of John Z., AA's expectation of existential change makes it the site of "more redemption, more actual healing and more transformation" than can be found in most churches.

AA's *atmosphere of acceptance and belonging* is a third dimension of the recovery ethos frequently mentioned in Christian tributes to AA. Many of the authors cited above contrast immersion in an AA fellowship with existence on the margins of a Christian congregation: Shoemaker remarks on the concerned calls placed to AA members who have missed a meeting, Buechner imagines alcoholics who travel abroad enjoying ready access to communities where people "take special responsibility for one another," and McDowell is struck by the number of strangers who offer him, an AA newcomer, their contact information and support. Other authors note a striking absence of judgment and self-righteousness in AA that is reinforced by the message that "we're all in this together." As Christian ethicist James B. Nelson writes of his own experience in AA, "you are accepted because there is only one requirement for membership in this group, and it has nothing to do with your achievements or your character."[21]

A fourth facet of the recovery ethos celebrated by Christian fans of AA is its *informality and lack of hierarchy*, a characteristic expressed in what has come to be known in the fellowship as Rule 62: "Don't take yourself too damn seriously!" Appreciation for AA's informality goes beyond its relaxed dress code and toleration of salty language to include its deemphasis on superficial personal details such as surnames and occupations. Envy of AA's nonhierarchical nature is highlighted in references to its lack of formal structures—for example, budgets, buildings, and employees—as well as to the absence of intermediaries, experts, and clergy "stars." The fellowship's own language for this commitment to spiritual equality can be found in Tradition 12's emphasis on "principles before personalities."[22]

AA's implicit understanding of *human nature* is a fifth aspect of the recovery ethos that is held up for praise in the literature of Christian AA envy. Animating John Z.'s bold claim that AA offers a better example of Christian community than can be found in most churches is his appreciation for the fellowship's conception of human beings as intrinsically impaired and spiritual growth as cyclical. AA's insistence that people in recovery are *sober addicts* is viewed as a reflection of the classical Protestant notion of the redeemed as being simultaneously justified and fallen. Others note that, by embracing relapse as part of the addictive process, Twelve-Step fellowships demonstrate that the spiritual life is characterized by progress, not perfection.

So, What's the Problem?

These authors, writing across a period of seventy years and representing a variety of theological traditions, claim that re-creating certain features of AA's recovery ethos could help the church enhance its ministry, extend its reach, reconnect with its spiritual roots, and reclaim its message. Given wide agreement on these points, why don't more churches look and feel like Twelve-Step fellowships? Answering this question requires us to acknowledge the distinctive cultures that exist within churches and recovery communities.

As Dale Ryan explains, even the church small groups that resemble recovery fellowships in size and informality differ fundamentally from Twelve-Step groups in terms of *composition* (church groups are typically open to all, while recovery groups are limited to people who claim a specific problem); *leader-*

ship (church groups value trained and creative leaders, while recovery group leaders rotate and adhere to group scripts); *goals* (recovery groups go beyond social networking and knowledge building to effect personal transformation); *group process* (church groups tend to be discussion-centered and cognitively focused, encourage advice-giving and emphasize in-group experience, while recovery groups are testimony-centered, discourage "cross talk," and require rigorous work outside group meetings); and *spirituality* (while the spiritual tenor of church groups mirrors the sponsoring congregation, recovery groups are spiritually eclectic, and group members are careful to avoid offending others' religious sensibilities).[23]

Ryan's elaboration of these asymmetries indicates that "making the church more like AA" is far from a simple matter. But even if we were able to overcome these cultural dissimilarities, we would have to account for the *attitudes* that hinder churches' efforts to emulate recovery communities. One of these is the long-standing association of church affiliation with *respectability*. Historian Ernest Kurtz notes that churches that have tried to mimic AA's "witness . . . to fault and frailty" have been frustrated by reigning assumptions about the "goodness" of churchgoing. James W. Fowler adds that although members of religious communities may desperately desire a place where their false selves can be "allowed to deflate," these communities' reactions to admissions of weakness often "exacerbate the dynamics of shame and false selfhood." A pastor I know learned firsthand how the need to project a façade of respectability can frustrate churches' efforts to be "more like AA." When he asked a former member why he had left his congregation, my friend learned that his church was not a place one could speak freely about problems like addiction. It was fine to generalize about sin, the man explained, as long as one was not "honest, real, and specific." His search for a community that valued "honesty, openness, and authenticity," the man told the pastor, had taken him to AA.[24]

Another attitude that interferes with efforts to make congregations resemble recovery fellowships, particularly in mainline churches in which most members are college-educated, is *intellectual sophistication*. From AA's beginnings, a tendency toward intellectualizing has been viewed as a barrier to recovery, with *Twelve Steps and Twelve Traditions* warning of the "intellectually self-sufficient" men and women who are too smart for their own good. Indeed, the more thoughtful Christians imagine themselves to be, the more disqualifying the simplicity of Twelve-Step recovery is likely to appear to them. A deep-seated problem like addiction, they reason, has to require a more complex solution than following steps and reciting truisms such as "one day at a time" and "let go and let God." AA describes these confident souls as men and women who "are certain that [their] intelligence, backed by willpower, can rightly control [their] inner lives."[25]

In his novel *Infinite Jest*, David Foster Wallace offers some indelible images of the barrier that sloganeering Twelve-Step culture represents for the intellectually inclined. The problem is personified in a character named Randy Lenz, a resident of Ennett House for Drug and Alcohol Recovery, the sober living facility at the center of much of the book's action. Lenz, the narrator informs us, views himself as "a hiply sexy artist-intellectual," and is thus far too sophisticated to submit to the simplistic program of recovery around which life at Ennett House revolves. He agrees to enter the facility only because the alternative is jail, and he cleverly outwits the Ennett House staff by hiding his stash of cocaine inside a hollowed-out copy of William James's *The Varieties of Religious Experience* (a text held in high esteem by thoughtful practitioners of AA).

Unwilling to take Twelve-Step recovery seriously, Lenz is forced to process his rage and resentment in "his own dark way." We soon learn that Lenz's peculiar method of "issue resolution" is dark indeed, as he begins killing animals on his walks back to Ennett House after obligatory Twelve-Step meetings. Lenz's killing spree begins with rats, then turns to cats, and finally to dogs. After the grisly deed has been done, he finds emotional relief by staring into the lifeless animal's face and saying, "There." This, I think, is Wallace's rather graphic way of reminding readers that, for the alcoholic or drug addict, the alternative to humble surrender is self-absorption and a wake of destruction.[26]

Another attitudinal obstacle that often keeps church people from recovery is their association of the Christian life with a *piety* that is incompatible with admitting personal struggles. For many religious folk—particularly longtime church members—it is difficult to imagine sacrificing one's hard-earned reputation for pious living by admitting powerlessness over a substance or behavior. For such Christians, the surrender implied in Step 1 ("we admitted we were powerless over alcohol and that our lives had become unmanageable") has to be preceded by an even more fundamental admission that might be called Step 0: "We admitted that, despite all appearances, we were not fine." A reluctance to take Step 0 for fear of fellow church members' reactions has kept many a pious Christian from reaching the threshold of recovery.

Then there are *theological* barriers that keep church people from embarking on the road to recovery. One is the assumption that, because they identify as Christians, their problem is unrelated to *belief*. Thus when they read in Step 2 that recovery requires them to *come to believe* in "a Power greater than [themselves]," they assume they can skip this Step. At this point, a good sponsor will say:

Not so fast. Your "belief" may be real, but it won't be enough to sustain your recovery. Because, here's the thing: while belief may have led you to do some good things—attend worship, teach Sunday school, serve in the soup kitchen, take on committee assignments, even pastor congregations—it did not keep you sober. In fact, it was your *belief* that kept you from acknowledging that you weren't sober. So let's start over on the whole belief thing. Trust the program. Before you realize it, your belief will be restored. *And* you'll be sober.

For many Christians the real theological challenge comes in Step 3—"we made a decision to turn our will and our lives over to the care of God as we understood Him." While persons socialized in church communities are used to assenting to propositions, reciting creeds, taking vows, and undergoing initiatory rites, they have rarely if ever been asked to surrender, to trust God utterly, which is what Step 3 requires. Because "turn[ing] our will and our lives over" is a difficult spiritual movement for one whose relationship with God has been based in intellectual assent, the results of Step 3 for Christians can be profound. In fact, according to the AA Big Book, by the time they have reached Step 5—"admitted to God, to ourselves and to another human being the exact nature of our wrongs"—people of faith often "become conscious of God as they never were before."[27]

If these observations about Christians and recovery are accurate, churches' failure to resemble Twelve-Step fellowships is a paradoxical result of their success in shaping people who are respectable, smart, pious, and believing, who desire to be *seen* as respectable, smart, pious, and believing, and who are encouraged to present themselves as such by other Christians pretending that they, too, are respectable, smart, pious, and believing. But as we have seen, these emblems of "churchiness" are direct antitheses of the Twelve-Step ethos that is admired by so many Christians.

What AA Envy Tells Us about American Christianity

Despite the obvious challenges of making a community of the pious and comfortable resemble a fellowship of the broken and desperate, American Christians' AA envy is real, persistent, and rooted in a suspicion that Twelve-Step culture possesses something the church *has lost and must get back*. This is hardly surprising when we consider AA's origins in the Oxford Group (OG), which are explored in a later chapter. It is even less surprising when we recognize that the OG, which initially promoted itself as "A First-Century Fellow-ship," embodied a long-standing Protestant impulse to forge contemporary church practice in the image of apostolic Christianity.

The American church's ongoing affinity for AA is evidence that the fellow-ship continues to reflect its Protestant inheritance by evincing vital aspects of primitive Christianity. This explains why Christians visiting recovery meetings for the first time often say they have experienced something like "true church," and why acute observers hear echoes in AA of what they imagine first-century Christianity must have been like. Frederick Buechner, for instance, judges that what goes on in Twelve-Step fellowships "is far closer to what Christ meant his church to be, and what it originally was, than much of what goes on in most churches I know," while James B. Nelson writes that in AA meetings he some-times wonders whether he is among "some first-century Christians freshly excited by the experience of the resurrection." Indeed, at their best, recovery fellowships are reminiscent of the informal Christian communities described in the early chapters of Acts, to which people were drawn by "many wonders and signs" (Acts 2:43). Is Christian AA envy, then, driven by a desire to dig beneath layers of tradition and cultural debris in search of the nondogmatic, preinstitutional bedrock of Christian faith?[28]

If so, this would explain why Christian tributes to AA typically envision something far more transformational than Christian recovery programs. They want to see the church as a whole retrieve something essential it has lost or forgotten, something that, like a dragonfly in amber, has been mysteriously preserved in the principles and programs of Twelve-Step fellowships. These tributes acknowledge that the project of recovering church—of reclaiming dimensions of authentic Christianity that are reflected in the ethos of recovery fellowships—will necessitate more than adopting informal dress and recovery jargon. It will require nothing less than letting go of respectability, reason-ableness, piety, and belief as the emblems of authentic Christian existence.

For those of us who are intimately familiar with church communities, such changes are difficult to imagine, in part because American Christianity is so wedded to its cultural identity as a home for righteous people untouched by stigmatizing problems like addiction. Perhaps the first step toward recover-ing church, then, will involve Christians with experience of Twelve-Step fel-lowships showing others what it means to have one's faith transformed by recovery. Luckily, this process is well underway in the memoirs of church leaders who have been forced to abandon the pretense of respectability and seek spiritual restoration "in the rooms," that is, in the anonymous spaces where recovering people gather. To their stories we now turn.

Do Christians Need Recovery?

(not until they do)

Several years ago I got to know a pastor who had written a memoir describing his descent into the pit of addiction and his long climb out. After reading the book, I began to wonder if there were similar stories of "professional" Christians who had found recovery. The results of my search for such stories, which are described in this chapter, answer the question "what can the church learn from AA?" from the perspective of pastors, authors, seminary professors, and members of monastic communities who discover in Twelve-Step fellowships healing that has eluded them in the church. Their stories render compelling testimony to Twelve-Step recovery's spiritual potential and offer tantalizing suggestions of how it might change American Christianity from the inside out.

"More Serenity Than I Have Ever Known"

Perhaps the first prominent Christian leader to publish a story of Twelve-Step recovery was J. Keith Miller, author of the 1973 best seller *The Taste of New Wine*, which sold over two million copies and made him a celebrity among American evangelicals. As Miller reveals in his memoir *A Hunger for Healing: The Twelve Steps as a Classic Model for Christian Spiritual Growth* (1991), several years into his career as a "Christian star" he found himself reeling from a failed marriage, suffering from stress-related cardiac issues, and feeling abandoned by erstwhile supporters. In desperation, he sought professional help and joined a Twelve-Step fellowship, where he was able to address his "workaholism" and compulsive behavior. As he moved through the Steps, Miller gradually experienced the sort of "spiritual awakening" alluded to in AA's Step 12:

I began to see that here in this "secular" program, a bunch of former drunks had taken some biblical principles, many of which the Church has largely neglected or eliminated, and had formed a spiritual "way." This path not only brought me into a deeper and more realistic relationship with Christ than I had ever known but has also turned out to be a way of calming and healing the driven compulsive life of intensity and fear that (after the first exciting "honeymoon" years) my Christian faith had not been able to touch.[1]

Miller writes that in Twelve-Step recovery he discovered "more self-worth in God, more serenity than I have ever known, and a way to deal specifically with the personal problems that have kept me anxious and afraid all my life," spiritual blessings that had evaded him during decades as a Christian leader. Miller stresses that the Steps did not nudge him back onto a well-established spiritual path but set him on an entirely new journey. As a result, when he reaches the point of surrender that signals the beginning of his recovery, Miller sees himself clearly for the first time: "I am a controller . . . I desperately need to be right, to control people, places and things to get what I think is the right outcome," he confesses. During nearly thirty years of serious commitment to Christ, Miller had somehow remained blind to this "basic Sin"— placing himself "in the center where only God should be."[2]

A crucial insight for Miller in the early stages of recovery is his chronic inability to trust God: "I hadn't been turning my life and my will over to God at all," he writes. "I had been making use of God as a sort of cosmic employee to help me do what I had already decided needed doing—which was my will for other people and myself." Eventually, this insight leads to a sobering realization about the God Miller brought into recovery:

I realized that after thirty years of being a speaker, eight years of graduate school, most of it in theology, being on the staff of a seminary, and later a writer about God. . . . *I needed to fire God.* . . . So I fired that God who was made in the image of my father and decided to believe in the God I saw living in the lives of recovering people in the Twelve-Step program, a God who operated exactly like the God of Jesus Christ in the Bible.[3]

Remarkably, working the Steps not only renews Miller's faith in Christ, but, as a result of being gradually "reparented" in Twelve-Step rooms, he is introduced to a God "who is honest and dependable and cares enough to confront

... my subtle attempts to get everybody to do it my way." To Miller's surprise, this "new" God turned out to be the God of the Bible.[4]

Looking back at Miller's earlier work through the lens of his recovery memoir, it is clear that even in 1973 he felt a "hunger for healing," as *The Taste of New Wine* encouraged Christians to acknowledge their brokenness as a first step to experiencing "the intimate love and forgiveness/acceptance of God." Thus, it is all the more remarkable that appropriating God's love and acceptance for himself required Miller to pursue a spiritual path cleared by a bunch of church-shy drunks.

"A Side Entrance to the Church"

In *Samson and the Pirate Monks: Calling Men to Authentic Brotherhood* (2006), former pastor Nate Larkin relates the exposure of his sexual indiscretions, the loss of his pulpit, and his subsequent discovery of "authentic brotherhood" in Twelve-Step recovery. As is often the case, Larkin's descent into the slavery of sexual compulsion begins with exposure to hard-core pornography. Oddly, however, Larkin's introduction to porn comes in a visit, organized by his seminary, to a Times Square sex shop. "Somewhere deep inside me," he writes of the experience, "I could feel a strange and beckoning fascination, as though a cellar door had been opened. Those images lit a fire in me that would burn uncontrollably for nearly twenty years, a fire that smolders still."[5]

Some years after this episode, Larkin is pastoring a church he started and playing the roles of "professional holy man" and "expert on all things spiritual." But convinced he will die without a porn "fix" and adrenalized by the risk of discovery, he continues to act out sexually until he reaches a humiliating "bottom" that involves paying for sex en route to a Christmas Eve service he is to lead. Determined to save his family and restore his reputation, Larkin "retires" from ministry at age thirty and sets out to become "a responsible Christian layman." But he soon learns that his mood-altering drug of choice can be safely and discreetly obtained at strip clubs and massage parlors; then, with the advent of the Internet, Larkin's problem becomes even easier to indulge, and to conceal. Eventually he logs thousands of hours acting out online and squanders $300,000 on porn and prostitutes (13, 41, 42).[6]

Hope appears on the horizon when Larkin and his family move to Nashville and discover a church where it is safe "to admit brokenness," led by a pastor who talks "about his own sin in the present tense." But the gift of desperation, as Larkin calls it, does not arrive until his wife discovers evidence of his infidelity and announces she is done with their marriage. At that point Larkin realizes that through some inscrutable providence he has relocated to "the center of the world for sex addiction recovery" and before long finds himself sitting in the basement of a local church, attending a Twelve-Step meeting (44).

Entering his first "S-group" meeting at age forty-two, Larkin needs to overcome an innate resistance to "secular" recovery, intensified by his assumption that any church hosting Twelve-Step meetings on a Wednesday night must be "liberal." Still, he is able to ignore these distractions long enough to listen as meeting participants take "turns describing [his] secret life." He receives a white chip symbolizing his desire to try this "way of life," shares a meal with group members, secures a temporary sponsor, and reads the AA Big Book into the wee hours. The next day Larkin attends his first AA meeting, where "the level of honesty [was] . . . startling, the wisdom exquisite." Yet he is troubled by feelings that are not uncommon among long-time Christians who find themselves sitting in "the rooms."

> My spirit was uplifted, but at the same time I was angry—furious—that never, in more than forty years of church attendance, had I experienced the safety, the honesty, the genuine concern and mutual respect that I had seen displayed by this community of recovering drunks. Even though the name of Jesus had not been spoken during the meeting, I had certainly sensed his presence there, and I had heard more echoes of his teaching during the meeting than in any sermon I could recall. These people were failures and outcasts, just the kind of losers Jesus had preferred to spend time with during his earthly ministry, but their fellowship was far removed from the Christian mainstream, their meeting relegated to a church basement in the middle of the day. Something didn't add up. (49, 54)

When he has been attending Twelve-Step meetings for several months, it occurs to Larkin that, rather than being banished to the church basement, AA had gone there voluntarily, "convinced that it must sever its formal ties with Christianity in order to fulfill its mission to alcoholics." In time Larkin comes to regard the basements where Twelve-Step groups meet as "side entrance[s]" to the church. He is surprised to learn, in fact, that many in his Twelve-Step circle are active Christians, that in this "quiet subculture of anonymous recovering addicts" nearly every local church is represented. This leads Larkin to wonder why Christians in recovery aren't more vocal about their faith. But when he shares his frustration at being unable to mention the name of Jesus "without getting funny looks," a fellow Christian points out that if Jesus were walking the earth today, he wouldn't "spend much time denouncing twelve-step groups on doctrinal grounds" (54–56).

Although Larkin finds a spiritual home in his newfound recovery community, he does not commit to working the Steps, and soon old behaviors begin to reemerge. In retrospect, he realizes he had been living in the pink cloud—"that fabulous feeling that felt like sobriety [but] had actually been a novel form of intoxication." So Larkin secures a new sponsor who insists he call him every day as if he were "calling God." "I mark the beginning of my recovery," he writes, "from the day I finally surrendered to the discipline of picking up the telephone each day to share the truth about my life with another guy and ask for honest feedback" (75, 76).

In exploring the roots of his compulsive sexuality, Larkin uncovers a familial history of addiction and a vale of secrecy designed to conceal it from outsiders. "As I understood it," he explains, "we needed to maintain a 'good witness' before the watching world, even if we sometimes had to lie a little to do it." Because his father was also his pastor, this concern with appearances—along with a quest for "holiness"—extended to Larkin's faith community as well. They didn't "drink, or dance, or play games of chance"; and, of course, they denied that Christians could be addicts. So, when the local Bible college hosted a singing troupe of ex–gang members called "The Addicts," it was implicitly understood that they were really "former addicts" whom Jesus had healed. As Larkin writes, this was a vital distinction in the world of his youth: "To us, an addict was a drug user who needed to get saved. Once he got saved, he was not an addict anymore" (27–28).

Of course, this assumption proved less than helpful when Larkin was compulsively cruising the streets near his church in search of prostitutes. Filled with shame and determined to find a "private solution to [his] private problem," he embraced traditional Christian wisdom, poring over books about holiness and victorious living, looking for the "magic combination of concepts and disciplines that would enable" him to reclaim his integrity. Ultimately, however, it is his commitment to attending recovery meetings, journaling, composing daily gratitude lists, and thinking honestly about his character defects that translates into real sobriety. The transformation in his character that results from these practices, Larkin concludes, is powerful evidence for God's existence (40, 106).

In part because suspicion of AA was a persistent theme in his religious upbringing, Larkin initially fancies himself a missionary to the Twelve-Step world. Like Paul in Athens, he feels called to testify to the true God in a group of curious but misguided seekers. Eventually, however, Larkin comes to regard himself as a missionary of recovery to the church. In pursuit of this calling, he founds the Samson Society, a Twelve-Step-inspired mutual aid group for Christian men with its own constitution, traditions, and meeting format. As Larkin writes, the society represents a challenge to the tacit agreement that there are "subjects that church people cannot talk about . . . activities that church people do not engage in . . . places we do not hang out, girls we do not call, hotel rooms where things do not happen, computers that do not show images that are not destructive, relationships that are not failing, abuses that are not stealing joy" (134–35).

"I Had Lost Hope"

T. C. Ryan's memoir *Ashamed No More: A Pastor's Journey through Sex Addiction* appeared in 2012. Like Larkin, Ryan is forced to resign his ministry as a result of compulsive sexual behavior. But in Ryan's case the precipitating event—his arrest in a public park where he is waiting to exchange pornography with other men—occurs after nine years of therapy and group support. Up to this point, Ryan's path to recovery from sexual compulsivity had coexisted uneasily with his identity as the leader of a prominent evangelical congregation. Keenly aware of his parishioners' high moral expectations, Ryan's shame was reinforced whenever he hinted at his dark secret—for instance, when a Bible study leader turned "beet red" at Ryan's disclosure that he struggled with lust. The message was clear: "This is something you don't talk about. You fix this on your own." So Ryan continued to lead a double life in which his disease and his faith went to war on the battlefield of his soul.[7]

Ryan does not directly credit Twelve-Step recovery with saving him from addiction and restoring his faith; the reality is more complicated. On the one hand, S-group meetings help him manage his problem by providing a place to tell his story, listen to others tell theirs, and experience "a piece of genuine community." On the other hand, Ryan's progress in recovery is impeded by his fear of identifying as a pastor, even in fellowships that prize anonymity. He finds himself in a classic double bind: While he desperately wants to reduce the secrecy and shame that fuel his sexual compulsion, he cannot risk professional humiliation and the loss of his livelihood. Thus, while admitting that "we have to change the thinking in the church," he stresses that "making martyrs" out of pastors is not a good way to do it. In the end, Ryan's healing requires not only the tools of Twelve-Step recovery but spiritual direction, "intensive restructuring psychotherapy," and the shock of arrest.[8]

Ryan writes with an awareness of evangelical suspicions toward recovery culture. For instance, he acknowledges that an issue for many churchgoers is whether the Twelve Steps belong in a Christian setting, given their concept of God as "a lowest-common-denominator 'Higher Power.'" Ryan's response is that the Steps' genius lies precisely in making God accessible to the desperate but unchurched addict, for whom they provide "a foot in the door of faith." Just as important, the Twelve Steps enhance the process of Christian spiritual transformation because recovery from compulsive behaviors involves the same "elemental reordering of human lives" that is at the heart of discipleship.[9]

Despite his complicated history with recovery and his care to avoid offending evangelicals' sexual sensibilities (the book is published by InterVarsity Press), Ryan wants the church to "fully embrace" the Twelve Steps because it "needs the honesty and the genuine acceptance of brokenness" that are the essence of recovery. Sadly, according to Ryan, the church too often conveys the message that "broken people . . . do not belong," or are welcome to participate "as long as they don't show their baggage." To overcome these attitudes, he writes, the church must model itself on recovery communities that understand we are "only as sick as our secrets."[10]

"I Was Thirsty Because I Was Feeling Incomplete"

Before his death in 2015, James B. Nelson was a highly regarded Christian ethicist who taught for many years at United Theological Seminary of the Twin Cities in Minneapolis. Nelson's story of recovery, published after his retirement from teaching, is titled *Thirst: God and the Alcoholic Experience* (2004). More than a memoir, *Thirst* is a theological reflection on addiction and recovery occasioned by the spiritual awakening Nelson experienced in AA.

Nelson relates that after some binge drinking in college, he swore off alcohol for two decades before becoming a social drinker in his forties. But by his fifties, he became a solitary, mostly functional, alcoholic whose drinking was of enough concern to his friends that they staged an unsuccessful intervention. Predictably, Nelson's problematic relationship with alcohol escalated until morning drinking and blackouts became frequent, "denial routine." Finally, on April 20, 1993, he hit bottom "after five and a half days in [a] hotel room two miles from [his] home."

The night before I had run out of vodka and it was too late to order more. Morning had come, and there was no morning drink to continue my escape. I looked into the mirror and saw defeat. The strange disease had me, and my efforts to conquer it had only wrapped the web more tightly around me.[11]

Finally at a point of surrender, Nelson enters alcohol rehab at Minnesota's Hazelden Center and, following a month of treatment and six months of "after care," becomes a regular participant in AA meetings.

In AA Nelson comes to the gradual realization that alcohol's anesthetic effects have helped protect him from deep-seated anxieties, including the fear that his professional mask will fall away to reveal "one with nothing left to say, no achievements worth noting, no contributions worth giving, little left in the inner bank with which to purchase self-respect, that is, manhood." Somehow, while in the grips of his alcoholism, Nelson has been reaching new heights professionally; however, regardless of what others think of him, he is unable to believe he is accepted by God. "I could give a decent lecture about the grace of God," he writes, "yet in my heart of hearts I wasn't sure it applied to me." In sobriety Nelson encounters with fresh eyes Paul's declaration in Romans 8 that for those who are in Christ there is "no condemnation." "I read those words time and again during that month in the treatment center," Nelson writes. "Each time I was moved to tears" (83, 124).

For Nelson, Twelve-Step recovery groups have a unique role in communicating the message of God's acceptance:

The welcome is always the same: *you are accepted.* You are the most important person in this room not only because you are particularly needy but also because you put everyone else back in touch with their own beginnings on the sobriety journey. You are accepted because there is only one requirement for membership in this group, and it has nothing to do with your achievements or your character. (137)

Eventually recovery effects a transformation in Nelson's self-understanding as a man (not surprising given that conceptions of masculinity and the male body are a major theme in his writing). If part of recovery is composing a "conversion narrative," he notes, for alcoholic men this often involves a changed conception of masculinity. While traditional masculinity deems emotional expression weak and feminine, the recovering man knows it is critical to his sobriety; while traditional masculinity encourages men to see each other as competitors, in sobriety they become sources of support (96).

Nelson testifies to the way recovery can effect a new intimacy between the addict and God. When he was in anxious denial of the pain caused by his alcoholism, God remained "distant and unreal." Sobriety, however, brings a keener sense of God's companionship, an experience he argues is typical:

> Without exception every alcoholic I know testifies that in the midst of their addiction the world was a markedly unfriendly place where God was either absent or felt like an enemy. And without exception, every sober alcoholic I know testifies that in the midst of their recovery a remarkable transition has occurred. The world and the world's Creator have become friendly. (162–63)

Nelson stresses that this shift in one's relationship with God must occur communally, that "saving requires a saving community, and healing requires a healing community" (182–83).

Although his basic theological orientation is unchanged (he remained a liberal Christian with a deep commitment to human liberation), recovery renews Nelson's faith and allows him to perceive more clearly what he has always believed to be true. Thus, it is no surprise that the aspects of his recovery community Nelson finds most meaningful—storytelling, vulnerability, grace, accountability, and mission—also represent the best of his church experience (182–83).

"Saved All Over Again"

In 2013 Heather Kopp published a poignant memoir of addiction and recovery titled *Sober Mercies: How Love Caught Up with a Christian Drunk*. The story begins as Kopp is in the depths of a twelve-year addiction to alcohol. Her mission "never to be without" her drug has led to mounting evidence of unmanageability—blackouts, trembling hands, booze hidden in a closet and toted around in an oversized purse, beer chugged in a toilet stall, drinks sipped while transporting her children. Nevertheless, Kopp has succeeded in keeping her alcoholism hidden from family and friends.[12]

Kopp reports that she began drinking with good intentions. Maturing out of a legalistic faith, she wanted to be "a different kind of Christian"—the kind who isn't sheltered from "the world," who drinks as a way of celebrating God's good creation. But eventually alcohol gets the upper hand, and she has to conceal her regular tippling from the people among whom she works in the

Christian publishing industry: "During all those years of drinking, I continued to write and edit Christian books," she confesses. "Publicly, I held forth on things like parenting and prayer, while privately I drank myself past sensibility." Predictably, Kopp's public religiosity made her reluctant to seek help. "Where do you turn for hope," she asks, "when you already have the answer, but it isn't working?" (14, 21, 22).

Kopp eventually hits bottom and enters a treatment facility as "a blubbering drunk in Banana Republic clothes." But she struggles to accept the idea that she has a treatable disease; in fact, she cannot turn off "old tapes" that deny her powerlessness and belittle the disease model of addiction as "an excuse to sin." Yet while she finds it difficult to give up "the simplicity and moral clarity of the sin paradigm," she recognizes that understanding her alcohol problem as a moral failure has fueled a vicious cycle of praying for deliverance, failing to get sober, and drinking to numb the guilt (44, 48, 49).

Although treatment does not solve the problem of how Kopp will "reconcile recovery with [her] battered faith," it does set her on a path to a new way of life. While she is dismayed to learn that this will involve attending AA meetings in a building that smells "faintly of burned coffee, used vacuum bags, and human desperation," she discovers she is not the only Christian in the fellowship whose addiction refuses to yield to "repentance and prayer." Like them, Kopp finds in AA "a tight-knit community that happen[s] largely outside of this room." This discovery is both exhilarating and sad:

> You'd think a close-knit community like this would feel at least vaguely familiar to me, that it might be reminiscent of church in some way, or of small groups I'd been part of. But the particular brand of love and loyalty that seemed to flow so easily here wasn't like anything I'd ever experienced, inside or outside of church.
>
> But how could this be? How could a bunch of addicts and alcoholics manage to succeed at creating the kind of intimate fellowship so many of my Christian groups had tried to achieve and failed?
>
> Many months would pass before I understood that people bond more deeply over shared brokenness than over shared beliefs. (63, 79, 80, 82)

In recovery, Kopp finds human connection that is fulfilling and sobriety-preserving, yet dependent on her continuing willingness to "pick up the phone." She learns to love people with whom she would not normally associate—"random, kind people who looked nothing like me on the outside but who turned out to be a lot like me on the inside." Still, Kopp has trouble relinquishing the assumption that as a "spiritual expert" the AA program should come easily for her. In fact, like other church folk who enter "the rooms," Kopp fancies herself a missionary to those whom she will help "get a better, more biblical grip on God." But this self-perception shifts as she observes transformation in individuals who, despite lacking her Christian background, possess more confidence in God's grace and goodness than she does.

Ultimately, Kopp concludes that her fellow alcoholics have things to teach *her* (85, 138, 140, 142), including that since the "God of her understanding" has not kept her sober, she needs a God she *doesn't* understand. The theological turning point arrives when her sponsor asks if she is willing to turn her life and her sobriety over to God. When she says "yes," she is asked to confirm her intention in typical AA fashion:

> Together we got on our knees and prayed. It was a short but heartfelt prayer of surrender, of peeling my fingers off my own life. I asked God to relieve me of the bondage of self, and I committed to seeking his will instead of mine.
>
> Walking down the steps of [my sponsor's] house to my car, I felt hopeful for the first time in a long time. I felt saved all over again—this time from myself. (137)

This experience is an initial step on what turns out to be Kopp's long journey toward true sobriety. At a family gathering, it becomes apparent that "alcohol hadn't created [her] personality flaws, it only exacerbated and magnified them." Reflecting on the roots of her excessive drinking, Kopp comes to understand that sneaking, cheating, and lying—survival skills she learned in childhood living with an absent, mentally ill father and a present, voyeuristic stepfather—had put her "in training to be a secret drunk." Along her bumpy path of recovery, she endures slips and full-blown relapses, not to mention the painful realization that she has missed out on having another child because she cannot imagine nine months without alcohol (117, 119).

An important part of Kopp's spiritual transformation in recovery is related to her years working in Christian publishing, a religious subculture that emphasizes "making sure every doctrinal dot is perfectly connected" and that is uncomfortable with experience-based faith. Helping her overcome her propensity to focus on belief to the exclusion of experience, Kopp's experience in AA reveals to her the difference between "ascribing to a set of Christian beliefs" and "clinging daily to an experience of God's love and grace" (142–43).

At the end of *Sober Mercies*, Kopp's project of reconciling recovery with her Christian faith remains unfinished. "Deep in my heart," she writes, "I knew that God wasn't calling me away from my faith to recovery, or away from recovery to my faith. Instead, I sensed I was being invited to walk forward in the sometimes scary tension I felt between the two." In this liminal space, Kopp discovers a ministry with addicts like herself—women from Christian backgrounds who "are mystified as to why their faith hadn't been able to save them," and who are seeking to merge their religious beliefs with the spiritual tenets of recovery (143, 145, 202).[13]

"My Spirit Came to Life Again"

Sister Molly Monahan is the pseudonym adopted by a Roman Catholic nun whose recovery memoir *Seeds of Grace: Reflections on the Spirituality of Alcoholics Anonymous* was published in 2001. At the time of the book's appearance, Monahan had seventeen years of sobriety from alcohol and was attending several AA meetings per week. But, unlike the other "professional Christians" whose memoirs are reviewed in this chapter, her entry into recovery is not the result of a lost job or public humiliation; rather, after thirty years in a Catholic religious order, Monahan finds herself "spiritually bereft," unable to pray and powerless to curb her drinking. On the advice of a fellow nun, she enters a rehab facility that stresses AA attendance and, after her discharge, follows a therapist's advice to "do 90 in 90" (attend ninety AA meetings in ninety days).

Monahan's initial response to Alcoholics Anonymous is predictable: "What could A.A. teach *me* about spirituality?" she wondered. In her mind, her uncontrolled drinking is unrelated to her troubled spiritual condition, which she understands as a temporary "dark night of the soul," an occupational hazard for those called to "the higher states of the contemplative life." But as Monahan continues in AA, she encounters "a startling kind of truth."

> Not dogmatic, or mathematical, or scientific truth, certainly. No, what I heard at meetings was personal truth, arising out of the experience of the speakers. It was a kind of "witnessing" . . . [in which] I heard the truth of my own feelings, faults, and sneaky motivations played back for me with uncommon honesty. And I began to know that I was not alone, and that I was not unique.[14]

Listening as others witness to the spiritual damage inflicted by alcohol, Monahan stakes out her own path of recovery. She works the Steps, secures a sponsor, sponsors others, and in due course discovers a "ministry" in AA. With the help of the fellowship, she not only addresses her unhealthy drinking behavior but gets in touch with the deep-seated fears that underlie her need to dominate and control others. Eventually Monahan comes to the realization that what AA says about recovery is true—that sobriety involves more than abstinence. "Even if I had managed merely to stop drinking . . . and had not dealt with the mental and spiritual aspects of the disease," she concludes, "I would still be miserable" (177).

Like other Christians who find recovery in AA, Monahan is perplexed to learn that her religious credentials—which in her case include monastic vows, theological training, and a devotion to Ignatian spirituality—had not protected her from the ravages of alcoholism. Just as surprising is the fact that after thirty years in a religious order, it is in AA that she discovers the "uniquely . . . rescuing and empowering community" that helps her recover her religious vocation. "When my faith in my Catholic religion, and sometimes even in the existence of God, is weak, my experience in A.A. comes to my rescue," Monahan writes. "I can literally see and hear the effects of faith in a roomful of people whose trust in a Higher Power has restored them to health of body, mind, and soul" (3, 45).

Monahan views AA—which she regards as universally relevant, since alcoholism is only "an emblem of the human condition writ large"—through the lens of the ancient Catholic distinction between "purgative," "illuminative," and "unitive" spirituality. According to this schema, the *purgative* stage of the spiritual journey, which involves being cleansed of sin and guilt, is reflected in the Steps' directions to acknowledge unmanageability, take moral inventory, admit wrongs, and make amends. The *illuminative* way, which in Catholic thought encompasses a "deepening knowledge and love of God within a contemplative experience," Monahan links to the quest for "conscious contact" with God described in Step 11. The *unitive* way, traditionally associated with mystical prayer and divine union, she identifies with the life of love and service implied in Step 12 (5, 36–40).

Yet for Monahan, the real attraction of AA is not its conformity to a familiar theological framework but its capacity to mediate a genuine *experience* of God's transformative grace. In AA, Monahan sees "the faces of people change from tortured to serene, from bleary-eyed and blotchy and flushed to clear and healthy"; and she watches people "change from bitter, angry, resentful, whining, and negative, as I was when I came in, to people of peace and humility and gratitude." One result of Monahan's experience of transformation in AA is a new perception of herself not as "a nice nun who drank too much," but as a sinner. "Having been gratefully saved," she has a new appreciation of Jesus as her redeemer (91, 96, 166, 155–56).

Spiritually reinvigorated, connected to "a God newly understood and loved," Monahan returns to her spiritual practice in a way that integrates Catholic and AA spiritualities. She engages in Ignatian meditation, reads from *Twenty Four Hours a Day* (a popular AA-themed devotional), recites the Third- and Seventh-Step prayers from the AA Big Book, prays the rosary, and each night takes a Tenth-Step inventory she says is as rigorous "as anything asked of me as a Catholic." Monahan even adopts the traditional AA practice of getting on her knees to pray (a posture from which nuns were liberated following Vatican II). She does so based on the conviction that "kneeling can and should express something—powerlessness, surrender, humility" (132, 54, 112).

Other Stories

Not surprisingly, briefer testimonies from recovering clergy reveal the same dynamics that animate these memoirs. Examples include a collection of stories by Lutheran clergy titled *Our Stories of Experience, Strength and Hope!* that describe recovery from addiction as "an amazing new way of life that fulfills all the promises of scripture." Typical of these recovering Lutheran pastors is Gary G., who after years of problem drinking encouraged by his denominational culture finds release from the compulsion to drink when he experiences freedom and acceptance in AA. "I am a different person today," writes Eric W., who discovers grace not in Christian fellowship or Lutheran theology but in jail and in AA meetings where Jesus was made "concrete in a way that the church did not."[15]

As John W. walks into his first AA meeting after a two-day drinking binge, he enters "the door that by God's grace would change [his] life," behind which he finds a kind of support he has never known in church. A stint in a treatment center allows Elwood R. to view himself "through new glasses, to see my daily need for God's grace." Al D. writes that AA introduced him to a spiritual way of living about which he had learned little in Sunday school, college, seminary, or graduate school. Ed T. admits giving up on the church in early sobriety after concluding that Jesus could be found "in 12 Step meetings where the broken are greeted and welcomed without condition and loved back in to life." Now the pastor rejoices that through AA he has peace, joy, and serenity.[16]

Such experiences are not limited to Lutherans, of course. In his book *Hope and Help for the Alcoholic*, Christian Reformed pastor Alexander C. DeJong tells of entering inpatient treatment for alcoholism after thirty years of pastoral ministry. While in rehab, DeJong visits the hospital chapel to perform familiar tasks—sitting quietly, reading the Bible, and praying. But for the first time in years he is able to experience intimacy with God:

> I was speaking to God *confidently*, because I trusted him; *hopefully*, because he had promised release; *calmly*, because I was no longer running. . . . During the early days of rehabilitation, my mind often went to biblical passages on which I had earlier written articles and delivered sermons. Now, with all my thinking being filtered through the experience of recovery, I had new insights into old stories. Fresh meaning colored old truths.[17]

Church of God pastor Bill Morris traces his own spiritual awakening in Twelve-Step recovery to working the first three Steps, which teach him the meaning of surrender, the process of daily denying his self-will, and allowing God "to do whatever work in my life needs to be done."[18]

Similar stories are related by laypeople with deep roots in the soil of the church. The daughter of a pastor reports undergoing a "second spiritual awakening" as she works the Steps of Al-Anon. In recovery, she writes, "I found that the Scriptures were coming alive for me." When her church will not endorse the call to ministry that emerges in the course of her recovery journey, she turns to her Al-Anon family, where she believes she has found the real church after all. A Sunday school teacher and choir member laments the lack of sympathy expressed by church members after she returns from addiction treatment. Discovering what she is looking for in a Twelve-Step program, she stops attending church and finds the "loving presence of Jesus" in her sponsor. A church outreach worker discovers in AA a spiritual home where "slowly, patiently, a group of strangers led me into warm personal relationships that I never thought were possible—with them, with God, and, after many months, with myself."[19]

A Spiritual Kindergarten for (Professional) Christians

These stories of recovery share a narrative arc in which Christians who struggle with addiction or dysfunction find in Twelve-Step fellowships a sort of "spiritual kindergarten," to use the phrase coined by AA cofounder Bill W. It is certainly counterintuitive to think of people with advanced degrees and extensive religious training beginning anew the process of spiritual formation; but the memoirs we have reviewed suggest this is often what recovery entails for "professional Christians." For such people the lessons to be learned in the Twelve-Step spiritual kindergarten appear to include *surprise, insight,* and *transformation.*[20]

According to these memoirs, the first *surprise* is often the realization that recovery fellowships are teeming with church folk. Nate Larkin is shocked to learn that the subculture of recovering addicts in his community includes representatives of "nearly every church in town," while Heather Kopp encounters Christian women in AA who, like herself, "are mystified as to why their faith hadn't been able to save them." A second surprise involves the unreliability of cherished assumptions about addiction—that real Christians do not become addicts, that addiction can be overcome through repentance and prayer, or that Twelve-Step fellowships have nothing to teach Christians. As these authors discover, not only has their faith failed to inoculate them against the ravages of addiction, but it actually presents an obstacle to their recovery. Deep-seated shame and fear prevent them from admitting powerlessness, confidence in their spiritual superiority makes it difficult to learn from other addicts, or an inner voice tells them the disease concept of addiction is nothing more than a sophisticated excuse for sin. Whatever form it may take, their Christian baggage becomes a serious impediment on the road to recovery.

A further surprise arrives when Christians who wrestle with addiction recognize that exposing themselves to recovery is not the same as "working" it. They come to learn that, despite their training, degrees, and titles, maintaining sobriety requires the sustained practice of mundane disciplines such as picking up the telephone, securing a sponsor, engaging in regular prayer and meditation, and spreading the message to "those who suffer." For Christians willing to do this work, surprise often yields to frustration and anger as they realize that the spiritual fruits of Twelve-Step recovery have eluded them in the church. Larkin is "furious" that, despite decades in various congregations, he has never known the safety, honesty, or mutual respect he finds in a "community of recovering drunks." Kopp is incredulous that the fellowship she discovers among addicts and alcoholics is not even "vaguely familiar" from her Christian experience.

In Christian recovery memoirs surprise eventually gives way to moments of deep *insight,* one of which reveals that recovery cannot begin in earnest until one "hits bottom," whether this means staring in the mirror at a face one loathes (Nelson), waking up unable to remember what happened the night before (Kopp), being arrested in a police sting (Ryan), facing the dissolution of a marriage (Larkin), experiencing frightening physiological symptoms (Miller), or becoming spiritually bereft in the midst of a monastic community (Monahan). In each case, "bottoming out" is the pivot point on which the arc of the narrator's life begins to shift in the direction of recovery.

Another insight that accompanies recovery in these memoirs is that the missionary impulse Christians often feel toward members of Twelve-Step fellowships is misguided. Kopp and Larkin recall with some embarrassment their desire to evangelize non-Christian members of their recovery communities although, to their credit, both come to view themselves as missionaries of recovery within the church. Insight into the character of God is another common theme in Christian recovery memoirs. Miller concludes that he must "fire" the God constructed in his father's image and embrace the healing force he encounters in the lives of recovering people. Kopp, meanwhile, realizes that because the "God of her understanding" has not kept her sober, she must seek a God she doesn't understand.

Given these hard-won spiritual insights, it is no wonder that Christian authors describe their recovery in terms of a *transformation* that involves nothing less than ceding control of one's life to God, fearlessly identifying character defects, reassessing priorities and values, restoring broken relationships, and choosing a life of humility and service. This transformation is often accompanied by the recognition that there is a profound difference between belief and experience, between statements of faith and "vital" religion. Nelson admits that prior to recovery he spoke often of God's grace while doubting that it applied to him. Kopp laments that her work in the Christian publishing industry made it difficult for her to appreciate that true faith had to be based in experience. Monahan learns to embrace an undogmatic, personal truth attested to in the stories she hears "in the rooms."[21]

Conclusion

These narratives of Christian leaders who experience healing and transformation through Twelve-Step recovery, as compelling as they are, raise a concern for those interested in recovering church: In such cases, is a recovery community destined to replace a Christian congregation at the center of one's spiritual life? If these memoirs are any guide, it appears that finding recovery is more likely to convince Christians to try to change rather than to leave their religious communities. But does this mean the spiritual awakenings occurring in recovery do not pose a threat to the church? To that question we now turn.

Are AA and the Church Allies or Competitors?

(maybe both)

I've related the circumstances through which I came to recognize the spiritual benefits of Twelve-Step recovery, traced the history of Christian AA envy, and reviewed the stories of Christians in crisis who discover in recovery fellowships spiritual resources that are unavailable in their churches. Now it's time to consider in more detail the relationship between American Christianity and Twelve-Step recovery. What is their historical connection? How has the relationship evolved over time? And should the two entities be viewed as allies or competitors? Answering this last question will require us to determine whether AA and similar fellowships can function as alternative religious communities for persons in recovery.

What Church Is This?

Several years ago, while attending a professional conference in another city, I was invited to an off-site meeting at a local church. Since the weather was mild and I had spent the day indoors, I decided to walk to the meeting. Naturally, given my poor sense of direction, I became lost. I kept walking until I came upon what I thought was the right building, but because I couldn't locate a sign I approached a young man who was locking his bike to a rail near a side entrance. "Is this First Presbyterian Church?" I asked. When he answered, "I have no idea," I said, "you must be here for a Twelve-Step meeting." "Yeah," he said. "How did you know?" It really wasn't a bold inference. The vast majority of Twelve-Step meetings are hosted by churches, and the vast majority of people who attend them are not members of those congregations and are unlikely to know a lot about them. It was surprising that the young man wasn't even aware of the church's name, but this only increased my certainty that he was headed to "a meeting."

It is to churches' credit that so many of them provide regular meeting places for recovery fellowships. In fact, when healing occurs "in the rooms," more often than not it is in rooms owned and maintained by Christian congregations. Yet within these churches, there is often an invisible firewall that prevents those in recovery meetings from learning much about the church, while keeping church members ignorant of what happens in those meetings. As a result, members of Twelve-Step fellowships rarely find a church home in the congregation that hosts their "home group," while church members who are in recovery rarely attend meetings in their home church. Understanding this odd state of affairs requires an exploration of the church's historical relationship with Twelve-Step recovery, beginning with AA's roots in the Oxford Group.[1]

Oxford Group Origins

The Oxford Group (OG) was the brainchild of Frank Buchman, an American Lutheran pastor, college chaplain, and foreign missionary who in 1921 founded "A First-Century Fellowship" with a mission to recall the world to primitive Christianity. The organization's name reflected the influence of Protestant restorationism—that is, the impulse to reform the contemporary church by retrieving the structure and practices of the earliest Christian communities. After achieving popular success in the United Kingdom, the organization rebranded itself as the "Oxford Group" in 1928.

Like other movements seeking to recover a preinstitutional church, the OG eschewed denominational shibboleths and sectarian squabbles in an effort to provide religion's cultured despisers with a fresh look at "mere Christianity." In this sense, the Oxford Group was a forerunner of the evangelical parachurch organizations that would proliferate in America following World War II, groups that were lay-directed, that targeted persons of influence, and that were a response to the perceived deficit of "vital religion" in the established churches. Rejecting the social gospel's inroads into mainline Protestantism, the OG identified a solution for the besetting problems of modern life in individual spiritual transformation—"world-changing through life-changing," as Buchman put it.[2]

Shaped by Lutheran Pietism and Protestant revivalism, the OG disseminated its message through testimonies of dramatic personal change. Such stories conformed to a theology of human transformation that was simple and systematic: people are sinners; sinners can be changed; confession is a prerequisite to this change; the changed soul has direct access to God; the age of miracles has returned; and those who have been changed are to change others. OG emissaries claimed this "changed life" was attainable by passing through five *stages* ("confidence," "confession," "conviction," "conversion," and "continuance"), a process aided by five *procedures* (giving in to God, listening to God's directions, checking guidance, making restitution, and mutual sharing).[3]

Glenn F. Chesnut argues that the Oxford Group cannot be understood apart from its roots in eighteenth-century Anglo-American evangelicalism, particularly the revivalist theologies of Jonathan Edwards and John Wesley, which shared the assumption that fundamental character shifts should be evidenced by objective changes in behavior. A more proximate influence, however, was the American collegiate evangelism movement shaped by Henry Drummond in the mid-nineteenth century and Henry B. Wright in the early decades of the twentieth. The "personal evangelism" practiced by Drummond, Wright, and other pioneer collegiate evangelists replaced mass evangelistic methods with efforts "to draw souls one by one . . . to read them off like a page of print, to . . . make them transparent." Adopting this approach as his own, Buchman's modus operandi became "personal contact of man with man."[4]

Alcoholics Anonymous

Among the Americans influenced by the Oxford Group in the second quarter of the twentieth century were Roland Hazard and Ebby Thacher, both of whom would become central figures in the emergence of Alcoholics Anonymous. Hazard was a prominent investment banker whose struggles with alcoholism led him in 1931 to Swiss psychologist Carl Jung, who told him the only cure for his destructive drinking lay in a "spiritual awakening." Jung conceded that such experiences were rare but believed they were worth pursuing because the void created by alcoholism could be filled only by a different sort of "spirit." In search of this elusive spiritual cure, Hazard sought out the Oxford Group, first in England and then in New York City at Calvary Episcopal Church.[5]

When Hazard heard that his friend Ebby Thacher's drinking had landed him in jail, he visited Thacer along with other OG members. Upon hearing Hazard's story of spiritual renewal in the Oxford Group, Thacher immediately stopped drinking and became involved in the OG himself. As he was eager to pass on the secret of his newfound sobriety, in November 1934, Ebby T. (as he is known in AA history) called on "the most hopeless and most self-destructive" drinker he knew, an old school friend named Bill Wilson. Wilson was initially unimpressed by Ebby's claim that he had "got religion," surmising that his "gin would last longer than [Ebby's] preaching." But as historian Ernest Kurtz notes, this unpromising meeting in Wilson's kitchen adumbrated two critical aspects of what would become the program of Alcoholics Anonymous: the centrality of one alcoholic talking with another, and a "self-conscious wariness" of religion.

Despite being put off by Ebby's attempt at outreach, a few weeks later Wilson would have his own spiritual encounter while "drying out" at New York City's Towns Hospital. Wilson described it as his "hot flash."

> All at once I found myself crying out, "If there is a God, let Him Show Himself! I am ready to do anything, anything!" Suddenly, the room lit up with a great white light. I was caught up into an ecstasy which there are no words to describe. . . . And then it burst upon me that I was a free man. . . . All about me there was a wonderful feeling of Presence, and I thought to myself, "So this is the God of the Preachers!"[6]

Unconvinced of the experience's authenticity, Wilson asked his physician William Silkworth whether he had suffered an hallucination. To Wilson's surprise, the psychiatrist suggested that Bill's "hot flash" may have been the sort of "spiritual breakthrough" that sometimes precedes a release from alcoholism. To help him make sense of the incident, Ebby brought Wilson a copy of William James's *The Varieties of Religious Experience*, which according to William White, provided just the interpretive key he required:

> It was in the pages of this book that Bill came to understand how out of calamity and pain could come surrender—"deflation at depth"—and an opening of oneself to the experience of a hope-infusing Higher Power. James' description of the elements of conversion validated for Bill what he later called "the sublime paradox of strength coming out of weakness."

Following Wilson's release from Towns Hospital, he and wife Lois began attending Oxford Group meetings at Calvary Episcopal Church as Bill sought out alcoholics at Towns and Calvary Mission. Gradually, Wilson envisioned a movement of alcoholics who would carry "the message of hope that Silkworth and James had brought him."[7]

A critical step toward realizing this vision took the form of a providential accident. In Akron on business in May 1935, Wilson sought out a local Oxford Group member to help him combat the impulse to drink. His search led eventually to Dr. Bob Smith, a chronic drunk known to one of the OG people Wilson had contacted. Wilson's five-hour meeting with Smith the next day laid the groundwork for what would become Alcoholics Anonymous, although AA's founding date is usually given as June 10, the day of "Dr. Bob's" last drink. Ernest Kurtz describes the essence of the fateful meeting between Bill W. and Dr. Bob by noting "four aspects of one critical idea": the alcoholic was "utterly hopeless, totally deflated, requiring conversion, and needing others."[8]

Wilson spent the summer of 1935 living with Bob and Anne Smith in Akron and working with a group of local alcoholics, a period of AA history described as "intensive Oxford Group living" guided by prayers and readings from the Bible and OG literature. When Wilson returned to New York at summer's end, he began recruiting alcoholics from the Oxford Group at Calvary Church in the hope of replicating the Akron experiment. But while these fledgling fellowships in Akron and New York would continue to meet within the framework of the Oxford Group, tensions were growing between alcoholic and nonalcoholic members. By late 1935, the New York group had formally split from the OG, and in 1937 men living in the Calvary Mission were forbidden from attending Tuesday evening meetings at the Wilsons' home.[9]

In fact, there were serious reservations on both sides. According to Wilson, the extended silence typical of OG meetings gave alcoholics "the jitters," and the publicity the group sought through reaching "up and outers"—its appeals to the wealthy and powerful led to the OG's caricature as a "Salvation Army for snobs"—seemed incompatible with the humility and anonymity that were becoming features of AA culture. There was also fear that the OG's evangelical ethos would scare away Roman Catholics or even cause the church hierarchy to prohibit their involvement. Furthermore, Bill W. concluded that an emphasis on OG's "Four Absolutes"—absolute honesty, absolute unselfishness, absolute love, and absolute purity—was counterproductive in working with alcoholics.[10]

Despite the mutually agreed separation, Oxford Group concepts and practices remained influential in early AA, particularly in Akron, where the sober alcoholics around Dr. Bob referred to themselves as the OG's "alcoholic squadron." Smith described this group as a "Christian fellowship," and membership required a profession of surrender to God. In fact, devotional reading, meditation for divine "guidance," and communal prayer remained hallmarks of weekly meetings in Akron even after AA's formal separation from the Oxford Group in 1939. Indicating the persistent influence of the OG, Dr. Bob and Bill W. both continued to practice a discipline of "quiet time" reading, in which Bible texts such as the Sermon on the Mount, 1 Corinthians 13, and the

Psalms were intensively read and studied. As devotional aids, Wilson preferred Oswald Chambers's *My Utmost for His Highest*, while Dr. Bob was committed to *The Upper Room*, an ecumenically flavored Southern Methodist publication that was a conduit for John Wesley's "religion of the heart." The early fellowship's affinity for Scripture is reflected in the fact that before it settled upon the name "Alcoholics Anonymous," a leading candidate was "James Club," a reference to members' fondness for the New Testament epistle.[11]

It is significant that despite AA's efforts to achieve an innovative amalgamation of spiritual, medical, and psychological knowledge, it was the group's overtly religious ethos that struck early commentators. In reviews of *Alcoholics Anonymous: The Story of How Many Thousands of Men and Women Have Recovered from Alcoholism* (the AA "Big Book" that appeared in 1939), medical journals drew attention to a "curious combination of organizing propaganda and religious exhortation," dismissing the book as a "rambling sort of camp-meeting confession of experiences . . . of various alcoholics . . . who have provisionally recovered, chiefly under the influence of the 'big brothers of the spirit.'" Yet despite lingering perceptions that AA's approach to alcoholism was nothing more than "religious fervor," Wilson himself never joined or regularly attended a particular church. Like the program he helped create, AA's cofounder is well described as "deeply spiritual, but not religious."[12]

Oxford Group Influence on AA

The strategy of attaining a changed life by passing through a sequence of stages is one obvious way the Twelve Steps of AA resemble the Oxford Group program. Both groups, furthermore, describe what Buchman called a "spiritual sickness" whose only cure is surrender before God, and both celebrate the "miracles" of personal transformation that follow from this act of surrender. AA's affinity for the language of miracle is particularly evident in "Bill's Story," chapter one of the AA Big Book, in which Wilson describes the sober Ebby T. as a man who "had been raised from the dead," "a miracle [sitting] directly across the kitchen table," just one piece of evidence that "the age of miracles is still with us."[13]

OG influence is also evident in AA's decision to meet in informal homelike settings, its expectation that Christian members remain in their own churches, its emphasis on helping others as a way of changing oneself, and its encouragement of "before and after" testimonials. Furthermore, "personal intimacy nurtured within an informal, non-professional atmosphere"—a phrase used to describe the core of the Oxford Group experience—could apply to early AA as well. One also detects in the OG belief that "the changed soul has direct access to God" the roots of AA's conviction that the fellowship's ultimate authority is "a loving God as He may express Himself in our group conscience." Another feature of the fellowship in which Oxford Group influence is evident is AA's "non-specific pietism." In their fateful 1934 meeting, Ebby T. explained to Wilson that in the OG he had learned to "pray to whatever God I thought there was, and if I did not believe there was any God, then [to] try the experiment of praying to whatever God there *might* be." The suggestion that Bill choose his conception of God, and his decision to do so, reflects the "pragmatic anti-doctrinalism" that characterized the OG and that became a defining characteristic of AA.[14]

In the 1950s, Bill W. downplayed AA's evangelical roots in the OG, saying the principles derived from the group "were ancient and universal ones, the common property of mankind." Nevertheless, OG was a direct conduit to AA of what scholars see as "a uniquely American expression of Evangelical Pietism." As Linda Mercadante notes, AA even adopted many of the OG's positions on key theological issues, including that conversion requires surrender, that sin is primarily self-centeredness, and that God seeks control of people's lives. According to Mercadante, while AA exchanged the OG's emphasis on human fallibility for a focus on the scourge of alcoholism, the fellowship held on to a quite traditional view of human beings' inability to break sin's bondage.[15]

In the final analysis, the OG's influence on AA was profound but paradoxical. The unmistakable similarities include a common emphasis on powerlessness, self-inventory, confession, and restitution; a stress on testimony that in the OG was known as "sharing for witness"; a pursuit of "God control" through men and women who have "surrendered" to the divine will; a reliance on uncompensated workers; a proclivity for slogans and "group language"; a pragmatic emphasis on how the program "works"; a belief that only by passing on the group's message can one maintain spiritual fitness; a pairing of established members and newcomers; and a focus on individual behavior that has led to charges of quietism. But the OG was also instrumental in teaching AA's founders what *didn't* work with alcoholics, even if they were sober, including aggressive evangelism, publicity-seeking, preference for members of the upper classes, and moral or theological claims that might repel those in need of the program.[16]

However we assess the Oxford Group's long-term impact on AA, it is important to note that many of the fellowship's features that are most admired by contemporary Christians are directly traceable to the OG's influence. In fact, participants' claims that OG meetings were places where "all pretense and hypocrisy faded," that the group "put to shame the accomplishments of the churches and conventional religion," that it was impossible to find "deeper Christian fellowship," and that the OG provided "joys . . . undreamed of by the conventional church-goer" resonate with the language of Christian AA envy explored in a previous chapter. In 1951, before the widespread success of AA, the Oxford Group was called "the most vital religious movement of [its] day." If many say the same of AA seventy years later, it is in part because the Twelve-Step movement has faithfully embodied the OG's legacy.[17]

The Church's Response

From its earliest days, AA received strong support from official representatives of American Christianity, Protestant and Catholic alike. Critical to winning acceptance for the fellowship among Roman Catholics was Father Ed Dowling, SJ, who perceived similarities between AA's Twelve Steps and the Spiritual Exercises of Saint Ignatius Loyola. In addition to helping the Big Book win approval in the New York archdiocese and bringing AA to Saint Louis, Dowling served as Bill W.'s unofficial spiritual advisor. Other early Catholic supporters of the fellowship included Sister Ignatia, a nun at Akron's Saint Thomas Hospital who helped Dr. Bob "smuggle" recovering drunks into her institution, and Father Vincent Haas, a young priest in Akron who noted the fellowship's resonance with the early Franciscan movement. But no one did more to translate AA principles into a Catholic idiom than Father Ralph Pfau, who between 1948 and 1967 wrote a series of fourteen AA-themed *Golden Books* under the pseudonym "Father John Doe."[18]

Among the Protestant clergy to publicly endorse AA in its early days were Dilworth Lupton, Sam Shoemaker, and Harry Emerson Fosdick. Lupton, pastor of Cleveland's First Unitarian Church, was one of the first to "preach on A.A." after reading the fellowship's Big Book in 1939. These sermons were covered by the *Cleveland Plain Dealer*, and one was reprinted in pamphlet form and widely distributed. Because he was intimately involved in the emergence of Alcoholics Anonymous in New York, Episcopal priest Sam Shoemaker embodied the close relationship between AA and the Protestant mainline in the group's early years. By the 1950s, Shoemaker had come to see the relationship as symbiotic, with AA needing the church for "personal stabilization and growth" and the church requiring AA "as a continuous spur to greater aliveness and expectation and power."[19]

Fosdick, the Baptist minister and prominent modernist, wrote one of the more positive reviews of the AA Big Book, in which he praised the group's "tolerance and open-mindedness" and characterized its program as containing "nothing partisan or sectarian." According to Fosdick, AA meetings were the only place Roman Catholics, Jews, Protestants, and even agnostics could "get together harmoniously on a religious basis." "I have listened to many learned arguments about God," he wrote, "but for honest-to-goodness experiential evidence of God, His power personally appropriated and His reality indubitably assured, give me a good meeting of A.A.!" Fosdick even claimed to be a regular reader of the *A.A. Grapevine* (the fellowship's monthly newsletter), whose stories he called "the most moving collection of testimonies to the possibility of personal transformation" of which he was aware.[20]

During the 1950s and 60s, American Christianity's relationship with AA was increasingly defined by mutual cooperation. Churches not only hosted AA meetings but provided pastoral assistance for alcoholics, particularly in helping them complete Step 5 ("admitted to God, ourselves and another human being the exact nature of our wrongs"). A 1949 article in the *Journal of Clinical and Pastoral Work* explored how pastors might collaborate with the fellowship, whose program it described as "religious," the Steps "fundamentally Christian." During this period, hundreds of ministers attended the Yale Center's Summer School for Alcohol Studies and many worked in the nascent alcohol treatment industry.

Symbolizing the role clergy could play in treating alcoholism, Hazelden, where the AA-based "Minnesota Model" was developed, established a pastoral training program to help clergy recognize and minister to alcoholics and addicts. According to the treatment center's pamphlet on "Christian Ministry and the Fifth Step," in responding to an alcoholic's story with the message that he or she is "still accepted despite anything [they've] felt, said, or done," the pastor becomes a "living sign of reconciliation." References to the role of clergy in helping alcoholics "take the Fifth" in AA would regularly appear in guides for ministry to alcoholics into the 1990s.[21]

Too Religious, Not Religious, or Not Religious Enough?

Eventually, the very qualities that made AA a natural ally of American churches gave rise to criticism that the fellowship was too intertwined with its Christian roots to effectively "carry the message" of recovery to alcoholics in a religiously pluralistic environment. As AA responded to this criticism by emphasizing its nonsectarian, nonreligious and generically "spiritual" character, visible church support was neither needed nor sought.

Yet despite AA's successful efforts to downplay its Christian origins, whether or not it is religious continues to be debated, with various factions claiming the fellowship is *too religious, not religious,* or *not religious enough.* The "too religious" charge has assumed different forms over time. In AA's early days, Roman Catholic leaders feared the fellowship was too "Protestant" in background and character to meet the needs of Church members. As this fear waned, it was gradually replaced by criticism that AA was too "Christian" to be of help to alcoholics outside, or alienated from, that religious tradition. This complaint continues to be lodged in one form or another by advocates of non-Twelve-Step recovery programs such as Rational Recovery, as well as by groups like Secular Organizations for Sobriety and LifeRing Secular Recovery.[22]

As Ernest Kurtz points out, the "too religious" perspective has always had its advocates within AA itself. In fact, preparation of the Big Book during the late 1930s led to the emergence of three internal factions: "conservatives" who thought the book ought to be Christian and should say so; "liberals" who were fine with the word "God" but wanted to eschew theological propositions; and a "radical left wing" of atheists and agnostics who wished to systematically avoid all references to the divine. As compromise measures, Wilson agreed to replace "God" in Step 2 with "a Power greater than ourselves," insert the words "as we understand Him" in Steps 3 and 11, and delete the expression "on our knees" from Step 7.[23]

Without pressing for further edits to the Big Book, AA's "radical" faction has sought over the years to ensure the group's program remains culturally sensitive. In 1975, for instance, AA members in Chicago formed Alcoholics Anonymous for Atheists and Agnostics, and in 2009 two Toronto AA groups—Beyond Belief and We Agnostics—developed the AA Agnostica website, to which the Greater Toronto Area AA Intergroup responded by removing them from its approved list of meetings. AA secularizers continue their efforts to make the group "safe for atheists," as well as the growing number of "nones" who report finding the fellowship too religious for their comfort. The organizational strength of these "modernizing secularizers" was revealed in 2014 at the first national gathering of an AA affinity group called We Agnostics, Atheists, and Free Thinkers (WAAFT).[24]

The "not religious" view of AA is the official position of the fellowship itself, which added the statement "Alcholics Anonymous is not a religious organization" to the foreword of the Big Book's second edition, published in 1955. This perspective is energetically advanced by recovery advocates who want to ensure that the religious-sounding concepts and language embedded in the Twelve-Step program do not deter the non- or antireligious from seeking recovery. Among them is clinical psychologist Joseph Nowinski, who argues that while "the God thing" has led some to mischaracterize AA as religious, to do so is inaccurate since "religions are governed by dogma, which is delivered by designated clergy who are monitored, in turn, via an authoritative hierarchy." Similarly, sex addiction expert Robert Weiss assures his readers that Twelve-Step groups are "spiritual programs, but not religious," and that references to God in Twelve-Step literature are "not in any way directed toward a specific religion or belief system."[25]

While it is important to reassure alcoholics that their recovery does not depend on adopting a particular religion, the "not religious" view of AA is not so easily sustained. First of all, there are committed members of non-Christian faith traditions who acknowledge and highlight Twelve-Step recovery's inherent religiosity. Some Jewish recovery advocates, for instance, are keen to convince skeptical Jews that AA and other seemingly Christian recovery fellowships are safe for them, despite meeting in churches, utilizing Christian prayers, and just "feeling" so Christian. They do so by explaining to their coreligionists that the religiosity of Twelve-Step fellowships is as compatible with Judaism as it appears to be with Christianity. In Carol Glass's version of this argument, Twelve-Step recovery "clearly echoes established beliefs found in mainstream Jewish liturgy and thought," its step-by-step process for altering addictive behavior bearing a striking resemblance to a Jewish perspective on changing "sinful" behavior and initiating a return to ethical living. In the thought of Jewish sages, in fact, Glass identifies "a guided spiritual journey" that is nearly identical to that outlined in the Twelve Steps.[26]

The American judicial system provides further reason to doubt the "not religious" view of AA and Twelve-Step recovery more generally. In recent years, as American courts have been called upon to assess the constitutionality of requiring probationers, parolees, or inmates to attend Twelve-Step meetings (a criminal justice practice that dates to the 1970s), many have determined that mandating meeting attendance violates the Establishment Clause of the US Constitution's First Amendment. In fact, between 1996 and 2007, five legislative jurisdictions—three federal circuit courts and two state supreme courts—ruled that, based on its Steps, prayers, and Big Book (which includes two hundred references to God), AA is indeed religious in nature. In *Griffin v. Coughlin* (1996), for instance, the Second Circuit's appellate court concluded that "doctrinally and as actually practiced," AA entails "religious activity and religious proselytization." In 2007, the Ninth Circuit Court of Appeals agreed, ruling that a parole officer who orders someone to attend AA or affiliated programs can be sued for damages.[27]

Desirous of keeping the path of recovery open for all who need it, Nowinski, Weiss, and other addiction professionals have the unenviable task of persuading men and women, many of whom have sustained deep psychological wounds in religious communities, to trust their lives to a program that not only sounds and feels religious but that more than likely meets in a church building. These authors are correct in pointing out that AA and other Twelve-Step fellowships lack many of the trappings of institutional religion—including clergy, dogma, and "specific belief system[s]." But given the frequent references to God in these groups' literature, their claim that sobriety depends on surrendering to a "Higher Power," and their self-presentation as a "way of life," one wonders whether denying the religious character of Twelve-Step recovery is mainly a semantic exercise.

Finally, if AA is "not religious," it is difficult to explain why it has given rise to emphatically nonreligious recovery programs and fellowships. Among them is Secular Organizations for Sobriety (SOS), founded by disaffected Texas Baptist James Christopher as an alternative to AA's "twelve-step theology" and its reliance on a mystical higher power he regards as a "substitute addiction." Determined to repudiate AA's "oppressive cultist atmosphere" and confident that sobriety can be attained through "self-reliance . . . and the choice of reason over religious superstition," Christopher started the first Secular Sobriety group in Los Angeles in 1986.[28]

The "not religious enough" perspective is represented within AA by Big Book fundamentalists and intra-group movements like Primary Purpose and Back to Basics, which seek to perpetuate spiritual practices developed in Akron and Cleveland during the first decade of the fellowship's history. While these AA fundamentalists give lip service to remaining "spiritual rather than religious," according to Ernest Kurtz and William White, in practice they "Christianize early A.A. history, elevate Christian literature on par with A.A.'s own literature, and assert Christian conversion as a central mechanism of A.A.'s effectiveness." The "not religious enough" perspective is also represented by explicitly Christian offshoots of AA, the most successful of which is Celebrate Recovery (CR).[29]

Celebrate Recovery was started by John Baker in southern California about the same time James Christopher was launching SOS. Despite the crucial role played by AA in his own recovery and his family's healing, Baker felt "mocked" in AA meetings when he identified Jesus Christ as his Higher Power; yet he could not find a Christian community where he was comfortable discussing his struggle with alcoholism. So he approached Saddleback Community Church pastor Rick Warren with the idea of initiating a Christ-centered recovery program based on a lightly edited version of AA's Twelve Steps and a thoroughgoing emphasis on the Steps' biblical basis. CR soon became one of Saddleback's signature programs and by 2020 had spread to thirty-five thousand churches, prisons, rehab facilities, and rescue missions worldwide.[30]

The programmatic efforts of Christopher and Baker, as different as they are, pose an implicit challenge to the notion that AA and other Twelve-Step groups are "not religious." After all, before they left AA to found their own recovery groups, both men had enough firsthand experience of the fellowship to draw informed conclusions about its religiosity. What they agreed upon (and it was perhaps the only thing) was that AA is religious *enough* to make both atheists and evangelical Christians uncomfortable. Of course, whether AA is *too religious* (Christopher and AA secularizers), *not religious* (Nowinski and Weiss), or *not religious enough* (Baker and AA fundamentalists) is a matter of opinion; but the longevity and ferocity of the debate belies any claim that the question has a simple answer.

Sect? Cult? Social World?

Perhaps AA religiosity is so difficult to pin down because the fellowship is more like a cult or sect than a traditional religious community. In 1970 Robert Kenneth Jones advanced this view, arguing in the journal *Sociology* that, based on what he described as its "totality of concern," AA should be regarded as a "sectarian organization." Assertions of AA's cultish character go as far back as 1963, when Arthur Cain described the group as "one of America's most fanatical religious cults" based on the way it invested the pursuit of sobriety with "religious flavor." For Cain, the question whether AA qualified as a cult was of more than theoretical interest. Because the group's members were convinced that "the Program" was a product of divine revelation, he argued, AA could only hinder scientific research on alcoholism.[31]

Since the 1980s, the "cult" accusation has been lodged against AA repeatedly and with increasing specificity. During that decade, professional sociologists claimed the group was an "unseen cult" that engages in brainwashing, while Jack Trimpey, founder of Rational Recovery, called AA a dangerous "religious cult" whose "12-step programming" creates fear, uncertainty, depression, and self-destruction. A more thoughtful assessment was offered by Charles Bufe in *Alcoholics Anonymous: Cult or Cure?* (1998). Bufe identified features of AA typical of modern cults, including religious orientation, discouragement of skepticism and rational thinking, self-absorption (that is, disinterest in research or other forms of treatment), mindless repetition of slogans and dogma, submission to the will of God, manipulation through guilt, and identification of "approved" literature. But Bufe also noted that AA lacks some distinguishing characteristics of cults—including charismatic leaders, a hierarchal authority structure, mechanisms to prevent members from leaving the group, mind-control techniques, prohibited contact with "outsiders," consciously deceptive recruitment techniques, violence, and exploitation for money. Nevertheless, he warned that "institutional" AA resembles groups such as Scientology, the People's Temple, and the Unification Church ("Moonies"), characterized by "brainwashing," "coercion and harassment," and "forcing false confessions."[32]

One way to avoid the thorny question of whether and to what extent AA qualifies as a "cult," "sect," or "religious group" is to label it a *social world*. In her description of AA, sociologist Annette R. Smith calls the fellowship "a universe of mutual response" whose boundaries are set only by "the limits of effective communication." Smith notes that "cognitive identification" with the AA social world—which is composed of local groups, area intergroups and assemblies, national and international conferences, AA literature, and AA-sponsored social events—is developed through shared stories and rituals, media "linking devices" (books, pamphlets, and periodicals), and informal exchanges in which AA language enters everyday discourse. As a social world, Smith observes, AA resembles an extended family in which "members who have never seen each other develop an instant rapport." Yet even from her sociological perspective, Smith is struck by the religious character of AA, noting that in it "adult re-socialization" is achieved through a process resembling religious "conversion" from which members derive a "sense of coherence about themselves and the world."[33]

Spiritual, but Not Religious?

One way of bypassing these definitional issues is to assume that Twelve-Step recovery is just what it claims to be: "spiritual, but not religious." The "spiritual" part of this formula would appear to be self-evident, since a foundational tenet of AA is that the hopelessness of alcoholism can be overcome only through a "deep and effective spiritual experience." That the fellowship places few limits on the term *spirituality* is indicated in "Many Steps to Spirituality" (2014), an AA publication that cites Buddhist, Jewish, Native American, Catholic, agnostic, and even atheist members in making the case that alcoholics can experience "spiritual awakening" in AA regardless of their type or degree of religiosity.[34]

Indeed, according to Ernest Kurtz and William White, it is possible to describe the spiritual values that animate AA using the thoroughly "nonsectarian" language of *release, gratitude, humility, tolerance, forgiveness,* and *being-at-home.* According to the authors, *release* refers to an individual's discovery, following an act of letting go, that he or she has been set free as well. *Gratitude* is based in appreciation for "the gift of sobriety," along with a recognition of "realities previously ignored or taken for granted or simply not seen." *Humility* refers to the acceptance that one is of some, though not infinite, value—in other words, that one is "not God." *Tolerance* entails viewing others' inanities in the context of what one is learning about oneself. *Forgiveness* is made possible by the experience of being forgiven, while *being-at-home* means finding connection with others "through mutually acknowledged flaws, weaknesses, inabilities."[35]

While none of these terms seems to imply allegiance to a particular religious tradition, Twelve-Step spirituality is far from a blank slate. In fact, a careful reading of AA's literature reveals that the fellowship's spirituality conflicts with a number of prominent cultural traditions, including self-help, positive thinking, New Thought, and New Age. As for "self-help," while it remains a standard description of Twelve-Step recovery, AA is emphatic that the source of deliverance from alcoholism lies *outside* the self and that recovery involves the replacement of self-sufficiency with God-sufficiency. Putting the matter quite succinctly, William White notes that AA is "the antithesis of self-help—an acknowledgment that all efforts at self-help have failed."[36]

AA spirituality must also be distinguished from the American positive-thinking tradition, which diagnoses failure as a lack of self-confidence, New Thought's emphasis on human beings' essential divinity (discussed in more detail in a later chapter), the neo-Gnosticism of the New Age movement, and even common assumptions about masculinity and market capitalism. As Trysh Travis explains, AA inverted the popular view that problem drinking was rooted in a lack of "manly self-mastery," claiming that, in fact, the alcoholic's problem was *too much* will-power. In the process it rejected middle-class norms of masculine autonomy in favor of a male self rooted in surrender and humility, one that predicated sobriety on the alcoholic's willingness to give up the fiction of self-mastery and "quit playing God." This countercultural vision was the basis for an "alcoholic equalitarianism" that replaced the autonomous masculine self with a "self-in-relation" that derived its identity from the community of sober alcoholics. Furthermore, according to Travis, this community operated according to a "gift economy" whose currency of exchange was a message believed to be transformative only when it was free.[37]

In a classic expression of what is distinctive about AA's view of the human condition, Ernest Kurtz and Katherine Ketcham employ the term "spirituality of imperfection" to indicate that acceptance and transcendence of limitation are the foundations upon which the alcoholic's transformation rests. According to Kurtz and Ketcham, an open acknowledgment that one is flawed means not only an implicit refutation of one's claim to godhood but also a recognition that "lack of wholeness is the essence of being human." To demonstrate that AA's "spirituality of imperfection" is rooted in traditions that are both ancient and universal, Kurtz and Ketcham cite stories and sayings from most of the world's great religions.[38]

Based on these considerations, it would appear that while the phrase "spiritual, but not religious" may be an accurate description of AA, it is not specific enough to capture the essence of Twelve-Step recovery. In fact, to the extent that Twelve-Step fellowships remain faithful to their AA lineage, they will view human beings as complexly flawed, while eschewing any spirituality rooted in celebration of the sovereign self.

Ally or Competitor?

Without doubt, by providing supportive spaces where people can work through their addictions and dysfunctions, Twelve-Step fellowships are allies of the church in their common quest for human healing. But these groups are the church's competitors inasmuch as they offer spiritual transformation through reliance on a power greater than the self. In fact, that Twelve-Step groups effect such change in an environment that is free from judgment or shame gives them a decided advantage among those who feel alienated from institutional religion.

Conversely, Twelve-Step groups would seem to be disadvantaged among those who seek religious communities' familiar rhythms of liturgy and ritual. But is this the case? As William White points out, despite its aura of informality, AA's program is structured by both "centering rituals," such as the reading of inspirational literature, prayer, meditation, and self-evaluation, and "mirroring rituals," such as meeting attendance, phone conversations with sponsors, group meals, storytelling, laughter (particularly "the boisterous, knowing belly-laugh of mutual identification and healing"), and slogans that become "the verbal equivalent of the secret handshake." Storytelling is another feature of Twelve-Step meetings that possesses both liturgical and ritual dimensions, as it allows addicts to translate their personal histories into "a meaningful and even sacred story," often animated by themes of sin and redemption, death and resurrection, despair, hope, and gratitude. Indeed, if Twelve-Step meetings "become church" for people in recovery, it is in part because the regular gathering times, familiar rituals, study of authoritative texts, and focus on shared spiritual principles are so reminiscent of church gatherings.[39]

Assuming Twelve-Step fellowships *can* function religiously in these ways, will they inevitably replace churches as communities of meaning and belonging? In most cases, probably not. But as David Rudy has argued, AA tends to be a "greedy organization" that is not satisfied by tentative or partial commitments. Thus, for people who find a home in a Twelve-Step fellowship, their church involvement is likely to suffer purely due to the demands that working recovery places on one's time and attention. Put simply, if people in recovery attend an average of 2.5 meetings per week (as is the case for AA members, according to the group's most recent membership survey), this is sure to limit their engagement in a church community. In this sense, the phrase that best captures the essence of Twelve-Step recovery may not be "spiritual, but not religious" but "way of life."[40]

This conception of AA was implicit in its Oxford Group origins and became explicit in Bill W.'s writings during the 1950s, in which he characterized the fellowship as "a new kind of human society" and "a vision for the whole world." The notion of recovery as a way of life has subsequently been embraced by other Twelve-Step fellowships, which in their own way emphasize the distinction between one who is "merely dry" (that is, abstinent without transformation) and one who is experiencing "true sobriety" (that is, has allowed the program to inform every aspect of their life).[41]

Similarly, to be "in recovery" is a comprehensive description of one's orientation to the world that resonates with the Pauline notion of being "in Christ." For it is used to indicate not only what one has stopped doing (i.e., self-medicating with a substance or process) but how one's life has changed as a result. Thus, when someone claims they are "in recovery," they are providing hints about how they spend their time, what they read, how they relax, the composition of their friend group, and the way they perceive themselves, others, and the world. If to "be religious" means to adopt a way of life shared by other members of a distinctive subculture, then the phrase "in recovery" undoubtedly has religious overtones.

Strains in the Relationship

Recovery fellowships' potential to fill the space traditionally occupied by religious communities may explain why the alliance between churches and Twelve-Step groups has loosened over the years. Another factor is the church's own forays into alcohol treatment, which during the 1960s included church-sponsored halfway houses, chaplaincies in hospitals and correctional facilities, a clinical pastoral education (CPE) movement that trained clergy to work with alcoholics, and rehabilitation programs for alcoholic clergymen. While many churches continued to host Twelve-Step fellowships, they no longer relied on them to bear the load of their ministry in the field of addiction.

But by 1970 federal and local governments were becoming increasingly involved in substance abuse treatment, and private options were rapidly expanding. What role would the church play in this complex ecosystem of public and private efforts to treat drug and alcohol abuse, an ecosystem dominated by professional providers and sustained by reimbursement from private insurance companies? Some denominational agencies and task forces worked alongside treatment entities toward the goal of "chemical health," developing print and video curricula, sponsoring workshops and classes, and launching education and prevention programs, and many congregations saw themselves as part of community networks designed to address addiction in its many dimensions.

But eventually the professionalization of addiction treatment created a gap between the church's perceived duty to aid alcoholics and addicts and its confidence in doing so. A 1979 survey of four thousand members of the United Presbyterian Church, for instance, found that 46 percent of laity and 83 percent of pastors believed the consumption of alcoholic beverages was a problem to which the church should attend. But when asked whether their own congregation was involved in programs that addressed alcohol abuse, 81 percent of laity and 76 percent of pastors answered negatively. By the end of the 1970s, the professionalization of addiction treatment had left the church to serve mainly as a referral agency.[42]

In the 1980s, Christian denominations shifted attention from the individual problem drinker, who seemed well served by AA, toward the public health implications of drinking habits in the general population. The approach was reflected in a 1986 document titled *Alcohol Use and Abuse: The Social and Health Effects*, in which the newly reunited Presbyterian Church (USA) brought to alcohol problems the social justice perspective it had begun to apply to other issues of public import. The study embraced a "broad public health perspective" on alcohol-related issues, which it considered "amenable to social control through public policy."[43]

Reflecting the symbiotic relationship between AA and mainline Protestantism that had existed during the previous half-century, *Alcohol Use and Abuse* acknowledged the fellowship's "pioneering and unique role" in the treatment and support of alcoholics, as well as its affinity with Christian faith and practice as understood by Presbyterians. The report affirmed AA's "compatibility with Christianity" and even encouraged congregations to "welcome Alcoholics Anonymous and other self-help groups [*sic*] into the church." But mainline ambivalence toward Twelve-Step recovery was evident in a collection of essays on "substance abuse and the church" published in 1992 in the Presbyterian Church (USA) journal *Church and Society*.

This special issue of the journal addressed a variety of matters, including addiction in women, drugs in racial/ethnic communities, AIDS, and "the war on drugs." But while some articles referred to Twelve-Step recovery and a few revealed an awareness of recent therapeutic trends in the treatment of codependents and "adult children" of alcoholics, there was little to suggest the historical alliance, let alone the common theological roots, shared by churches and Twelve-Step fellowships. In fact, an article that did foreground Twelve-Step recovery—"The Feminine Face of Addiction" by Jane Searjeant Watt—illuminated women's struggles with AA's male-oriented spirituality, particularly among victims of "abusive fathers, brothers, husbands, employers, ministers, physicians, or counselors."[44]

Conclusion

Let's return to my encounter with the young man who was headed to a recovery meeting at a church he knew nothing about. What Twelve-Step fellowship was he preparing to attend? Time was, one could assume he was headed to AA. But in 2016 his destination could have been any number of groups—Al-Anon, Narcotics Anonymous, Sexaholics Anonymous, Sex and Love Addicts Anonymous, Overeaters Anonymous, Gamblers Anonymous, Codependents Anonymous, or Adult Children of Alcoholics, to name a few. It is possible, in fact, that several of these groups were meeting in the church on that very night. For those who want the church to be more like AA, this would appear to represent progress in the direction of recovering church. But as we will see in the next chapter, it is far from certain that the young man's recovery meeting would have been recognizable to Bill W. and Dr. Bob.

What Is Recovery Anyway?

(it's complicated)

My first visit to a Twelve-Step fellowship occurred shortly after I joined a therapeutic group that required its members to attend at least two recovery meetings per week, a requirement I generally fulfilled during the eight years I was part of the group. As a result, from the beginning my recovery has been mediated by a combination of Twelve-Step and therapeutic work, a recipe that is standard in the contemporary treatment of addiction. In fact, what is colloquially referred to as "rehab" consists mainly of therapeutic interventions, group processes, and Twelve-Step meetings, on-site and off. Furthermore, the detailed aftercare plans that patients receive upon leaving inpatient treatment typically call for participation in one or more local recovery fellowships, often with a prescription to attend ninety meetings in the first ninety days after discharge. According to a 2019 analysis, 73 percent of substance abuse treatment services in the US are informed by Twelve-Step philosophy.[1]

AA membership surveys provide another picture of this overlap between Twelve-Step recovery, inpatient and outpatient treatment, and ongoing psychotherapy. AA's 2014 membership survey, for instance, indicated that nearly 19 percent of members had been introduced to the fellowship through a treatment facility. Furthermore, 59 percent reported receiving treatment or counseling related to their drinking *before* attending AA, and 74 percent of those said it had played an important role in directing them to the fellowship. Finally, 58 percent of AA members continued to receive treatment or counseling *after* coming into AA. The efficacy of this treatment-recovery nexus has been confirmed in studies demonstrating that professional therapy is useful in initiating and sustaining Twelve-Step involvement and that making Twelve-Step recovery a focus of therapy increases its effectiveness.[2]

However, although there is strong evidence that Twelve-Step recovery can function symbiotically with professional treatment in the attainment of long-term sobriety, the influence of therapeutic culture on the recovery movement has led some to conclude that the program pioneered by AA has become hopelessly contaminated by alien concepts. In this chapter, we will define "Twelve-Step recovery" as conceived by AA and describe some of the therapeutic currents that have begun to influence it in recent years.[3]

Therapy Informing Recovery: A Personal Story

Today recovery overlaps with psychotherapy and other forms of professional treatment in part due to a growing awareness of the ways trauma and mental illness affect addiction. In my case, working with a therapist has helped clarify the roles of childhood trauma and chronic depression in my addictive processes. Using parts of my own story, I'll try to explain how these things intersect.

When I began working with the therapist who pushed me toward recovery, my initial diagnosis was "major depressive disorder." This was no surprise. I had experienced intermittent bouts of depression since childhood and had been taking antidepressant medication since a debilitating mental health episode fifteen years earlier. But while pharmaceuticals had worked well for many years, they were no match for the crises I was experiencing when I sought professional help. My wife had departed unexpectedly for inpatient treatment in another state, leaving me with our three-year-old child, and I barely saw or heard from my older children, both teenagers, who had succumbed to my ex-wife's efforts to alienate them from me, their brother, and their stepmother. Major depression, indeed.

What I came to see in the course of therapy was that over time, I had learned to medicate my depression—and anxiety, fear, and rage—with a variety of chemicals and processes that were culturally acceptable but spiritually deadening. To explore this connection between my depression and my addictive tendencies, I followed my therapist's recommendation and began attending a Twelve-Step fellowship. As my reluctance to admit I had a problem dissipated, I came to identify with the stories being told in recovery meetings and eventually dared to share my own. Over time, I noticed that people sometimes spoke about how their early experiences had set them up for addiction. Curious whether the same might be true for me, I began to explore this question with my therapist.

Eventually, I came to identify childhood neglect as one root of my chronic depression and addictive behavior. Doing so was not easy for me, as I have an emotional investment in the image of a happy family of origin in which I play the role of hero child. But in therapy, stories I had long regarded as humorous tales of growing up in the '60s were revealed to be traumatic and character-shaping. For instance, as a toddler being watched by my grandparents, I discovered a container of dishwashing powder beneath their kitchen sink, picked up the scoop that rested in the open bin, and imbibed enough of the detergent to sustain serious burns and require gastric suction ("stomach pumping"). Around the same time, I wandered away from home on my tricycle and found my way onto a four-lane thoroughfare. Somewhat miraculously, I was recognized, rescued, and returned home safely by our milkman.

I have no distinct memories of these events, and in neither case was I seriously harmed. But they resonate with experiences I do recall and that contributed to an abiding childhood sense of feeling unsafe and unseen. One of these experiences involves getting to school each morning. When I was five, my family moved to a major metropolitan area, where I, the oldest of three children, would attend first grade. Because my father was starting medical school and my mother was working outside the home and wrangling two toddlers, I was left on my own to walk to the local bus stop, where, along with other neighborhood kids, I waited with a dime in my hand for a chartered city bus. But since many buses passed that corner each morning, it was paramount that we board the one bearing the designation "SPECIAL."

Until I began group therapy, I had never talked much about this part of my childhood because nothing bad had ever happened to me as a result of taking a city bus to and from school. For four years, I managed to board the right bus, end up at school safe and sound, and excel academically. As I grew older, having been left on my own to negotiate that bus stop barely registered in my memory. But as I learned in therapy, it had registered deeply in my psyche and in my body. When fellow group members pointed out that first graders in urban areas are generally not left on their own to negotiate city transit systems—and that having to discern whether a bus was "special" would have been stressful for a child just learning to read—I was able to acknowledge the traumatic impact of this experience for the first time.

Regardless of whether my bus stop story qualifies as what today is known as an adverse childhood experience, for me it has come to represent a period of my life during which I often felt alone, afraid, and uncomforted. Perhaps the other kids at that bus stop were fine; but I needed more from the adults in my life—more supervision, more support, more comfort. I know my parents did the best they could in their circumstances and had no malicious intent. And yet, this and other situations in which I was left to negotiate unfamiliar situations without adult guidance fed a childhood need to self-soothe that eventually contributed to an adult attachment disorder. I have revisited that bus stop many times in therapy and have sculpted the scene with the help of group members; each time I experience profound feelings of fear and help-lessness. "You're still terrified of getting on the wrong bus," my therapist has commented more than once. And he is right.

This part of my story indicates how therapeutic insight into one's early ex-periences can change how one engages in recovery. And it raises a question: If childhood neglect does underlie my adult problems, isn't it reasonable that my caregivers share some of the blame? This is a question faced by those whom therapy leads to view their difficulties in the light of family dysfunction and learned coping mechanisms. They may also be encouraged to do so by some of the recovery trends that have emerged since the 1970s.

The Recovery Revolution

In part because of AA's success in helping alcoholics find and maintain sobriety, and in part because problem drinking is a requirement for membership in the fellowship, over the years hundreds of nonalcoholic groups have adapted AA's program to fit their own needs. The process began in 1951 with the founding of Al-Anon and Alateen, Twelve-Step fellowships that addressed alcoholism's impact on spouses and adolescent children. The next two decades witnessed the birth of Twelve-Step groups for those struggling with problems beyond alcohol abuse, including Narcotics Anonymous (1953), Potsmokers Anony-mous (1968), and Emotions Anonymous (1971). Then, beginning in the mid-1970s, a new wave of AA adaptations gave rise to two groups—Adult Children of Alcoholics and Dysfunctional Families (ACA, 1978) and Co-Dependents Anonymous (CoDA, 1986)—that subtly revised the Twelve-Step model. As Trysh Travis summarizes this development, these groups combined Twelve-Step recovery with a humanist self-actualization project that drew recovery into "the floodlit mainstream of popular discourses of the self."[4]

ACA and CoDA emerged as part of what came to be known as the recovery revolution, which was powered not only by an expansion in the variety and character of recovery fellowships but also by explosive growth in the number of therapeutic professionals and the availability of public and private funding to support addiction treatment. Responding to and accelerating these changes was a deluge of recovery-themed publications, a phenomenon *Publisher's Weekly* in 1990 called "the rage for recovery." But because the new generation of recovery writers behind this phenomenon had shallow roots in AA and mutual-aid spirituality, their work tended to conflate recovery with self-help, a movement that at the time was addressing conditions as far flung as hair loss, transvestitism, narcolepsy, and inflammatory bowel disease.[5]

In the wake of this revolution, much of what passed as "recovery" located the roots of adult dysfunction in childhood trauma and faulty socialization rather than characterological deficiencies such as selfishness and grandiosity, which were emphasized in AA. Because my own therapists were committed to Twelve-Step philosophy, they were able to illuminate the role played by emotional abandonment in my addictive process while insisting that I take responsibility for my adult character defects and the behaviors that issued from them. In this respect, they were carrying on the legacy of their teacher Sharon Wegscheider-Cruse, who applied Twelve-Step principles to treatment of the alcoholic family during the 1970s. In *Another Chance: Hope and Help for the Alcoholic Family* (1981), Wegscheider-Cruse described the dynamic system that coalesces around chemically dependent persons, including the family roles, rules, and scripts that serve to maintain equilibrium in the system. But she insisted that addiction was not a symptom of family dysfunction, but a primary disease that treatment professionals should work hand-in-hand with Twelve-Step groups to address.[6]

Through the work of Wegscheider-Cruse and others, family systems theory brought a sharper focus to addiction's impact on coaddicts and led to family treatment becoming a standard part of recovery from chemical dependency. In the 1980s, however, concern for coaddicts in the alcoholic family was displaced by attention to a generalized condition called "codependency" (based on the notion that someone affected by another's dependency, whatever its nature, is codependent). Codependency thus lost its unique association with substance abuse and was applied to an expanding range of maladaptive behaviors and relationships to which much of the population could seemingly relate. As codependency theorists focused on the ways dysfunctional families shape the behavior and self-image of adults, many in recovery began to ask the question I faced as part of my own therapeutic process: Were my addictive issues problems for which I was responsible, or did their roots in my family system take me off the hook, so to speak?[7]

Twelve-Step Philosophy, Therapeutic Culture, and Humanistic Psychology

An excellent resource for tracing how the therapeutic insights driving the recovery revolution stretched and altered the Twelve-Step paradigm is John

Steadman Rice's *A Disease of One's Own: Psychotherapy, Addiction and the Emergence of Co-Dependency* (1996), which explores how the philosophical underpinnings of the codependency movement that burst into popular consciousness during the 1980s subtly affected the Twelve-Step model.

Key to the codependency movement's success, according to Rice, were best-selling books by Melody Beattie, John Bradshaw, and others that invested the term *codependency* with cultural currency, publishing and marketing networks that popularized these authors' ideas, and an exponential increase in the number of support groups where baby boomers learned and enacted the movement's scripts. Since the 1980s the concept of codependency has been much maligned—for diagnostic imprecision, a lack of empirical support, assertions that it affects nearly everyone, and claims that it explains the problems of communities and even whole societies. But Rice's critique is focused on the way the codependency movement effected subtle but fundamental changes in the concepts of addiction and coaddiction that stemmed from AA and the twentieth-century alcoholism movement (discussed in a later chapter).

According to Rice, the codependency movement advanced three novel ideas. First, it conceived codependency as an addictive disease in its own right, rather than a condition caused by intimacy with an addict. Second, it imagined a reversal in the causal relationship between addiction and coaddiction, viewing codependency as the cause rather than the effect of addictive behavior. Third, it located the ultimate source of codependency, and thus of addiction, in repressive socialization practices. In this sense, the movement conformed to what Rice calls the discourse of "liberation psychotherapy," whose cardinal principles are the innate benevolence of human nature, the repressive character of societal structures, and the latter's role as a source of psychological and social ills. In this sense, codependency became infused with the ethos of humanistic psychology, which asserted that, despite a collapse of stable values outside the individual that left "no place else to turn but inward, to the self," self-actualized persons could be trusted to "do right."[8]

Rice emphasizes that despite its portrayal as a culmination of insights about addiction stemming from AA and family alcoholism treatment, the codependency movement's foundational ideas actually represented a significant defection from Twelve-Step philosophy. Most crucial was its reversal of AA's understanding of the relationship between self and society. According to Twelve-Step philosophy, the addict harms others, inevitably but unintentionally, in behaviors that are both symptoms and consequences of his or her disease, and self-justifying explanations for these behaviors are considered examples of the denial that is one manifestation of the disease process. But, according to Rice, in displacing AA's emphasis on taking responsibility for wrongs done *to* others with a focus on identifying wrongs inflicted *by* others, the codependency movement fostered "a qualitative reversal" in the logic of recovery.[9]

In other words, the codependency movement's utilization of Twelve-Step language contributed to a fateful confusion of therapeutic and recovery cultures. Rice identifies a major site of this confusion in Adult Children of Alcoholics and Dysfunctional Families (ACA), a fellowship through which codependency's "truth rules" were introduced into the Twelve-Step world. Inasmuch as it explained how childhood roles learned in alcoholic families could affect adult experience, ACA was a natural extension of Al-Anon, Ala-teen, and family systems theory. But what appeared to be a natural evolution in the Twelve-Step paradigm brought about a radically new understanding of the self-society relationship. As Rice puts it, while traditional Twelve-Step practice encouraged addicts to review the past in order to identify and address the ways one had harmed others "in disease," ACA counseled "adult children" to locate the source of their disease in the "repressions meted out in the course of primary socialization."[10]

The next step in therapeuticizing Twelve-Step culture came in 1986 with the founding of Co-Dependents Anonymous (CoDA), a fellowship that spread like wildfire across the American landscape, spawning over two thousand chapters in a single year. Since CoDA was chiefly concerned with the psychic wounds inflicted in dysfunctional family systems, it furthered what Rice calls the "qualitative reversal of the mood in which recovery is conceived and exercised." That is, CoDA encouraged those recovering from codependency to focus on experiences of "abandonment and abuse" that, in the parlance of John Bradshaw, contaminate the innocent "inner child" with "toxic shame." And since codependency theory locates the source of adult problems in the dysfunctional family broadly conceived, CoDA members did not have to identify addiction in themselves or their families of origin. Indeed, when the range of early experiences deemed abusive includes divorce, self-righteousness, and even "rigidity," any family can operate like an alcoholic family.[11]

Attending a variety of CoDA meetings in the 1990s, Rice found that participants had assimilated the codependency movement's ethos, particularly the conviction that addiction's roots are to be found in childhood shame that "binds" codependents to ways of living that are incongruous with their true selves. Comments in CoDA meetings, Rice found, reflected shared experiences of childhood abandonment expressed in phrases such as "rigid standards," "criticism," and "emotionally unavailable fathers." Based on his experience as a participant-observer in CoDA meetings, Rice concluded that the fellowship had more in common with conventional group therapy than with traditional Twelve-Step groups.[12]

Feminism and Post-Twelve-Step Recovery

Further perspective on late twentieth-century developments in recovery culture is offered by Trysh Travis's *Language of the Heart: A Cultural History of the Recovery Movement from Alcoholics Anonymous to Oprah Winfrey* (2013). Travis agrees with Rice that the "hybrid psycho-spiritual discourse" adopted by ACA and CoDA reflects a thorough commingling of therapeutic and Twelve-Step principles. But her chief focus is the broader "feminization" of AA traditions in which these groups participated, a trend more fully realized in what she calls "post–12 Step recovery."

According to Travis, the feminization of Twelve-Step culture and the emergence of "post–12 Step recovery" were products of the "women's alcoholism movement" of the 1970s, which reflected the reality that women had begun to benefit from expanded treatment options, as well as federal addiction money targeting special populations. Like codependency theory, the women's alcoholism movement significantly revised Twelve-Step philosophy, according to Travis, in this case by claiming that in women the etiology of alcoholism is not an effort to "run the show ourselves" (as in AA) but a lack of self-esteem, making the condition's antidote not humble surrender but increased empowerment. Among those whose contributions to the women's alcoholism movement Travis details are Jean Kirkpatrick and Karen Casey.[13]

In 1975 Kirkpatrick founded Women for Sobriety (WFS) as an alternative to AA. Anticipating the logic of the yet-to-be-born codependency movement, WFS effectively reversed the direction of the self-society relationship assumed in AA, claiming that the "feelings of inadequacy and unhappiness" that cause women to drink result not from their own failings and character defects but from "distorted expectations placed on them by a male-dominated society." While AA's emphasis on *powerlessness* encourages a woman to surrender her problem to a Higher Power, Kirkpatrick wrote, WFS's emphasis on *control* leads her to think "about why she drank." Accordingly, WFS's "13 Steps" stress self-empowerment rooted in women's natural capacities to analyze the thoughts, feelings, and behaviors that underlie problem drinking (195, 196, 197).

Casey, who became managing editor of Hazelden's publishing division in 1979, is key for understanding the treatment industry's role in bringing feminism and codependency theory to bear on the recovery movement. In 1982 Hazelden released Casey's *Each Day a New Beginning*, a collection of daily recovery devotions for women that portrayed alcoholism less as a disease than as a by-product of low self-esteem resulting from women's internalization of patriarchal culture and its discounting of their worth and capabilities. According to Travis, Casey's thorough revision of AA's description of alcoholism as a result of "self-will run riot" amounted to a "radical rewriting of the etiology of addiction" (151, 155, 159).

In 1986 Hazelden entered the codependency market when it released Melody Beattie's *Codependent No More*, which defined as codependent anyone affected by another person's behavior to the point of becoming obsessed with controlling that person. Like other writers influenced by the women's alcoholism movement, Beattie perceived the basis of addictive patterns in low self-esteem; and like other codependency theorists, she believed these patterns were rooted in the unfinished business of childhood. Thus, she located the cure for adult women's "low self-worth or self-hatred" in efforts to nurture the "frightened, vulnerable, needy child inside us." According to Beattie, recovery for codependency was not to be found in active fellowship with other sufferers (as in AA) but in individuation and autonomy, a fact startlingly clear in her dedication of *Codependent No More* to herself. Because the book's relentless self-focus makes it difficult for Travis to imagine "a more thorough inversion of the 12-Step philosophy," it is ironic that *Codependent No More* became a main vehicle for recovery's entry into the US cultural mainstream (170).

Another cultural conduit for post-Twelve-Step recovery was Alice Walker's *The Color Purple* (1982), which Travis calls "perhaps the most important feminist recovery text to appear in the early 1980s." Travis refers to Celie's story as a narrative of "self-recovery," a journey "from a place of spiritual darkness into a full and happy humanity" made possible by shedding the internalized norms that oppress her. Celie's self-liberation, in other words, is not a project of surrender, self-scrutiny, and amends-making, but of "acceptance, forgiveness and the healing power of love." Travis notes that *The Color Purple*'s remarkable success revealed a considerable market for this sort of feminist recovery narrative among well-educated and affluent female baby boomers (209, 211, 224, 225, 226).

The most effective evangelist for post-Twelve-Step recovery was no doubt the woman who played Sophia in the movie version of *The Color Purple*— Oprah Winfrey, who beginning in the late 1980s used her television show, magazine, and book club to develop and disseminate her own version of "recovered selfhood." During its first season in 1986–87, "The Oprah Winfrey

Show" became a showcase for post-Twelve-Step culture by providing a platform for "adult children" suffering from a host of substance and process addictions. By the 1989–90 season, Winfrey was devoting a program each month to addiction and was increasingly open about her identity as a compulsive overeater and a survivor of childhood sexual abuse (232, 168, 230).

Winfrey's struggle with food provided the background for her 1996 book *Make the Connection* (coauthored with Bob Greene), in which she offered her own vision of recovery that blended traditional Twelve-Step philosophy and therapeutic insights. Reflecting the feminist assumptions of the post-Twelve-Step movement, Winfrey identified low self-esteem as the precipitating factor in her food addiction and prescribed a solution for emotional eating that included "10 Steps to a Better Body." The last of these—"a ritual for recognizing the falsity of negative ideas . . . and focusing on the true self and its desires"— was a tribute to the influence of New Thought on Winfrey's brand of recovery. The appearance of New Thought themes in this context was hardly a coincidence. In fact, the phenomenon is so fundamental to post-Twelve-Step culture that an appreciation of the recovery revolution's ambiguous relationship to AA spirituality requires that we explore it more thoroughly (235).

New Thought and Recovery Spirituality

For decades, AA's roots in the Oxford Group kept Twelve-Step recovery tethered fairly closely to what Ernest Kurtz and Katherine Ketcham call "the spirituality of imperfection." But these ties began to loosen with the advent of the women's alcoholism movement, codependency theory, and the discourse of personal recovery celebrated by Alice Walker and Oprah Winfrey. The philosophical thread connecting these iterations of the recovery revolution was New Thought, a nineteenth-century American religious movement rooted in the convictions that Infinite Intelligence (God) is everywhere, that true human selfhood is divine, that the powers of the universe are directly respondent to one's needs, that one's thoughts are forces, that sickness originates in the mind, and that "right thinking" has a healing effect.[14]

Women for Sobriety, the woman-centered alternative to AA founded by Jean Kirkpatrick in 1975, became one conduit for New Thought's entry into post-Twelve-Step culture. A member of the New Thought–influenced Unity Church, Kirkpatrick exhorted WFS members to create the world in which they wanted to live using the "power of mind." For instance, WFS taught women to control their alcohol consumption by *thinking* about why they drink. As Travis points out, New Thought's emphasis on the healing power of one's mental state was explicit in several of WFS's New Life Program Acceptance Statements, particularly 2 ("negative emotions destroy only myself") and 5 ("I am what I think"). New Thought's influence on Casey, another adherent of the Unity School of Christianity, was evident in *Each Day a New Beginning*, the recovery devotional in which AA's masculine Higher Power was replaced by "a feeling of presence . . . something to tap into—always accessible, not judgmental." According to Travis, Casey's advice that women heed a "special 'inner voice'" placed the self at the center of the recovery process, thus "effectively inverting [AA's] critique of self-will and self-centeredness."[15]

As we have seen, another point of entry for New Thought into the recovery mainstream was *The Oprah Winfrey Show*, which went national in 1986. Winfrey's connection with this tradition was explicit in declarations such as "I am Spirit come from the greatest Spirit," "I am highly tuned to my Divine Self," and "once you tap into [the God force that lives inside us] you can do anything." Among the New Thought voices Winfrey featured in the show's first season was Unity Church pastor, author, and future presidential candidate Marianne Williamson. Winfrey's message that "changing your life . . . [is] about really changing the way you think" moved even further into the forefront in subsequent seasons of *The Oprah Winfrey Show*.[16]

As Winfrey's quotes in the previous paragraph suggest, a common trope in New Thought–inflected recovery discourse is the association, and even identification, of the self with God. Among the earliest recovery guides to promote this discourse was *The Twelve Steps for Everyone Who Really Wants Them* (1975), which encouraged members of Emotional Health Anonymous to discover "ourselves and the God within us" and "live our lives according to the guidance of this spiritual Self." The recovery toolbox offered by *The Twelve Steps for Everyone* contained fifteen principles of emotional and spiritual development, including engaging in "an ongoing search toward my spiritual center" and coming ever closer to "the Higher Power that is partially within me."[17]

Another recovery guide animated by New Thought sensibilities is Christina Grof's *The Thirst for Wholeness: Attachment, Addiction and the Spiritual Path* (1993), in which the author combines transpersonal psychology, Eastern mysticism, holotropic breathwork, perinatal experiences (memories from before, during, and after one's biological birth), and Twelve-Step principles in forging "a path to the deeper Self." Along this path, Grof writes, we tap into "the sacred force" people refer to as "God." While Grof appears to endorse the surrender emphasized by traditional Twelve-Step recovery, it is only as a means of achieving awareness of the deeper Self that "swim[s] in the glory of

Cosmic Consciousness." According to Grof, God is not "outside us"; rather, the "power greater than ourselves" named in Twelve-Step recovery *is* the deeper Self—a "divine reservoir within us [that] is literally our Higher Power." "God dwells within you as you," Grof is told by her Indian guru, a view she seems to recommend as the key to recovery.[18]

In *One Journey, Many Roads* (1992), Charlotte Davis Kasl offers a Quaker-inspired version of recovery that is permeated by the divine self motif. Kasl understands human beings—addicts included—as sacred persons who are born holy and in whom "God or Goddess or Spirit" resides. Thus, the goal of recovery is to achieve not a self "deflated at depth," as AA would have it, but one "continually merging with awareness and compassion." Viewing oneself as "one-down" relative to a God "out there," Kasl claims, discourages us from finding our own voice and articulating our "authentic, creative Self." As an alternative, Kasl touts a life-loving version of spirituality that perceives "God, Goddess, and the Great Spirit" as residing within us and interprets this Being's healing work as a "cooperative union between the power of the Universe and [our] own will."[19]

Leo Booth is another author whose vision of recovery is shaped by New Thought's emphasis on the self's "essential divinity." In *The Happy Heretic*, Booth offers a mash-up of Pelagius, Rumi, and "noetic science" designed to revise traditional understandings of spirituality. Booth's central claims are that God's creativity "exists in each of us" and that we live the good life when "we express and participate in the divine." Because people in Twelve-Step programs remain unaware of their "essential divinity" and innate perfection, Booth explains, they ask God to do "what they should be doing or creating for themselves." Thus, Twelve-Step recovery encourages the "religious codependence" fostered by traditional Christianity, whose "crippling teaching of sinfulness" causes believers to mistrust themselves and look outward for guidance. Since Booth is convinced that spirituality involves "discovering me . . . [and] God working with me," it is not surprising that he decided to leave the Episcopal Church for the Unity School of Christianity.[20]

As these examples suggest, in the wake of the recovery revolution the divine self theme associated with New Thought has become ubiquitous in the literature of "recovery." In *Beyond the Twelve Steps*, Lynn Grabhorn lays out "a path . . . to reconnect us with our own divinity." In *Freedom from Addiction*, Deepak Chopra and David Simon assert that the Higher Power required to escape the grip of addiction is actually "the higher self." In *Recovery: The Twelve Steps as Spiritual Practice*, Rami Shapiro argues that addiction results from the "optical delusion that we are apart from, rather than a part of, the Whole that is God." He maintains that behind the addicted you there is a greater you "that Hindus call *atman* and Westerners call soul, a unique manifestation of God that is your true self." Thus, Shapiro writes, recovery entails "the discovery that you are part of the Divine."[21]

And then there is *A Course in Miracles*, the neo-Gnostic spiritual franchise to which some advocates of recovery refer as the "thirteenth step," and which has generated Step-course parallels analogous to the Step-Scripture lists produced by Christians. We could go on and on, but by now it should be clear that the influence of New Thought on recovery culture raises an important concern for those interested in recovering church. In an environment where New Thought and New Age principles have taken root like kudzu on a southern hillside, how do Christians determine what strains of recovery spirituality are compatible with their faith commitments and which are not?[22]

Before turning to this question, we should note that the discernment process is particularly challenging when New Thought assumptions make their way into explicitly Christian adaptations of Twelve-Step spirituality. A good example of this phenomenon is Vernon J. Bittner's *Twelve Steps for Christian Living* (1987). Bittner claims the Steps contain "the basic concepts of the Christian faith," but his view of recovery resonates more with New Thought than with Christian anthropology. The keys to recovery, according to Bittner, are "affirm[ing] our power," finding our "true self," developing "self-trust," "grow[ing] in self-esteem," and "making amends with" and "affirming" ourselves. All this is in the interest, Bittner writes, of allowing "the 'Christ' within to come forth," a process impeded by the "fear many people have . . . of their own DIVINITY."[23]

Twelve-Step Spirituality vs. Recovery Mind-Cure

Without doubt, illuminating the spiritual roots and fruits of post-Twelve-Step culture raises discernment issues for Christians. Where is the boundary between Christian theism and New Thought pantheism? Between Christian anthropology and belief in divine selfhood? Between the doctrine of providence and "Cosmic Consciousness"? We may disagree about whether or not the exotic spiritual concepts endorsed in recovery literature are consistent with Christian faith; but if they are incompatible with Twelve-Step philosophy, churches seeking to emulate AA should be wary of them.

Even within AA, of course, it has sometimes been difficult to distinguish Oxford Group–inspired religiosity from popular mysticism. This is in part because Bill W. and Dr. Bob both were avid spiritualists who were influenced by esoteric religious traditions associated with New Thought, including Sweden-borgianism, which was Lois Wilson's family religion, and Christian Science, which Bill explored in the years prior to AA's founding. Indeed, although the Pietist inheritance of the Oxford Group predominates in AA's printed litera-ture, what Travis calls New Thought's "expansive mysticism" can be detected in AA pioneers' confidence in a beneficent moral order and their belief in an accessible, personal, and nonjudgmental Higher Power that works in the lives of the faithful.[24]

Yet William James's reflections on the "varieties" of American religiosity are helpful in distinguishing traditional Twelve-Step spirituality from versions of recovery informed by New Thought. In *The Varieties of Religious Experi-ence*, James refers to New Thought as "mind-cure" or "the gospel of healthy-mindedness," his names for an idealist tendency that speaks "to persons for whom the conception of salvation has lost its ancient theological meaning, but who labor nevertheless with the same eternal human difficulty." According to James, the question asked by the healthy minded is "what shall I do to be clear, right, sound, whole, and well?" Their answer? "You are well, sound and clear already, if you did but know it. . . . You must awaken to the knowledge of your real being." For these souls, whom James describes as "once born," redemption is achieved through right thinking and confidence that "the powers of the universe" will respond to one's needs.[25]

In addition to the mind's ability to transform reality, advocates of "mind-cure" or "healthy mindedness" emphasize the soul's innate perfection and divinity. James refers to New Thought's "decidedly pantheistic" perception of humans' higher nature as "already one with the Divine without any miracle of grace, or abrupt creation of a new inner man." We are not only "partakers in the life of God," asserts a mind-cure advocate whom James cites, but "in essence the life of God and the life of man are identically the same." When we realize "our oneness with the Infinite Spirit," the man continues, we learn that to turn inward "is to live in the presence of God or [our] divine self," to "recognize our own divinity."[26]

As we have seen, the discourse of the divine self that James identifies as essential to New Thought is a common theme in recovery spirituality. But any version of recovery controlled by this discourse would seem to be incompatible with the Twelve-Step principle that the chief pitfall on the addict's journey toward God, not to mention sobriety, is the expansive self. As *Twelve Steps and Twelve Traditions* reminds us, earnest religious beliefs remain barren when we try to play God. Or as historian Ernest Kurtz puts it, the fundamental and first message of Alcoholics Anonymous is that human beings "are not infinite, not absolute, *not* God." In fact, according to Kurtz, AA has only two things to say on the subject of God: "First, there *is* one. And second, you're not it. From there, you're on your own." Obviously, this excludes any notion of recovery as a process of accepting and embracing one's essential divinity.[27]

As Kurtz goes on to remind us, AA's founders not only rejected New Thought's discourse of the divine self; they dissented from the entire worldview of healthy mindedness. In fact, Bill W. and Dr. Bob represented a variety of religious experience James attributed to "sick souls," whose conception of existence as "morbid" and "pessimistic" made them the antitype of the healthy minded. Believing "the evil aspects of our life are of its very essence," James wrote, these "twice-born people" seek a supernatural remedy for the "wrongness or vice in [their] essential nature." In the view of these sick souls, the self is not so much divine as divided, riven by "inner instability, tension, and conflict." In Jamesean terms, as the product of sick souls' efforts to get and remain sober, AA's program is not a "mere reversion to natural health" but a "religion of deliverance" that offers a "second birth."[28]

Those who can acknowledge their "sickness" and accept their limits live by what we have called the "spirituality of imperfection." In doing so, they embody the idea—captured and amplified by AA—that to be human is to be essentially *mixed*, finite, and limited, that is, not God. Their acknowledgment of finitude becomes an antidote to the self-centeredness and grandiosity that drive addiction and makes way for the humility that is among the chief signs of the spiritual life. While the purportedly divine self refuses to acknowledge its essential weakness and insists on becoming its own Higher Power, the spirituality of imperfection at the heart of Twelve-Step recovery denies the self's ability to direct its own play, as the Big Book puts it.[29]

Based on this analysis, it is clear that recovery forsakes Twelve-Step spirituality when it denies that human beings are in need of a power who comes to save them from outside, who challenges their efforts at control, and who relieves them of their grandiose notions of identity with the divine. Indicative of Twelve-Step spirituality's biblical roots, recovery that opposes the discourse of the divine self also corresponds with a scripturally informed theological anthropology. As Dietrich Bonhoeffer writes in *Creation and Fall*, there is a fundamental difference between God creating humankind "in God's image" (*imago dei*) and humanity's seeking to be "like God" (*sicut deus*). For Bonhoeffer, these represent distinct and opposing modes of existence before God:

Imago dei—humankind in the image of God in being for God and the neighbor, in its original creatureliness and limitedness; sicut deus—humankind like God in knowing out of its own self about good and evil, in having no limit and acting out of its own resources, in its aseity [self-sufficiency], in its being alone.

As "the human being who is God incarnate," Bonhoeffer writes, Christ is sacrificed on behalf of humankind *sicut deus*, "in true divinity slaying its false divinity and restoring the imago dei."[30]

Conclusion

The historical review undertaken in this and the previous chapter illumines two facts that will guide us as we consider the ways American Christians have responded to and adapted Twelve-Step recovery. First, AA and the Twelve-Step fellowships based on it have been conduits for a broad range of spiritualities, from evangelical Pietism, to the "spirituality of imperfection," to New Thought pantheism. Second, the recovery revolution that began in the 1980s, and whose influence continues to be felt, presents both promise and peril for the church's efforts in the area of recovery.

On the one hand, the Twelve-Step model's recent accommodation of process addictions, codependency, and family dysfunction has made recovery attractive to church folk who may assume they have nothing in common with "real addicts." On the other hand, the mixing of therapeutic and recovery cultures in the wake of the recovery revolution makes it difficult to assess how much of what passes as "recovery" is consistent with the Twelve-Step tradition. This has encouraged Christian critics of Twelve-Step recovery to associate it with ideas and trends to which it is quite foreign. To that problem we now turn.

Is Recovery Anti-Christian?

(nope)

I recently taught an online course for seminary students called Spirituality and the Twelve Steps. In one of her weekly posts, a student wrote that some of her ministry peers had expressed strong feelings about her decision to enroll in the class. "Every single one of them gave me what I call 'the warning,'" she wrote, which was essentially that although Twelve-Step recovery may have begun on a solid spiritual basis, at some point, in an effort to be "progressive and politically correct," God was "taken out" of the Twelve-Step program and replaced with vague references to a Higher Power. This perspective, which is not uncommon in the more conservative precincts of the Christian world, has existed in some form since AA's emergence. This chapter explores the arguments of those who claim the Twelve-Step model is fundamentally anti-Christian ("rejecters"), while those who believe it must be revised for use in the church ("adapters") are the subject of chapter 7, and Christians who believe the gospel message is incorporated in, or implied by, Twelve-Step recovery ("embracers") are treated in chapter 8.

The Rejecters

Christian rejection of Twelve-Step recovery can take many forms, including *silence*. For instance, Calvary Chapel's "One Step to Freedom" curriculum avoids any mention of the Steps since, according to the program, "it only takes one step to Jesus to set you free." Another rejection strategy is *disassociation*, exhibited in Addiction Recovery Ministry's claim that it is not a "program" and involves no steps, meetings, or sponsors. Rejection can also take the form of *warning*. This is the approach taken by the pastors who cautioned my student about studying Twelve-Step spirituality, as well as by organizations like Recovery Reformation, whose website spells out "5 Ways That Alcoholics

Anonymous and the Twelve Steps Insult Jesus Christ." Even renting space to such groups carries spiritual danger, according to the group. For if your congregation allows AA to meet on its premises, "the Devil is running rampant in an orgy of destroying souls in your own Church."[1]

A more common, and more subtle, strategy for rejecting Twelve-Step recovery is *replacement*. Uncomfortable with the Twelve-Step program but recognizing the need to compete with it for the minds and hearts of hurting people, Christian authors and groups have developed dozens of alternative recovery schemes. As they generally include a short list of steps or principles, these plans share formal similarities with the AA program; but it is important that they be easily distinguished from it as well. This means that if substitute programs include steps, they will not number twelve; and if they do number twelve, they will not be referred to as steps. Thus, Neil T. Anderson offers seven "Steps to Freedom in Christ" and Michael Wren describes "Ten Biblical Steps to Freedom," while Russell Willingham marks the path to "breaking free" from sex addiction with "Twelve Essentials," "Sinners Anonymous" identifies twelve "Crisis Points" along "the path to spiritual healing," and Pam Morrison develops twelve "soul-healing" Bible studies for recovering addicts.[2]

Ten is a popular number in these alternative schemes, perhaps because of its biblical resonance. For instance, Reformers Unanimous offers "Ten Principles for Overcoming Stubborn Habits," principles 6 ("those who do not love the Lord will not help us serve the Lord") and 8 ("it is not possible to fight a fleshly temptation with fleshly weapons") communicating the group's suspicion toward secular recovery programs. Meanwhile, Edward T. Welch's "Ten Steps Away from Addiction" endorse the Twelve-Step themes of unmanageability, insanity, selfishness, resentment, humility, and surrender, but concludes that AA's program is theologically deficient.[3]

Seven, another number with biblical significance, is also popular in Christian alternatives to the Twelve Steps. The "Seven Stages on the Path" are the creation of Nate Larkin, the former pastor and recovering sex addict whom we met in an earlier chapter. These stages are designed for use in the Samson Society, a mutual aid fellowship for Christian men desiring to "live their lives together openly as equals, playing as a team." Samson Society meetings reflect Twelve-Step philosophy and practice in several ways, for instance, by rotating leadership, standardizing readings, prohibiting advice-giving, and using the Lord's Prayer as a closing ritual. But the "Seven Stages on the Path" are Larkin's attempt to "retranslate" the Twelve Steps, "appropriating the principles that AA had borrowed from the Bible and rephrasing them in an effort to recover them for the church."[4]

Another seven-fold Christian recovery plan is Mark Laaser's "7 Principles of Living in Everyday Freedom." Principle 1 ("admit that your life has become unmanageable") is a reiteration of Step 1, while principle 2 ("believe in God, accept the grace offered through His Son Jesus Christ, and surrender our lives and our wills to Him on a daily basis") restates Steps 2 and 3 in Trinitarian language, and principle 3 ("become aware of your own sins and weaknesses, and confess them to a safe group of spiritual people") encompasses the actions in Steps 4–6. As Laaser's program is essentially a reiteration of the Twelve Steps, one naturally wonders why he found it necessary to restate them as "7 principles."[5]

The same question arises when one examines the "Eight Principles" of Celebrate Recovery, which represent a rewording and reshuffling of the Twelve Steps with little effort to disguise this fact. For instance, principle 1 ("I am powerless to control my tendency to do the wrong thing and . . . my life is unmanageable"), principle 2 ("earnestly believe that God exists, that I matter to Him and that He has the power to help me recover"), and principle 3 ("consciously choose to commit all my life and will to Christ's care and control") are only slightly revised versions of Steps 1–3. Instead of reinventing the Twelve Steps as "Eight Principles," why not acknowledge that they are serviceable in a Christian context? The answer, as we will see in the next chapter, is tied up with a perceived need to establish the "biblical" character of Christian recovery programs.[6]

Why Reject Twelve-Step Recovery?

Why ignore, disassociate from, warn about, or replace the Steps? Some Christians offer reasoned arguments for their dismissal of Twelve-Step recovery, often echoing the complaints of secular critics. These include charges that AA treats symptoms rather than underlying causes, that its program is ineffective, that its notion of alcoholism as a life-long condition is needlessly stigmatizing, that people in AA substitute one dependency for another, and that the fellowship ignores environmental factors that contribute to addiction. But the charge that has found the most resonance among Christians who are suspicious of Twelve-Step recovery is that AA regards alcoholism as disease rather than sin, and thus cannot hold alcoholics responsible for their behavior.[7]

Stanton Peele's *Diseasing of America: How We Allowed Recovery Zealots and the Treatment Industry to Convince Us We Are Out of Control* (1985) is an influential attack on the so-called disease model of addiction that foregrounds this concern with responsibility. Peele emphasizes individuals' active agency in addiction and claims that the disease model excuses crime while depriving human beings of the opportunity for growth. In *Heavy Drinking: The Myth of Alcoholism as a Disease* (1989), Herbert Fingarette expands on Peele's critique and argues that the "scientifically discredited" disease concept is propped up by powerful institutions, including the health care industry. In *Rational Recovery: The New Cure for Substance Addiction* (1996), Jack Trimpey maintains that the conception of alcoholism as a disease "systemically absolves addicted people of responsibility" for their addictions. Refusing to view addiction as "habitual vice," Trimpey argues, removes addicts' "willful, purposeful immoral conduct" from the reach of moral judgment.[8]

Attacks on Twelve-Step recovery by these and other like-minded critics of the disease model of addiction reassert the efficacy of human agency, will-power, and self-awareness. Emphasizing the addict's ultimate responsibility for his or her behavior, they reclaim disfavored terms—including *habit, sin, vice,* and *immorality*—that describe addiction in terms of moral failure. Given their own investment in upholding free will and personal responsibility, it is easy to understand why Christian opponents of Twelve-Step recovery have relied on these criticisms of the disease model. But are they accurate, and do they apply to Twelve-Step recovery?[9]

AA and the Disease Model of Addiction

Defending Twelve-Step recovery from these charges requires that we examine the emergence of the disease model and the process by which it came to be associated with AA. For much of American history, the dominant cultural lens for perceiving the abuse of alcohol and other substances was the moral model, which viewed such abuse as sinful behavior for which one was personally cul-pable. Beginning in the nineteenth century, however, the moral model began to loosen its hold on the public consciousness as medical conceptions of in-ebriety led some to interpret habitual intemperance as a result of regular alco-hol consumption and the strong, perhaps uncontrollable, desire it created.

By the 1940s, the disease model was becoming ascendant in America under the influence of the so-called alcoholism movement. The movement dissem-inated its message—that as a treatable disease alcoholism was a public health issue—through a variety of education and advocacy programs, including the Yale Center of Alcohol Studies and the National Council for Education on Alcoholism (NCEA). Other institutional arms of the alcoholism movement were the Yale Summer School of Alcohol Studies, which educated community leaders in the burgeoning study of alcoholism, and the Yale Plan clinics, where outpatient alcoholism treatment was pioneered. The disease model received scientific backing in the *Quarterly Journal of Alcohol Studies,* which propagated editor E. M. Jellinek's view that the disease of alcoholism was "progressive, characterized by increased tolerance, craving, loss of control and a bottoming out that made treatment impossible."[10]

Within the scope of a few years, research and advocacy associated with the alcoholism movement resulted in wide acceptance of the disease model. In 1951, for instance, the World Health Organization declared alcoholism a disease, and by the early 1960s around 65 percent of Americans concurred with this assessment. They included President Lyndon Johnson, who in 1966 assured Congress that "the alcoholic suffers from a disease which will yield to scientific research and adequate treatment." As the alcoholism movement provided a scientific and medical basis for understanding chronic alcohol abuse, the moral model's influence steadily eroded among mainline Christians. Its displacement was already evident in midcentury denominational pronouncements, including a 1946 statement by the Presbyterian Church (USA) calling alcoholism "a disease which requires treatment." The denomination's General Assembly reiterated this view in 1949 and 1950, a full decade before the American Medical Association declared alcoholism a "medical problem."[11]

Yet despite these indications of the disease model's ascendancy in American culture, the moral model would remain firmly entrenched in some quarters of the Christian world. In 1967, for instance, when the Cooperative Commission on the Study of Alcoholism (a panel of experts financed by the National Institute of Mental Health) released a report that adopted a public health approach to alcohol problems, it was endorsed by ecumenical church organizations. But because the report called for responsible alcohol consumption and a lowering of the legal drinking age, official Christian responses varied. The flagship evangelical publication *Christianity Today,* for instance, criticized the commission for seeking to replace spiritual guidance with legal controls on drinking and concluded that "the Gospel of Jesus Christ is the only sure cure for alcoholism and every other sin." The stubborn persistence of the moral model was still in evidence two decades later when Billy Graham referred to drunkenness as "one of the oldest sins."[12]

AA's success paved the way for the alcoholism movement, just as it benefited from the movement's disease model advocacy. Representing the symbiosis between AA and the movement was Marty Mann, a prominent and attractive female member of the fellowship who was heavily involved in both the Yale Summer Schools and the National Council on Alcoholism (successor to the NCEA). As an unofficial spokesperson for the alcoholism movement, Mann personified the link between the disease model and AA, despite the group's refusal to take a public stand on matters of medical debate. AA's association with the disease concept was further strengthened by the encouragement that clients of Yale Plan clinics received to join AA, by Jellinek's use of AA members as research subjects, and by official AA publications that compared alcoholism to heart disease, diabetes, and cancer, medical analogies that commended themselves because in each case the disease's progress was easily observable although its origins remained obscure. Local AA groups even adapted and published assessment tools developed by alcoholism movement experts.[13]

But while AA program literature employed terms such as *illness, malady,* and *allergy* that tapped into a growing public consensus that alcoholism was better conceived as sickness than as sin, AA leaders were careful to avoid pulling the fellowship into medical controversy. Thus, despite AA cofounder Dr. Bob's conviction that the language of disease was necessary to communicate alcoholism's hopelessness, the closest the main text of the AA Big Book came to heeding this advice was in describing alcoholism as an "illness which only a spiritual experience will conquer." Careful use of language was particularly evident in public appearances by AA cofounder Bill Wilson, who called alcoholism a "complex malady" whose exact nature he left to the medical community to describe. When Wilson testified in 1969 before the Hughes Commission, which would prove to be crucial in lending government support to the disease model of alcoholism, he studiously avoided the terms *disease, illness,* and even *sick.*[14]

There was less caution on display during the 1970s, when AA publications took a perceptible turn toward endorsing the disease model. As many AA members became involved in alcoholism treatment, there was a "significant if not systemic overlap" between the fellowship and the rapidly expanding treatment industry. Because industry advocates were tasked with convincing medical, governmental, and insurance authorities that alcoholism was a genuine illness, the barrier between AA and the disease concept became further blurred. As Trysh Travis summarizes the situation, AA was "intimately involved in the legitimation and spread of the disease concept and in the development of the education/treatment/policy network that elaborated and institutionalized it." Thus, cultural forces tended to fuse the two in the popular mind.[15]

Christian Rejection of the Disease Model

Because this association endures, whenever there is pushback against the disease concept of addiction, AA and other Twelve-Step fellowships become natural targets of criticism. Already suspicious of "secular" recovery and lacking a nuanced understanding of the Twelve-Step program, Christian opponents echo and amplify the claims of critics like Peele, Fingarette, and Trimpey. Thus, theologian David Wells complains that Twelve-Step philosophy replaces the concept of sin with sickness, treating rebellious sinners as "innocent and injured children," while physician William Playfair argues that Twelve-Step groups put into practice "the principles of the disease model" by treating criminals as patients.[16]

Since Playfair has offered the most robust Christian critique of AA and Twelve-Step recovery, we will carefully review his case. In *The Useful Lie: How the Recovery Industry Has Entrapped America in a Disease Model of Addiction*, written in 1991 at the height of the recovery revolution's influence in American Christianity, Playfair emphatically rejects what he calls the "medical" model of addiction as unbiblical and unscientific, argues that addicts are driven by bad behavior rather than bad genes (at the time there was hope of discovering a genetic basis for alcoholism), and describes "Twelve Stepdom" as a counterfeit faith that endangers people's souls. Playfair further warns that, among American Christians, a moral understanding of addictive behavior was gradually being displaced by the view that compulsive behavior is the result of sickness. In Playfair's mind, this development signaled a fateful "diseasing of Christianity" (a phrase with clear echoes of Peele's "diseasing of America").[17]

Playfair assails the disease concept he identifies with Twelve-Step recovery, claiming it is an "open secret" that both are rooted in "bad science." Without a solid scientific basis, why does the "disease myth" persist? It does so because it is a *useful* lie, as it sustains the lucrative recovery industry and its army of Twelve-Step supporters. What really concerns Playfair, however, are the inroads the disease model has made into the American church as a result of its openness to Twelve-Step recovery. Playfair complains not only that churches have become home to addiction support groups he regards as extensions of the secular recovery industry but that Christian publishers have encouraged this trend.

Playfair has particular disdain for books by "Christianized Compromisers" Alexander DeJong, Dennis Morreim, and Tim Timmons—authors who tout AA's philosophy as being compatible with Christian faith and even "biblical." In contrast, Playfair contends for a return to the traditional, "common sense" view that drug users become addicts because they abuse drugs, that they are immoral because their addiction results from immoral behavior. Since the Bible describes addictive behaviors as "willful acts of iniquity," Playfair argues, the only truly "biblical" view is that the *sin* of abuse precedes and underlies the *sinful condition* of addiction. From this perspective, the cure for addictive behavior is rather straightforward: "Just as habits are made, so they can be broken and replaced. Say 'no' enough, and it increasingly becomes easier."[18]

Although few Christian critiques of Twelve-Step recovery are as thorough-going as Playfair's, many echo his uncompromising rejection of the disease model as a way of defending a "biblical" view of personal culpability for sinful actions. For instance, Addiction Recovery Ministry (ARM) offers "Christ Centered Recovery" for those seeking an alternative to Twelve-Step programs, which, the group claims, rely on the disease model as their "basic foundation." In contrast, ARM asserts, the Bible teaches that "self-destructive behavior is sinful and that each person who commits a sin is personally responsible before a Holy God." Similarly, "The Ten Principles for Overcoming Stubborn Habits" of Reformers Unanimous affirm personal responsibility for addictive behavior by endorsing the "simple law" of sowing and reaping: sow destructive behavior and reap destruction; sow good behavior and reap blessings from God. Separate oneself from any behavior God considers wrong, the group advises, and "the thought of using or engaging in our addiction is not even a remote possibility."[19]

According to C. Wayne Marshall, the apparent intransigence of compulsive behavior should not tempt Christians to deny its sinfulness because the Bible teaches that, regardless of how serious or overwhelming sin might seem, it can always be overcome "if one follows God's plan for all of life and living." Similarly, Edward Welch recommends that Christians take their cue for understanding addiction from the Bible's descriptions of persistent sinful behavior as rebellion, false worship, idolatry, voluntary slavery, and "folly"—none of which implies a disease against which one is powerless. Though his arguments are not rooted in Scripture, Anglican layman Peter Hitchens claims that a medicalized view of addiction is inimical to the Christian conception of free will. Because it implies "a power greater than the will," Hitchens says, he is distressed whenever he hears Christians promoting a disease model of addiction.[20]

Addiction, Disease, and Responsibility

Assuming that the Twelve-Step model implies viewing addiction as a sickness that absolves the addict from responsibility for his or her destructive behavior, Christian rejecters have declared that any endorsement of the Steps on the part of the church contributes to the "diseasing of Christianity" (Playfair) by treating sinners as "innocent and injured children" (Wells) and pardoning "unconditionally and in advance, all the self-indulgences you can think of"

(Hitchens). But these allegations are based on a grave misunderstanding of the relationship between addiction and responsibility in Twelve-Step recovery.

The crucial fact is that AA and the fellowships modeled upon it offer an explanation of addiction that is more characterological than medical. That is, recovery focuses not on the physical manifestations of the condition that are beyond one's control but on the defects of character—especially selfishness, defiance, and grandiosity—that are. The implications of this fact are easily deduced from the AA Big Book, which is authoritative in AA, as well as in most other Twelve-Step fellowships. Directly relevant to the question of personal responsibility is chapter 5, "How It Works," which explains that alcoholics' troubles "are basically of [their] own making." As "extreme example[s] of self-will run riot," the Big Book says, alcoholics who want to recover must search out "the flaws in [their] make-up which caused [their] failure."[21]

If the roots of the alcoholic's problems lie in "self, manifested in various ways," the method for extirpating them is the "personal housecleaning" undertaken in Step 4. The "'number one' offender" in this regard—the ultimate source of the alcoholic's "spiritual malady"—is resentment, an obsession with the "wrong-doing of others, fancied or real," that retains the power to kill. Recovery requires that the alcoholic master these resentments, in part by recognizing that one's offenders are "spiritually sick." "Putting out of our minds the wrongs others had done," the Big Book explains, "we resolutely looked for our own mistakes . . . where were we to blame?" The recovering alcoholic is specifically warned against casting blame upon family members, even though "their defects may be glaring."[22]

In the Big Book's instructions for working Step 4, a similar approach is recommended with regard to sexual behavior. Questions to be asked in reviewing past conduct include: "Where had we been selfish, dishonest, or inconsiderate? Whom had we hurt? Did we unjustifiably arouse jealousy, suspicion or bitterness? Where were we at fault, what should we have done instead?" Remaining focused on these questions, we "sweep off our side of the street." Where do those we feel have wronged us come into the equation? If sex is a particularly troublesome issue for us, we throw ourselves into helping them. "We think of their needs and work for them," which allows us "to be of maximum service to God and the people about us."[23]

That alcoholics are ultimately responsible for their behavior is reiterated in *Twelve Steps and Twelve Traditions*, which identifies blaming others as a common excuse for avoiding Step 4's personal inventory-taking. The "Twelve and Twelve" warns that if we delude ourselves into thinking that our troubles are "caused by the behavior of other people—people who *really* need a moral inventory," we will "resentfully focus" on their wrongs in order to escape looking at our own. The correct approach is rather to admit what we have done, "meanwhile forgiving the wrongs done us, real or fancied." When assessing relationships that bring us recurring trouble, the crucial questions to be asked are "can I see where I have been at fault?" and "did these perplexities beset me because of selfishness or unreasonable demands?" Alcoholics are advised, in fact, "to drop the word 'blame' from [their] speech and thought," since "it is a spiritual axiom that every time we are disturbed, no matter what the cause, there is something wrong *with us*."[24]

AA's program literature is clear, then, that whether alcoholism is characterized as an illness, malady, allergy, spiritual disease, or mental obsession, the alcoholic is a collaborator in the condition. In this sense, the Twelve-Step program attempts to thread a conceptual needle in the narrow space between the moral and disease conceptions of addiction. On the one hand, the physical element in AA's view of alcoholism reduces *shame* by rejecting a moral explanation of the condition; on the other hand, AA's emphasis on the characterological element in alcoholism places it within a moral framework that underscores *responsibility*. Alcoholism may be a physical malady beyond the individual's control, but alcoholic behavior is a product of "alcoholic thinking" that is rooted in selfishness, fear, resentment, and a lack of humility for which the alcoholic alone is responsible. In other words, although AA confirms that alcoholism is in some sense a physical illness, it prohibits using this as an alibi.[25]

Christians who find recovery in Twelve-Step fellowships confirm that coming to see addiction as a condition that has preceded their behavior in no way removes their accountability. As Sister Molly Monahan writes, in AA,

> admitting that you have a disease doesn't let you off the hook. It doesn't absolve you from taking responsibility for the person you were when you were drinking or for the things that you did. You cannot use your disease as an excuse. Once you admit that you are powerless over alcohol, your recovery depends on getting into action. Far from the comforting bromide "I'm OK, you're OK," the program tells you, in effect, "I'm not OK, you're not OK. But we can get better."[26]

In his own recovery memoir, pastor T. C. Ryan makes a similar point, stressing that anyone who works through recovery will face "the real consequences of his actions with genuine, profound and life-changing remorse. More than you can imagine."[27]

Thus, with regard to how addiction is understood in AA and other Twelve-Step fellowships, two points are paramount. First, AA conceives of alcoholism as a condition with physical, psychological, and spiritual dimensions whose solution lies in rigorous adherence to its program. Second, despite suffering from a complex and debilitating malady, alcoholics must assume responsibility not only for their thinking and behavior but for their consequences as well, making amends where appropriate. In short, the Twelve-Step approach to recovery assumes that while addicts cannot be blamed for their condition, they are solely accountable for arresting it and repairing any damage it may cause.

What about the Newer Twelve-Step Fellowships?

Unfortunately, confusion about Twelve-Step recovery's stance on personal responsibility has been sown by therapeutically informed Twelve-Step groups such as Co-Dependents Anonymous (CoDA) and Adult Children of Alcoholics and Dysfunctional Families (ACA), in which recovery entails thorough exploration of the childhood traumas, deprivations, and dysfunctions that are believed to cause addiction in adults. As we have seen, some argue these groups have effected an inversion of the Twelve-Step model, displacing AA's emphasis on wrongs committed with a focus on wrongs suffered. Obviously, if these programs encourage people to interpret their addictive behavior as a result of others' actions, the issue of responsibility can become hopelessly muddied. But let's let these groups speak for themselves on the matter.

A careful reader of *Co-Dependents Anonymous*, CoDA's Big Book published in 1995, will notice therapeutic concepts that seem out of place in a Twelve-Step context, including inner child, self-parenting, healthy boundaries, enmeshment, shame, and authentic self. Another notable departure from Twelve-Step tradition is CoDA's rejection of self-deflation as a prerequisite to recovery. In fact, in place of familiar AA images like "self-centeredness," "self-propulsion," and "self-will run riot," the CoDA Big Book emphasizes "learning to love the self," "believ[ing] in [one's] own capabilities," making amends to oneself, and having confidence that "goodness dwells within us."[28]

Indeed, the path to recovery in CoDA is marked not by surrender but by a restoration of self-worth and a refusal to allow previous abuse to shape one's "sense of self and well-being." This is because CoDA assumes the sources of codependent behavior are "the abuse and neglect . . . experienced in our significant childhood relationships," as well as the "emotional conflicts and survival patterns" brought into adulthood. Thus, working Step 1 in Co-Dependents Anonymous involves interrogating one's childhood with such questions as: "What neglect and abuse did I experience growing up?" and "When . . . did I learn to deny my own thoughts, feelings and needs?" Posing these questions is crucial, we read, because "codependence is born out of . . . dysfunctional family systems."[29]

Nevertheless, CoDA's assessment of responsibility for behavior performed "in disease" remains within the parameters of traditional Twelve-Step recovery. In fact, those who "act out" on the basis of childhood socialization nevertheless bear ultimate responsibility for the "codependent behaviors which reinforce patterns of devastation in [their] lives." Growing in humility and owning their defects of character, those in recovery from codependency must "strive on a daily basis to maintain accountability for [their] own behavior." This same stress on personal responsibility informs the CoDA Big Book's guidance for taking moral inventory in Step 4, which is to focus not on one's grievances or resentments but on one's codependent behaviors and those who have been affected by them. Recovery from codependency, we are instructed, involves constant reminders that "if you want to heal, you must learn to forgive."[30]

We find a similar relationship to the Twelve-Step model in *Adult Children of Alcoholics/Dysfunctional Families*, the ACA Big Red Book first published in 2006. Since ACA emerged from Alateen in 1978, a central feature of its program has been "The Laundry List," a litany of "14 Traits of an Adult Child" that include feelings of isolation, fear of authority figures and angry people, approval seeking, attraction to compulsive personalities, harsh self-criticism, fear of abandonment, and a tendency to confuse love with pity. According to the Big Red Book, these character traits are symptoms of a progressive spiritual disease called "para-alcoholism," whose roots lie in "traumatic childhoods" lived in "neglectful and abusive homes" with "sick people who were never there emotionally for us."[31]

As the Big Red Book makes clear, there was initial reluctance in ACA to adopt AA's Twelve Steps, particularly Steps 4 ("made a searching and fearless moral inventory of ourselves") and 5 ("admitted to God, to ourselves, and to another human being the exact nature of our wrongs"), which were thought to direct attention away from family dysfunction and its role in the adult child's behavior. Steps 8 and 9 (which call for making amends to "people we had harmed") were also seen as problematic, inasmuch as they could be interpreted as directing adult children to humbly approach "violent or abusive parents still in denial about the harm they had rained on the adult child." Ultimately, however, ACA adopted the Twelve Steps in their entirety, with the single exception that "alcohol" in Step 1 was changed to "the effects of alcoholism or other family dysfunction" (xxxv, 93).

Nevertheless, ACA's interpretation of the Steps departs in some important ways from the AA model. In Step 1, for instance, the fact over which one is expected to acknowledge powerlessness is the dysfunctionality of his or her family. Similarly, the guidelines for Step 4 focus on identifying family secrets, shame, abandonment, trauma/neglect, and stored anger, and recommend "praise work" in which the adult child confronts his or her habit of pushing away compliments. Similarly, Step 5 involves recognizing the ways adult children have harmed themselves, while Steps 6 and 7 distinguish character defects from the Laundry-List traits that develop as survival strategies in dysfunctional homes. As the Big Red Book explains, coping skills learned in childhood are the branches of a tree whose ripened fruits are adult character defects (201, 111, 211).

Another feature of ACA that stands out against the background of traditional Twelve-Step recovery is its emphasis on rescuing, nurturing, and affirming the self. While AA decries the inadequacy of self-knowledge and locates the alcoholic's problems in the baleful effects of self-propulsion, self-will, and self-sufficiency, hyphenates of the self play a very different role in ACA. Indeed, self-esteem, self-worth, self-discovery, and self-forgiveness are identified as keys to recovery, while self-doubt, self-abandonment, self-hate, self-blame, self-rejection, and self-harm are named as blocks to healing. Since adult children working the ACA program must "reparent" themselves and embrace their inner child, "focus on oneself" is a chief recovery strategy (61).

Other departures from Twelve-Step philosophy in ACA are instructive as well. Shame, not resentment, is regarded as "the number one offender" and the adult child's source of identification with other sufferers is "abandonment, shame and abuse." Further, in working the ACA program, one's problematic relationship to a substance or process must share attention with the trauma inflicted by family dysfunction in the form of ritualistic beliefs, harsh punishment, secretiveness, covert or overt sexual abuse, perfectionism, shaming, and mental illness. The prominence of therapeutic language in the Big Red Book is also noteworthy. It is recommended that adult children pursue therapy and clinical treatment, while family systems theory is used to illuminate the generational nature of addiction and the roles assumed by family members in addictive systems (73, 168, 172, xiv, xxxi).

However, on the crucial question of responsibility for actions carried out "in disease," ACA's approach is summed up in the slogan "Name It, Don't Blame It." On the one hand, adult children are survivors who cannot be held responsible for their reactions to a dysfunctional upbringing, which after all are instinctive repetitions of "what was done to [them]." Furthermore, people in ACA recovery must remember that harsh self-judgment is one of the harmful legacies of "abusive and hypercritical parents" that has led them to feel overresponsible as adults. On the other hand, a goal of Step work in ACA is to conduct a "blameless inventory" of one's parents, balancing an awareness that "our mistakes probably have their origin in the abuse we endured as children" with the necessity of taking responsibility for our adult misdeeds. After all, the Big Red Book counsels, "we must realize that our parents passed on what was done to them" (8, 113, 15, xvi, 160, 109, 25, 202, 52).

Acknowledging that at times adult children are criticized for focusing on their parents' purported failures, the Big Red Book emphasizes that ACA principles require "owning your truth, grieving your losses, and being accountable today for how you live your life." We may not be at fault for our responses to family dysfunction, the book concedes, "but we are responsible for our recovery." Indeed, the emphasis on personal responsibility in ACA is progressive. If in Step 1 we weigh an accounting of our own behavior against an inventory of our family system, in Step 4 we "balance our knowledge of the effects of family abuse in our lives with our own troublesome behavior as adults," and in Step 8 we scrutinize our behavior more than that of our parents (xiii, 156, 158, 159, 457, 231, 242, 251).

As this survey of their program literature makes clear, neither CoDA nor ACA excuses adult dysfunction as an inevitable result of childhood trauma. To this extent, they share with other Twelve-Step fellowships an implicit endorsement of free will, personal responsibility, and moral accountability. Identifying Twelve-Step recovery with a disease model of addiction that undermines responsibility, then, is to ignore the self-descriptions of Twelve-Step fellowships, even those that have therapeutized the AA paradigm in the wake of the recovery revolution. In all its expressions, this paradigm regards addicts as victims of an illness that may have physical dimensions, but for whose symptoms they are accountable.[32]

Other Objections

Christian rejecters of Twelve-Step recovery have targeted many features of its popularity among the faithful. One is the claim that AA's founders were orthodox believers who established the fellowship on biblical principles. Strongly resisting this notion, William Playfair writes that there is no evidence Bill W.

or Dr. Bob were "Christians in the Biblical sense." In his view, to call AA's founders Christians is tantamount to claiming the same for a Buddhist—or a Mormon! Other Christian opponents of Twelve-Step recovery charge that Wilson's search for sobriety drew him into occult activities and that the Steps, "written through an automatic writing process similar to New Age techniques," are a "cleverly disguised counterfeit of real biblical truth."[33]

Another basis for Christian attacks on the Twelve Steps is the fear, considered in an earlier chapter, that recovery is in effect a rival religion that often becomes a surrogate for involvement in the local church. Lamenting the fact that for recovering addicts Twelve-Step fellowships can become "their family, their church, their job," Edward Welch relates a cautionary tale about a man who loses interest in church after discovering AA. His thinking about alcohol abuse is shaped, according to Welch's portrait, by "an eclectic combination of AA, Scripture and the chip he had carried on his shoulder for years." As his struggle for sobriety becomes disconnected from his knowledge of Scripture, Welch explains, the man begins to define himself more as an alcoholic than as a Christian and he is lost to the church.[34]

Some Christian critics of Twelve-Step recovery express caution about the endorsement of meditation in Step 11 ("sought through prayer and meditation to improve our conscious contact with God"). Despite the practice's long history as a Christian spiritual discipline, for many believers meditation conjures images of Eastern or, worse, New Age practices. Other Christians resist what they see as the glorification of sinful behavior in the stories told in recovery meetings. And there is concern with the mingling of recovery and ecclesial cultures in church-based recovery ministries. Playfair refers to these groups as examples of "Christianized Compromise," and Welch calls them a mash-up of AA, pop psychology, and scriptural prooftexts. It is bad enough that AA's "sub-biblical worldview" seeps into Christian minds through therapy, rehab, and the wider culture, Welch writes; it is worse when the church accelerates this process.[35]

Conclusion

Although their criticisms vary, what Christian rejecters of Twelve-Step recovery share is a conviction that the ultimate solution to the problem of addiction is the transformative power of God in Jesus Christ, and that this truth is ignored or diluted in approaches that adopt all or part of Twelve-Step philosophy, even if they claim to be Christ-centered. On this view, the Steps are at best an unhelpful distraction, at worst a demonic trap. In the next chapter, we will explore how a much larger group of Christians has responded to these lingering concerns about "secular" recovery with efforts to Christianize—or re-Christianize—Twelve-Step philosophy and practice.

CHAPTER 7

Is Recovery Biblical?

(sort of)

My first experience of the church-based AA spin-off known as Celebrate Recovery (CR) came in 2017, at a Presbyterian church in Florida I had visited with my mom and dad a handful of times over the years. When they learned that I had begun attending Twelve-Step meetings, my parents sent me a collection of CR texts, courtesy of a friend who led the group at their church (the church I was now visiting). When I showed up on a weeknight in December, I was met by a long table cluttered with the sort of dishes that comprise a typical church potluck, some of them easily identifiable, others not.

After dinner, I moved along with thirty or so others into a small auditorium to participate in a worship service consisting mostly of praise songs. Group singing was punctuated by announcements, communal readings, and a lesson from the CR curriculum. Afterward, we were invited to attend one of a number of share groups that were segregated by gender and problem type. But since it was my first visit to CR, I was directed to a newcomer's meeting along with another newbie. A lay leader speaking from an outline explained to us that recovery "is just a twenty-first-century word for sanctification." I wasn't sure whether this was an official CR position, but it shed light on something I had overheard at dinner—that only about a third of CR participants claim substance addictions. Presumably, the other two-thirds are seeking relief from unspecified "hurts, habits, and hang-ups," CR's catchall description of human dysfunction.

Our group leader told us that in CR self-introductions follow a consistent formula: "My name is Steve, and I am a believer in Jesus Christ who struggles with. . . ." She said her own reason for seeking recovery was "judgmentalness"—a legitimate flaw, I thought, though something Twelve-Steppers would classify as a common character defect. Even so, I inferred from what she and others said that within the church community there was some stigma attached to CR involvement, whether one identified as a dope addict or a judgmental church lady. While group leaders I spoke with reported at least verbal backing from the church's staff, they also said they sometimes felt dismissed as "those people with problems."

Over the next several months, I attended four other CR meetings in four states, in a wide array of church settings. The hosting congregations were Baptist, Methodist, Pentecostal, and nondenominational; suburban and urban; predominantly white, predominantly black, and predominantly Latinx. Meetings were held in family life buildings, one-room cinder-block sanctuaries, and, in one case, a storefront space nestled between a tax preparation service and a dry cleaner. Food offerings varied from hot dogs and potato chips to delivery pizza to potluck. Music and testimonies were sometimes live, sometimes recorded. Lessons were conducted with varying degrees of adherence to CR-supplied scripts. In one case, all five people in attendance gathered in one open-share meeting; in another, attendees joined one of two gender-specific groups; in still another, break-out options were tailored to a bewildering array of problems, including codependency, sexual addiction, cosex addiction, adult children of family dysfunction, sexual, physical, and emotional abuse, eating disorders and food addiction, anger, chemical dependence, love and relationship addiction, same-sex attraction, and "mixed issues."

What was consistently true at every CR meeting I attended—from Florida to California—was the care taken to create a welcoming atmosphere. I was particularly appreciative of this effort to welcome strangers, since I was a newcomer to each group I visited. Honesty was another part of the CR ethos that was consistently on display. In plenary sessions leaders unfailingly introduced themselves as "believers who struggle with X." Small groups invited participants to disclose their failures and fears as honestly as they wished. After every CR experience I came away feeling like I had been to a good Twelve-Step meeting. In this sense, Celebrate Recovery represents a programmatic response to the question, Why can't the church be more like AA? Under the right conditions, it would appear that it can.

But certain features of these CR gatherings set them apart from the Twelve-Step meetings with which I am familiar. One was the explicit prohibition of profanity ("offensive language has no place in a Christ-centered recovery group," according to CR's small group guidelines), which anyone familiar with Twelve-Step culture knows is one of their regular, often humorous, features. Also, no matter how few people were in attendance on a particular night, each part of the CR program was led by members of the church staff or trained volunteers. In other words, leadership in CR is not a rotating service role but a privilege limited to those who have been properly trained.[1]

Finally, at each of these meetings, I was reminded of CR's penchant for a form of Bible prooftexting in which each Step, principle, or point is bolstered by a biblical citation, usually without any reference to its canonical context. This biblicizing of recovery is reflected in the list of "Steps and Biblical Comparisons" that was read at every CR meeting I attended. Pairing each Step with a Bible verse (or part of a verse), this litany of comparisons creates an impression of natural correspondence, even derivation. Yet if one takes the time to examine these pairings, it becomes evident that many are artificial.

Of course, it is difficult to fairly assess a movement as large as Celebrate Recovery on the basis of such limited experience. But my brief exposure to this recovery ministry serves as a useful introduction to the promise and peril of adapting Twelve-Step recovery to the rhythms, rules, and leadership models of the American church.

Adapting the Steps

In 1993, evangelical writer Tim Stafford summed up the ambivalence many Christians feel toward Twelve-Step recovery, writing that "the 12 Steps are Christian, but A.A. is not." Stafford's appraisal identified the middle ground eyed by those who believe the church has a genuine claim on the Twelve Steps but are reluctant to sanction what they regard as a secular recovery program. Seizing this space requires Christian adapters to demonstrate that the Steps can be utilized in a church setting without endorsing the therapeutic and spiritual baggage that often comes with them. So how do adapters approach this task?[2]

The process begins as it always has for AA spin-offs —with a revision to Step 1 that replaces "alcohol" with another addictive substance or process, such as "lust," "gambling," "food," or "cocaine." Christian adapters, however, favor replacing alcohol in Step 1 with references to more inclusive conditions. Examples are "our addictions," "our addictions and codependencies," "our addictions and dysfunctional behaviors," "certain areas of our lives," "the effects of our separation from God," "our dependencies," "our problems," "our human condition," and "our sin." The broader the net that is cast in this revision of Step 1 the better, since, as one Christian guide to "addictive lifestyles" claims, people can be victimized by "an almost endless number of substances, activities, emotions, and objects."[3]

A second alteration to the Steps typical of Christian adapters grows out of theological concerns. It involves clarifying references to the divine in Steps

2, 3, 6, 7, and 11, typically by adding explicit references to Jesus Christ or the "God of the Bible." For instance, one Christian program for addressing chemical dependency changes "Power greater than ourselves" in Step 2 to "God as we know God in Jesus, through the power of the Spirit," and "God as we understood Him" in Step 3 to "God as we know God in the Crucified and Risen One." Another program alters each reference to God in Steps 2, 3, and 11 to read "Jesus Christ" or "God, through Jesus Christ."[4]

A third move common among Christian adapters underscores the Steps' "biblical" character by bolstering each with Scripture references. The first Step-Scripture list seems to have been assembled by Alcoholics Victorious (AV), a network of Christian support groups for chemically dependent persons, and published in 1975. But AV's Step-Scripture pairings underwent significant revisions in the list presented in *The Twelve Steps for Christians* by Friends in Recovery (FIR) in 1988. Then, in 1992 FIR's Step-Scripture list was itself revised in Terry Webb's "Twelve Steps of Christian Living." Variations in the three lists are indicated in the following chart, with commonalities noted in bold:[5]

	Alcoholics Victorious (1975)	Friends in Recovery (1988)	12 Steps of Christian Living (1992)
Step 1	**Romans 7:18**	**Romans 7:18**	**Romans 7:18**
Step 2	2 Corinthians 12:9	Philippians 2:13	Mark 9:23
Step 3	Luke 9:23	Romans 12:1	Jeremiah 29:11-13
Step 4	**Lamentations 3:40**	**Lamentations 3:40**	Psalm 139:7
Step 5	**James 5:16**	**James 5:16**	Proverbs 28:13
Step 6	Isaiah 1:19	James 4:10	1 John 5:14
Step 7	James 4:10	**1 John 1:9**	1 Peter 5:6-7; **1 John 1:9**
Step 8	Matthew 5:23-24	**Luke 6:31**	**Luke 6:31**
Step 9	Luke 6:38	**Matthew 5:23-24**	**Matthew 5:23-24**
Step 10	Romans 12:3	**1 Corinthians 10:12**	**1 Corinthians 10:12**
Step 11	Psalm 19:14	Colossians 3:16	Psalm 1:1-3
Step 12	**Galatians 6:1-2**	**Galatians 6:1**	Mark 10:42-45; Matthew 5:16

Two things stand out about this table. First, all three lists cite the same Scripture passage only in connection with Step 1. Second, in the cases of Steps 2, 3, 6, and 11, the lists of Bible citations do not overlap at all. In addition to this lack of consistency, these Step-Scripture lists fall short in the area of validity, as some of the connections they indicate are quite tenuous. Consider, for example, the pairing of Step 6's preparation for God's removal of character defects with Isaiah's promise that "you will eat the best from the land," Step 9's direction to make "direct amends" with Jesus's admonition to "give and it shall be given you," and Step 10's charge to take daily inventory and promptly admit wrongdoing with Paul's warning that *"if you think you are standing firm, be careful that you don't fall!"*[6]

Such dubious connections indicate that these lists tell us less about the Steps' relationship to the Bible than about American evangelicals' penchant for using it as a catalogue of prooftexts. Specifically, the assumption that the truth of each Step can be verified with a single Bible verse reflects the evangelical belief that any spiritual truth must also be biblical. Celebrate Recovery offers an instructive example of the way this assumption plays out in Christian adaptations of Twelve-Step recovery. CR's "Eight Recovery Principles," which appear below, represent a consolidation of the Twelve Steps in explicitly Christian language. But CR presents these principles as distillations of the Beatitudes, which are referred to as Jesus's "eight principles for healing and happiness":

Realize I'm not God; I admit that I am powerless to control my tendency to do the wrong thing and that my life is unmanageable. (Step 1) "Happy are those who know that they are spiritually poor." Matthew 5:3a TEV.

Earnestly believe that God exists, that I matter to Him and that He has the power to help me recover. (Step 2) "Happy are those who mourn, for they shall be comforted." Matthew 5:4 TEV, NIV.

Consciously choose to commit all my life and will to Christ's care and control. (Step 3) "Happy are the meek." Matthew 5:5a TEV.

Openly examine and confess my faults to myself, to God, and to someone I trust. (Steps 4 and 5) "Happy are the pure in heart." Matthew 5:8a TEV.

Voluntarily submit to any and all changes God wants to make in my life and humbly ask Him to remove my character defects. (Steps 6 and 7) "Happy are those whose greatest desire is to do what God requires." Matthew 5:6a TEV.

Evaluate all my relationships. Offer forgiveness to those who have hurt me and make amends for harm I've done to others when possible, except when to do so would harm them or others. (Steps 8 and 9) "Happy are the merciful." Matthew 5:7a TEV; "Happy are the peacemakers." Matthew 5:9 TEV.

Reserve a daily time with God for self-examination, Bible reading, and prayer in order to know God and His will for my life and to gain the power to follow His will. (Steps 10 and 11)

Yield myself to God to be used to bring this Good News to others, both by my example and my words. (Step 12) "Happy are those who are persecuted because they do what God requires." Matthew 5:10 TEV.[7]

CR's recovery principles and the Twelve Steps they paraphrase do not appear to be incompatible with Jesus's words in Matthew 5; but to imply that these principles have been derived from them is disingenuous. Because CR claims its program is based in "the actual words of Jesus rather than psychological theory," it is obliged to locate its "Eight Principles" in the Gospels. But its attempt to do so reveals that these principles (not to mention the Steps) do not correspond very well to Jesus's Beatitudes. This is particularly clear in principle 2 ("earnestly believe that God exists, that I matter to Him and that He has the power to help me recover"), which is paired with Matthew 5:4 ("happy are those who mourn, for they shall be comforted") and principle 8 ("yield myself to God to be used to bring this Good News to others, both by my example and my words"), which is linked to Matthew 5:10 ("happy are those who are persecuted because they do what God requires"). Like other adaptation schemes that claim to harmonize the Steps and Scripture, this one is visually impressive, but substantively disappointing.[8]

Recovery Bibles

Over the past thirty years, efforts to establish the Twelve Steps' scriptural bona fides and bring the Bible to bear on recovery have led to the emergence of a novel publishing phenomenon—the recovery Bible. First on the scene was *Serenity: A Companion for Twelve Step Recovery*, published by Thomas Nelson in 1990. *Serenity* included the New Testament, Psalms, and Proverbs in a red-letter New King James version that featured numerical marginal references to the Twelve Steps, "recovery meditations," and about eighty pages of front matter. An "early recovery version" of *Seren-*

ity appearing in 1997 added instruction in evangelical theology, a twelve-week day-by-day guide to spiritual growth, and a list of "practical scripture references."[9]

The *Recovery Devotional Bible* (*RDB*), published by Zondervan in 1993, was the first recovery Bible to include the entire Christian canon. In addition to marginal notations indicating a passage's connections with specific Steps, the *RDB* featured articles on the Twelve Steps' spiritual and biblical roots, as well as daily meditations by authors well known in the world of recovery, including Melody Beattie, John Bradshaw, Sharon Wegscheider-Cruse, Gerald May, Pia Mellody, and M. Scott Peck. Reflecting the recovery Bible's lineage as an offspring of the life application Bible, the *RDB* was the first to include recovery-oriented textual annotations called "life connections."[10]

Competition in the recovery-Bible market intensified in 1998 with Tyndale House's publication of *The Life Recovery Bible* (*LRB*), which included articles on "The Twelve Steps and Scripture," "The Twelve Laws of Life Recovery," and "The Twelve Gifts of Life Recovery." Among the *LRB*'s in-text features were a "Twelve Step Devotional Reading Plan," "recovery profiles" of sixty Bible figures, and hundreds of "Recovery Notes" positioned at the bottom of each page. The *LRB* even addressed Christian resistance to "secular" recovery, taking on common misconceptions such as "turning my life over to Christ is the only step I need," "Twelve Step groups that don't talk about Jesus aren't worth my time," and "if I follow the Bible, I don't really need to work the Twelve Steps."[11]

Over the past fifteen years, the recovery-Bible market has become significantly more crowded. In 2006, the International Bible Society published the *Journey to Recovery New Testament* (*JRNT*) in the New International Version. Although lacking recovery-themed annotations, the *JRNT* featured extensive front and back matter, including testimonies by men and women who describe their participation in Twelve-Step fellowships. The *JRNT* also included self-tests for chemical dependence, sexual addiction, eating disorders, and codependence, and a seventy-five-page study guide titled "The Twelve Steps: A Process of Healing, Repentance and Growth." Even more than other Bibles in this genre, *JRNT* portrayed recovery as a natural part of the Christian life and encouraged anyone seeking to heal from addiction or codependence to join a recovery group and secure a sponsor.[12]

In 2007, Zondervan released the *Celebrate Recovery Bible* (*CRB*, republished in 2016 as the *NIV Celebrate Recovery Study Bible*). Designed to supplement Celebrate Recovery's curriculum and programming, *CRB* was more likely to refer to the CR program than to Twelve-Step recovery per se (for instance, marginal numbers linked Bible passages to CR's "Eight Principles" rather than to the Steps). In addition to expositions of these principles, *CRB* included introductions to each book identifying its recovery themes, Bible character studies ("My Name Is Eve," etc.), testimonies from Celebrate Recovery participants, lesson studies tied to key words in CR's principles, and daily devotionals.[13]

In 2015, Christians Against Substance Abuse (CASA) published *Journey to Recovery through Christ (JRTC)*, a Twelve-Step study Bible comprising the New Testament, Psalms, and Proverbs in the New American Standard Version. *JRTC*'s front matter included an article titled "The Biblical Basis and Background of the 12-Steps," an unedited list of AA's Steps with an overview of each, and references to associated Scripture passages. In-text annotations took the form of recovery insights and reflections on the Steps. Like the *CRB*, *JRTC* mirrored the priorities of its parent organization, a Texas-based ministry operating primarily in jails and prisons and dedicated to helping people overcome addiction "through a belief in Jesus Christ and applying biblical truths."[14]

While the material in these Bibles is vast and varied, there are three general problems with the way they adapt recovery to the concerns of Bible readers. First—and hardly surprising given our review of the Step-Scripture lists produced by adapters—there is little consistency in the way these Bibles relate recovery to particular passages. Second, these Bibles broaden the concept of recovery to such an extent that one wonders why recovery Bibles are not simply called life application Bibles. Third, recovery Bibles routinely engage in a form of interpretation (technically known as eisegesis) that brings more *to* the text than it takes *from* it.

Consistency

It is surely unfair to expect commentaries composed by separate editorial teams to agree on the meaning and relevance of any canonical passage. But inasmuch as these recovery Bibles purport to view Scripture through a common lens, it seems reasonable to expect from them a degree of interpretive consistency. To gauge how much consistency is present, let's compare their treatments of Matthew 5:3–12, which as we have seen is cited by Celebrate Recovery as a source for the Twelve Steps. Here is a table of the Beatitude-Step connections claimed by these Bibles:[15]

	Serenity	RDB	LRB	CRB	JRTC
v. 3 (poor in spirit)		Steps 1–3	Step 9	Steps 1–3	
v. 4 (those who mourn)		Steps 1–3	Step 9	Steps 1–3	
v. 5 (the meek)		Steps 1–3	Step 9	Steps 1–3	
v. 6 (those who seek righteousness)		Steps 1–3	Step 9	Steps 1–3	Step 7
v. 7 (merciful)		Steps 8–9	Step 9	Steps 8–9	
v. 8 (pure in heart)	Step 10	Steps 4–7	Step 9	Steps 4–7	
v. 9 (peacemakers)	Step 9	Steps 8–9	Step 9	Steps 8–9	Step 9
v. 10 (persecuted)			Step 9		
v. 11 (reviled)			Step 9	Steps 8–9	
v. 12 (rejoice!)			Step 9		

Based on this chart, we see that each of these Bibles identifies parallels between Jesus's Beatitudes and the Twelve Steps and that the *RDB* and *CRB* do so with some specificity. But when we examine these pairings, striking discrepancies emerge. For example, at least three of the Bibles fail to link verses 10–12 with any Steps, and of the verses linked to one or more Steps by at least three Bibles, there is consistency only in relation to verses 7 and 9. This does not mean, of course, that comparing the Twelve Steps with Jesus's Beatitudes is fruitless—only that doing so yields few self-evident connections, even when one is looking for them.

Redefining Recovery

Recovery Bibles do more than claim "striking parallels" between the Twelve Steps and Scripture; they insist that the Steps themselves are "biblical," that they "capture principles clearly revealed in the Bible," that they are "taken from the New Testament," that working them "is following the Bible." In fact, these Bibles assert that since every book of the Bible "touch[es] on recovery issues," it is "a book about recovery," perhaps "the greatest book on recovery ever written." Delivering on these claims, however, requires these Bibles to cast recovery in extremely broad terms.[16]

At times the Bibles describe recovery as being "a lot like living the Christian life" (*RDB*) or "the process of daily seeking God's will for our life instead of demanding to go our own way" (*LRB*). In these cases, recovery appears to be used as another name for Christian discipleship. At other times these Bibles treat recovery as a synonym for God's work of redemption. The *LRB*, for instance, asserts that when humans rejected God's original "program," God offered a "plan for recovery . . . a program for reconciliation and healing." Adopting a similar view, the *CRB* notes that Jesus "did the ultimate in 12-step work by doing for us what we cannot do for ourselves," that is, offering a means for "recovery from sin and its destructive effects."[17]

In other places these Bibles associate recovery with the ethos of transparency and trust that has led Christians to wonder why church can't be more like AA. As *JRTC* explains,

> Recovery includes being honest about past hurts so they can be healed, gaining insights about destructive patterns of behavior so they can be changed, developing trust in God as the source of wisdom and strength, and finding hope to replace shame and despair. And through this process a person can be recreated to live the way God intended.[18]

Each of these conceptions of recovery conveys the message that Christians need not regard the concept as foreign or threatening. But one gets the sense that these Bibles want to make church more like AA by applying the name recovery to what already goes on there.

Recovery Lessons?

A third problem endemic to recovery Bibles is that, in their effort to find recovery on every page of Scripture, "lessons" become divorced from Scripture's historical and literary contexts. Of course, in order to reach people who speak the language of recovery, these Bibles must employ the specialized vocabularies of medicine (*addiction, compulsion,* and *dependency*), therapy (*codependency, shame, boundary setting, low self-esteem, inner child, adult children, dysfunctional families,* and *healthy ways of handling conflict*), the Steps (*powerlessness, unmanageability, coming to believe, a Power greater than ourselves, restored sanity, moral inventory, character defects, turning our will and lives over to the care of God,* asking God to *remove our shortcomings,* developing *conscious contact with God,* and *carrying the message*), and the literature and traditions of Twelve-Step fellowships (*working the Steps,* finding a *Higher Power, attending meetings, finding a sponsor,* recognizing the *things we cannot change, hitting bottom, faking it to make it, living one day at a time,* and believing that *it works if you work it*).

But these modern idioms are rarely a good fit for the ancient texts they are being asked to interpret. How well do recovery Bibles balance the quest for relevance with respect for the historical and literary integrity of canonical texts? Editorial comments in the five Bibles that introduce or annotate Scripture can be placed into three general categories. In the first, the recovery language applied to a biblical passage, though anachronistic, neither distorts nor illuminates it to any meaningful extent. In a second category, recovery language highlights something of permanent value in the text. In a third, the recovery lesson claimed to reside in a scriptural passage distorts its original meaning by bringing something foreign to the text.

In the first category of comments, the almost gratuitous use of recovery jargon provides little of interpretive value: After hiding from God, Adam began the "road to recovery" (*CRB*, 9); deception was habitual in Isaac and Rebekah's "dysfunctional family" (*LRB*, 35); in prison, Joseph lived according to "God's program" (*LRB*, 58); the plague on Egypt's firstborn caused Pharaoh to "hit bottom" (*LRB*, 124); the sacrifices described in Leviticus were a way for the Hebrews to "make amends" (*RDB*, 110); Elijah was a "perfectionist" (*LRB*, 443); 1 Samuel describes David's "possibly codependent" relationship with Jonathan (*RDB*, 288); Josiah was not perfect, "but he was a true champion of recovery" (*LRB*, 561); Ezra recorded "the recovery experienced by those returning from Babylon" (*CRB*, 548); "King Herod apparently never heard the saying, 'There is a God and you ain't Him'" (*JRTC*, 194); Jesus's command to "seek first [the] kingdom" was his way of saying "one day at a time" (*RDB*, 1042); the Corinthians had "hurts, hang-ups and habits just as we do" (*CRB*, 1419); Paul's letter to the Philippians spoke to those whose lives had "become unmanageable" (*LRB*, 1423); Timothy and Titus were Paul's "sponsees" (*RDB*, 1347). These bits of commentary do not meaningfully elucidate the passages to which they are applied; but neither do they constitute interpretive violence.

In a second category of comments, something of enduring value in the biblical passage is brought to light through a connection with recovery: "Abraham's journey into the unknown at age 75 provides a recovery model to all of us who have had to leave familiar surroundings or unhealthy patterns" (*RDB*, 16); "David demonstrates the humility needed for Step Seven" ("humbly asked him to remove our shortcomings") (*JRTC*, 365, on Ps. 25); "our addictions became the idols of our own making" (*JRTC*, 448, on Ps. 115); Solomon's experience suggests "we are most vulnerable to relapse when life is going well" (*LRB*, 414); Christ knew the same "abuse, shaming and abandonment that many of us did" (*DRB*, 1076); "coming out of our addictions, many of us feel unclean, untouchable" (*JRTC*, 82, on Mark 1:40–42); like Jesus, we may find that "those who are most skeptical about our recovery are our own family" (*DRB*, 1088); "most addicted people identify with the dilemma spelled out by Paul [in Rom. 7]" (*JRTC*, 222); for someone recovering from alcoholism, "being around others who are drinking might be dangerous" (on the "weak" and "strong" in 1 Cor. 8; *DRB*, 1263); "If we've taken Step One, we've named a 'thorn in our flesh'" (*JRTC*, 258).

These comments ring true from a recovery perspective without interpreting the biblical text in a way that is jarringly anachronistic. Perhaps the best examples of comments in this category are to be found in *Serenity*. On Matthew 16:25, we read that Jesus voices the central paradox [of recovery] when he says, "For whoever desires to save his life will lose it, and whoever loses his life for My sake will find it" (27). Similarly, comments in the *RDB* liken addiction to idolatry and spiritual enslavement in insightful ways: Jeremiah decries the Hebrews' "addiction to idolatry" (*RDB*, 815, 869); Jesus's statement that "everyone who sins is a slave to sin" (John 8:34) means "we are all addicted—to sin" (*RDB*, 1169); and Paul's image of slavery to sin in Romans "sounds a lot like our experience of slavery to addiction or codependency" (*RDB*, 1239). The *JRTC* also relates Bible passages to recovery in provocative ways, asking, "What do Jesus' words in Matthew 18 ('if your eye causes you to stumble, pluck it out and throw it from you') have to say about the use of pornography?" (64) and "In what ways were you a slave to your addiction before you took Step One?" (263, on Gal. 4).

In a third category, recovery jargon rings hollow because it distorts a passage's content or context beyond recognition. Here too the *RDB* deserves special mention: "Change the spelling of Pharaoh to a-d-d-i-c-t-i-o-n," we read, "and we see a clear picture of what addictive behaviors do to us" (*RDB*, 68). Many editorial comments in this category equate addiction or codependency with existential threats faced by the ancient Hebrews. For instance, those who suffer from having been raised in a dysfunctional family are said to "feel a lot like the exiles in Babylon felt" (*LRB*, 942); in addiction we can be overcome by fear, just as "the people of Judah lived under the threat of Assyrian attack" (*LRB*, 1070); Joel's "day of the Lord" [a future apocalyptic judgment] is similar to "the day we hit bottom" (*DRB*, 973).

Although it is common to describe dependency on a substance or behavior as spiritual slavery, comments in this third category liken addiction to a state of actual forced servitude: "like the Hebrews, we were once slaves—to a dysfunctional family system, and later to our addictive and codependent behaviors" (*RDB*, 214); "just as the Israelites were powerless as slaves in Egypt, we are slaves to our human tendency toward sin and its destructive consequences"

(*LRB*, 128); "people who are addicted have created their own lands of slavery" (*JRTC*, 14). As James B. Nelson has noted, "there are expressions of sin for which the recovery model is of little relevance. War is one example." Human thralldom would seem to be another.[19]

Recovery Bibles can be useful in demonstrating that "the struggles we face today have been common for thousands of years" (*CRB*, xiv). But their efforts to prove that the Bible is "a book about recovery" obliges them to uncover recovery-themed messages in all sixty-six books of the Christian canon. Given the enormity of this interpretive task, it is not surprising that many of their "lessons" ring hollow, or worse.

Adapter Programs

The desire to make Twelve-Step recovery serviceable in church contexts has given rise to a wide variety of recovery programs adapted from AA and touting themselves as Christ-centered. One of the first such adapter groups was Alcoholics for Christ, which emerged in the Detroit area in the mid-1970s when two born again alcoholics met at an AA retreat. Alcoholics for Christ remains active, hosting weekly meetings in seventeen states. The organization's focus is "Bible believing denominations, independent churches and Christian ministries," where it uses a revised version of AA's Steps in supporting addicts with "God's Word and the 12-step process."[20]

The Twelve Steps: A Spiritual Journey (1988) lays out a thirty-week recovery program that combines "the tested wisdom of Bible truths and the proven effectiveness of Twelve-Step principles" and signals the Steps' compatibility with Scripture by citing dozens of Bible passages. *Rapha's 12-Step Program for Overcoming Chemical Dependency* (1990) is an adaptation of Twelve-Step recovery based on AA's "originally Bible-based twelve steps." Ron Keller's *The Twelve Steps and Beyond: A Transforming Journey through the Gospel of John into Life in Christ* (1989) is a resource for church recovery groups using Keller's "Twelve Steps for Life in Christ," in which references to the divine have been replaced with "Jesus Christ" and the Steps have been turned into a series of faith statements.[21]

Living Free: A Guide to Forming and Conducting a Recovery Ministry (1992) by Ron Halvorson and Valerie Deilgat describes a "Living Free" program of Christ-centered support meetings for persons raised in "addictive, emotionally repressive, or dysfunctional families." The authors view the Twelve Steps as embodying "the Bible's core teachings" concerning God's relationship with humankind:

[The Steps] begin with an admission of human shortcomings and a profession of faith in God's power, love and forgiveness—the essence of justification. The Twelve Steps go on to encourage continual confession of wrongdoing, submission to God's control and proper conduct toward others—the principles of sanctification. Finally, they encourage habits of devotion, responsiveness to God's will and sharing the message of recovery with others—the basics of biblical Christian living.

The Living Free program combines Scripture with a lightly revised version of AA's Twelve Steps designed "to help participants rely on Jesus Christ for guidance in resolving troublesome personal issues."[22]

Overcomers Outreach (OO) is an international network of Christ-centered Twelve-Step support groups that use the Bible and AA's Twelve Steps to address substance and process addictions, compulsive behaviors, and other dependencies. Viewing itself as a two-way bridge between evangelical churches and traditional Twelve-Step programs, OO points Twelve-Steppers to Christ while providing a safe space for church people who are reluctant to attend or share in community recovery meetings. In the group's experience, the spiritual awakening that results from Twelve-Step recovery often paves the way for men and women to "return to the church of their childhood."[23]

Christians in Recovery (CIR) is another group that seeks to provide spaces where recovering Christians can share their faith. Unlike other Christ-centered recovery programs, however, the spaces created by CIR are primarily virtual. As the only online "full featured Christian recovery community," CIR offers anonymity and security for those "too afraid or ashamed . . . to approach conventional ministries and recovery groups." Like other adapter organizations, CIR casts the net of recovery quite widely: the "trials, problems, addictions and dysfunctions" addressed by the group include abuse, anxiety, eating disorders, substance abuse, gambling, sexual addiction, and mental health issues.[24]

Christians against Substance Abuse (CASA), founded in 1988, is committed to the view that the Twelve Steps are "based directly on biblical principles" and contain nothing "not found in the Bible." According to CASA, Twelve-Step fellowships cannot fulfill all one's spiritual needs, since they ignore "life after death and an eternal future residing with God." Nevertheless, the organization does not edit the God-language in Steps 2, 3, or 11, claiming that AA's "Higher Power" enables it to reach atheists and agnostics. *Journey to Recovery through Christ: CASA's 12-Step Bible Study* includes multiple references to AA slogans and program literature, but reflects a biblicized concept of addiction in which temptation and the work of Satan are highlighted.[25]

The majority of these programs came into being in response to the recovery revolution, whose influence was also felt in the church small group movement. Beginning in the 1960s, Serendipity House published a series of works applying small group theory to youth ministry, Bible study, and "serendipity groups," but it was only in the late 1980s that the publisher began offering guides for Twelve-Step-based church groups. Serendipity's *12 Steps: The Path to Wholeness* (1989) blended Bible study aids and group activities with Twelve-Step principles, which it assured readers were "based directly on the teaching of the New Testament." *12 Steps* was quickly followed by small group guides dealing with addictive lifestyles, codependency, eating disorders, sexual addictions, and adult children. Meanwhile, a 1988 revision of the *Serendipity Bible* added outlines for "recovery courses" on a variety of topics, including getting in shape, healing significant relationships, recovering from divorce, dealing with grief and loss, and moving past the pain of abuse.[26]

Conclusion

How do we explain the varied and long-standing phenomenon that is Christian adaptation of Twelve-Step recovery? There seem to be three factors. One is the well-documented envy of Christians for AA, and for the Twelve-Step movement's impressive results in helping people overcome besetting problems and find spiritual fulfillment. A second factor driving adaptation is the desire of Christian leaders, particularly evangelicals who place a high value on cultural relevance, to capitalize on recovery's popularity, which has been steadily expanding since the 1980s. And then there are the efforts of Christian publishers to respond to the forces aforementioned. For several decades, these publishers have been involved in a careful balancing act that involves monetizing recovery's cultural capital while reassuring evangelical readers that the Twelve Steps are solidly Christian.

But it is precisely this emphasis on recovery's Christian character, affirmed by every adapter author and organization we have reviewed, that limits the adapters' ability to make church more like AA. For the Step-Scripture lists and biblical annotations that characterize adapter literature (dubious though many of them are) have the paradoxical effect of convincing Christians that the church can appropriate the trappings of recovery without embracing the unfamiliarity or messiness of Twelve-Step fellowships. Christ-centered adapter groups rarely present themselves as replacements for these fellowships; but because they make them unnecessary in practice, Christians who join them are unlikely to leave the familiar confines of their churches to experience Twelve-Step recovery firsthand.

The replacement function of adapter groups is particularly evident in Celebrate Recovery, where there is much borrowing from Twelve-Step culture but very little attribution. For instance, the testimonies that make up a good portion of CR founder John Baker's *Life's Healing Choices: Freedom from Your Hurts, Hang-Ups, and Habits* are rife with the shibboleths of Twelve-Step recovery—"powerlessness," "unmanageability," "working the program," "using," "relapse," "clean and sober," "surrender," the impotence of "willpower," "God [doing] for me what I couldn't do for myself," "chips," "sobriety birthdays," "denial," "attitude of gratitude," "dry drunk," "fearless and thorough moral inventory," facing "life on life's terms," "hitting bottom," and "keep coming back."[27]

Yet despite its obvious debts to Twelve-Step culture, *Life's Healing Choices* is reluctant to give it credit, even referring to the Serenity Prayer made famous by AA as the Prayer for Serenity. In fact, virtually the only references to Twelve-Step fellowships in *Life's Healing Choices* appear in the testimonies of CR converts who flounder in secular recovery until they find liberation "up the hill" at Saddleback Church. "I managed to stay sober by going to [AA] meetings, but it wasn't till I started attending Saddleback Church that the other miracles started happening," writes Carl. "Within weeks of attending Celebrate Recovery, I stopped sexually acting out," Tina testifies. Bob adds, "From my first [CR] meeting, I knew this was home." The message is clear: those who start out thinking they need recovery eventually realize that they need a church recovery program.[28]

An implicit but persistent message of *Life's Healing Choices* is that AA and similar fellowships should hold little if any ongoing value for committed Christians. In this sense, CR and other adapter groups seem to view Twelve-Step recovery much the way Paul views the law in his letter to Christians in Galatia—as a "tutor" to bring people to Christ—or at least to Christ-centered recovery. By accommodating children and families, limiting leadership roles to church staff and trained volunteers, and providing a safe space where one can avoid profanity and insults to one's faith, Christ-centered recovery makes AA more like church without making church any more like AA.[29]

In any case, these programmatic expressions of Christian adaptation have had have little impact outside the evangelical orbit. More conservative Christians continue to criticize them for overstating Twelve-Step recovery's compatibility with the Bible, while mainline Christians view them as importing evangelical theology and culture into a movement that functions quite well without it. We turn now to consider some outspoken representatives of the latter perspective—the Christian embracers.

Can Christians Embrace Recovery?

(apparently)

Just north of Delray Beach, Florida—a location that has been called America's recovery capital, as well as an epicenter for drug overdose and insurance fraud—lies the city of Lantana. Given the ubiquity of treatment centers and halfway houses in Palm Beach County, local residents driving along Lantana Boulevard are probably not surprised to see a banner advertising something called Recovery Church. But most are likely unaware that the name refers not only to a congregation but to a church brand.[1]

The Recovery Church movement is the brainchild of Philip Dvorak, a youngish-looking minister and licensed therapist who relocated to south Florida from the Midwest to start a "Christian track" in one of Delray Beach's residential treatment centers. When another facility in the area hired him to develop a similar program, Dvorak and his team began a midweek church service for residents called Drunk Church. The name was suggested by a client. "You've been to church drunk," Dvorak remembers the man saying. "But you've never been to Drunk Church." Over time, the weekly service began to function as an independent congregation and was growing at the rate of ten to twenty adult baptisms per week. Although uneasy staff members scheduled activities to compete with Drunk Church, the service thrived and eventually outgrew the treatment center.

In 2011, Drunk Church relocated to Lake Worth's Bamboo Room—an aging blues hall that was unoccupied during much of the week—and changed its name to Recovery Church. Services at the Bamboo Room attracted up to three hundred people, but when rent went sky-high following the venue's revitalization, Recovery Church was forced to find a new home. Dvorak identified a local Lutheran congregation in the process of going under and offered to fund renovations to its building in exchange for rent credit. By the time I visited Lantana Recovery Church in 2019, it was occupying the renovated building on Lantana Boulevard.

The first Recovery Church plant was Drunk Church in Knoxville, Tennessee, established in 2013, and by 2020 ten sites were in operation across the eastern half of the US, in Florida, Tennessee, Missouri, New Jersey, Texas, Michigan, and Minnesota. Congregations affiliated with Recovery Church endorse a set of core values that reveal the movement's commitment to Twelve-Step recovery. These include *unity* ("We are united with the church and all 12-Step fellowships. We are for the church. We are for recovery, and we encourage the Recovery Church family to be active in both."); *Steps* ("We work and believe in the 12-Steps. They embody many of the Bible's core teachings and will lead a person closer to God."); *rotation* ("We serve with a spirit of [leadership] rotation, with humility at the center of all efforts."); *rawness* ("Recovery Church is raw, unrefined, and with no pretense."); and *discipleship/sponsorship* ("We see both sponsorship and discipleship as essential to our life.").

Recovery Movement churches also commit to a set of processes that include self-support, team leadership, gospel- and recovery-centered teaching, celebration of sobriety anniversaries, open sharing, and anonymity. Worship follows a pattern well known in evangelical circles in which the words to praise songs are projected onto large screens. Interspersed between songs are film clips, personal testimonies, announcements, and a reading of the Recovery Church movement's core principles. Sobriety milestones are marked by small crosses that function like chips in Twelve-Step fellowships. All this is followed by a sermon, after which attendees break into small groups according to gender and topic.

The night I visited Lantana Recovery Church, Dvorak's message was an unambiguous endorsement of Twelve-Step recovery. Using phrases from the AA Big Book such as "half measures availed us nothing" and "rarely have we seen a person fail," he emphasized that Christian faith and recovery each require "all-in" commitments. The sermon concluded with an altar call in which newcomers were invited to dedicate their lives to Christ, pray a prayer of acceptance, raise their hands indicating they had done so, and come to the front of the sanctuary for prayer. The five persons who responded to the call were charged with the words "God bless you, and stay sober." About half of the sixty to seventy people present for worship stayed to attend open-share groups that resembled Twelve-Step meetings in nearly every respect. Familiar guidelines were reiterated—no fixing others' problems, no cross-talk, no foul language, no violations of anonymity. Those who spoke introduced themselves using the well-known AA formula ("I'm Steve, and I'm an alcoholic or addict").

My visit a few weeks later to Recovery Church Vero Beach—about ninety miles up Florida's Atlantic coast—revealed a problem that any loose association of churches must eventually face: Since each Recovery Church is hosted by a sponsoring congregation, it inevitably reflects that church's distinct ecclesiastical character. Recovery Church's host in Vero Beach is Overflow Church, an independent charismatic congregation associated with the Vineyard movement that was founded, according to its literature, "through dreams and words" received directly from the Spirit. Dvorak works hard to ensure that such denominational quirks do not deter those seeking recovery. But managing such things is challenging in a network of churches that are connected by loose bonds and separated by considerable distances.[2]

In many ways, the Recovery Church services I visited felt and sounded like Celebrate Recovery meetings. But while they share the familiar CR rhythm of meal, service, message, and group share, Recovery Churches are distinctive inasmuch as they do not Christianize or otherwise adapt Twelve-Step recovery to the sensibilities of church folk. This is clear in the organization's pitch to potential donors, whom they ask to provide not only Bibles but also the basic texts of Alcoholics Anonymous and Narcotics Anonymous. In its own words, Recovery Church is not a Christian adaptation of "secular recovery" but "a church created by the recovery community for the recovery community." Nor is Recovery Church a substitute for involvement in Twelve-Step fellowships. As Dvorak puts it, "we need Christians 'in the rooms.'"

Recovery Church also differs from most adapter programs in its narrow focus on substance addiction. Because many involved in the movement are employees or former clients of residential addiction treatment centers, churches affiliated with Recovery Church tend to focus on the problems that send people to rehab. This means that in Recovery Church services one is more likely to hear references to interventions, relapses, and overdoses than to family dysfunction, codependency, and the sorts of "hurts, habits, and hang-ups" that attract many people to CR. The way Dvorak sees it, codependents need recovery, too; but RCM is called to work with the addicts and alcoholics "who need God or will die."

Finally, because Recovery Church views itself as a *church* rather than a *program*, it generally avoids the us/them dynamic that can leave people in church-based recovery groups feeling like a congregation's stepchildren. Recovery Church is neither an outreach ministry nor a time set aside for "those people" to use church facilities. As a congregation of recovering addicts, it reflects the singleness of purpose for which Christians have long admired AA and other Twelve-Step fellowships.

The Embracers

Like Dvorak and other members of the Recovery Church movement, embracers are Christians whose endorsement of Twelve-Step recovery is virtually unqualified. It is not predicated on revising the Steps to make them better reflect Christian principles, compiling Scripture passages to indicate the Steps' biblical character, or otherwise attempting to make Twelve-Step recovery "Christ-centered." Whatever other labels can be applied to them—conservative or liberal, Roman Catholic or Protestant, low church or high—embracers view Twelve-Step recovery as eminently compatible with Christian thought and practice in their own traditions.

However, different embracer groups arrive at their positive assessments of Twelve-Step recovery on different paths. For evangelical embracers, their confidence is rooted in a conviction that, as part of a recovery program nurtured by the theological commitments of the Oxford Group, the Twelve Steps are eminently Christian. Nonevangelical embracers, meanwhile, tend to view the Steps as compatible with Christian spirituality but also as a distillation of an "ancient wisdom" that reflects "the teaching of spiritual thinkers from all ages and all traditions." For the first group, Twelve-Step recovery belongs in church because it was "born in the cradle of Christianity"; for the second, because it represents a "spiritual journey [taken] throughout the ages" that embodies a perennial "spirituality of imperfection" echoing Christianity's own deepest truths.[3]

Evangelical Embracers

Because so many adaptation schemes have arisen from within American evangelicalism, it is tempting to conclude that conservative Christians' engagements with Twelve-Step recovery fall exclusively into that category. But as the Recovery Church movement indicates, this is not the case.

Claire W. is an evangelical embracer who in *God, Help Me Stop!* (1988) calls the Twelve Steps "a path to freedom" that is relied on by people "to solve all kinds of addictive and compulsive behavior." While she utilizes dozens of Bible verses to elucidate the Steps' Christian meaning, with the exception of replacing "alcohol" with "our compulsion" in Step 1, Claire W. adopts them in their entirety. Nor is she concerned with the lack of theological content in phrases such as "God as we understood Him." For Claire W., a former atheist raised as a Jew, the Steps' theological openness is an acknowledgment that, when it comes to God, personal experience is more reliable than "the conflict-ing doctrines over which men argue." With regard to the Steps' evangelistic potential, she claims that the search to improve their conscious contact with God has led many in recovery "to know His Son Jesus."[4]

Evangelical publications belonging in the embracer category include the Life Recovery Guides authored by Dale and Juanita Ryan and published by InterVarsity Press between 1990 and 1993. These brief (sixty-page) work-books treat recovery from family dysfunction, distorted images of God, shame, bitterness, abuse, loss, addictions, and codependency. In their ap-proach to illuminating the Bible's relevance for recovery, these guides differ markedly from the recovery Bibles reviewed in the previous chapter. Rather than claiming to find a recovery message on every page of Scripture, the Ryans view selected biblical texts in the light of Twelve-Step concepts such as powerlessness, unmanageability, restoration to sanity, and turning one's will and life over to God. In the process, they show that while the Bible can be fruitfully explored with recovery in mind, it is "not a book of quick fixes and simplistic solutions."[5]

In 1999, the Ryans offered a more focused biblical exploration of the Steps that highlights their usefulness in facing difficulties beyond addiction. In *A Spiritual Kindergarten: Christian Perspectives on the Twelve Steps* ("spiritual kindergarten" is a description of the Steps coined by Bill W.), the Ryans com-mend the Steps as "building blocks for a saner, freer, more grace-full way of life" for all whose problems include patterns of behavior hurtful to themselves and others. Even more so than in their Life Recovery Guides, in *A Spiritual Kindergarten* the Ryans utilize the language of the Steps as a hermeneutical key for unlocking the Scriptures. For example, their chapter on Step 1 is divided into sections titled "we," "admitted," "we were powerless," "over alcohol," and "our lives had become unmanageable."[6]

In *A Spiritual Kindergarten*, the Ryans also note places in the Steps where Christians often become hung up, particularly the God-language in Steps 2, 3, and 11. They emphasize that while some are tempted to replace phrases such as "power greater than ourselves" and "God as we understood Him" with refer-ences to Jesus Christ, in recovery it is important to "keep the door of spiritual kindergarten open." "We won't get very far," the Ryans remind us, "if we must pass an examination in theology" before we start working the Steps. In this spirit, they suggest that after completing Step 11 readers observe how different is their concept of God from when they began recovery. Crucially, the Ryans emphasize that most Christians continue to find participation in secular re-covery groups essential to maintaining their recovery.[7]

The Path to Serenity: The Book of Spiritual Growth and Spiritual Change through Twelve-Step Recovery was coauthored in 1991 by psychologists Robert Hemfelt and Richard Fowler and psychiatrists Frank Minirth and Paul Meier, all staff members at the Minirth-Meier Clinic in Dallas. The authors' unqualified advocacy of Twelve-Step recovery as a "unique approach to spiritual and emotional healing" is reflected in their decision to recommend an unedited version of the Steps, as well as in their repeated references to AA program literature. *The Path to Serenity* even presents the Steps as a boon to Christian discipleship, connecting AA's "promises" with "the fruits of the spirit" and the message-carrying emphasis in Step 12 with "lifestyle evangelism." Like the Ryans, Hemfelt and his coauthors claim that anyone who works the Steps will grow gradually closer to God, although the "invitation to move into the presence of the all-powerful God who is available in the person of the Lord Jesus Christ" may only be fully realized in Step 11. Like the Ryans, Hemfelt and his coauthors encourage readers to join Twelve-Step groups as they "embark on their journey to recovery."[8]

In 1993, Minirth and Fowler combined with Brian Newman and Dave Carder to once again give Twelve-Step recovery the Minirth-Meier Clinic's imprimatur. *Steps to a New Beginning: Leading Others to Christ through the Twelve Step Process* is a plea for placing the Steps at the center of the church's life—as a spiritual discipline, a foundation for recovery support groups, and a guide to personal evangelism. The physician-authors of *Steps to a New Beginning* recommend the Steps not only for those suffering from obsessive-compulsive disorders such as addiction, but for all Christians. And since the Steps are "a distillation of profound Christian truths" that serve their purpose "exactly as written," adaptation is unnecessary.[9]

Mike O'Neill's *Power to Choose: Twelve Steps to Wholeness* (1991) is a workbook designed to assist those "taking the Twelve Steps" as part of the Power to Choose program, a Christ-centered Twelve-Step support ministry. Like other embracers, O'Neill sees no need to adapt or revise the Steps, particularly since working them as "originally described" brought him into "a relationship with Jesus Christ that [he] had never had before." While O'Neill regards Jesus Christ as "the highest power," he defends the Steps' emphasis on "God as we understood Him" and does not recommend altering their language. O'Neill's frequent citations of the AA Big Book and his claim to find "the gospel of Jesus Christ in the Twelve Steps" are indicative of *The Power to Choose*'s unflinching embrace of Twelve-Step recovery.[10]

Bill Morris is another evangelical author who sees a central place for Twelve-Step recovery in the church's ministry. In *The Complete Handbook for Recovery Ministry in the Church* (1993), Morris presents the Twelve-Step movement as a spiritual revolution the church should embrace:

> The church helped to begin and offer to the world one of God's most life-changing ministries, one that has done miracles in the lives of millions of individuals and families, and let it slip away because of its judgmentalism and legalism. . . . I believe it is time for the church to reclaim and restore the truth of Scripture reflected in the Twelve Steps, and to offer once again the life-changing power of Jesus Christ that they point to and offer to all people.[11]

Morris's affirmation of the Steps, though couched in explicitly Christian language, is unequivocal. Without editing or adaptation, he writes, they comprise "a form of discipleship" that instructs people "how to begin and how to live the Christian life." In fact, because the Steps "reflect the central message of the Bible and the gospel of Jesus Christ," Christians who follow them can be confident they are following Christ himself.[12]

The most prominent of the evangelical embracers is probably J. Keith Miller, whose story of recovery was described in an earlier chapter. In *A Hunger for Healing: The Twelve Steps as a Classic Model for Spiritual Growth* (1991), Miller relates how he discovers Twelve-Step recovery in the wake of a divorce and professional treatment for "compulsive and addictive behavior." As a "Christian star" who is forced to acknowledge that the failure of his marriage was caused in part by his work addiction, Miller feels abandoned by erstwhile fans and supporters. But this experience of "hitting bottom" ends up precipitating a spiritual awakening through the Steps, which he comes to regard as perhaps "the most important spiritual model of any age for contemporary Christians."[13]

While Miller connects each Step with verses from the New Testament, he does not do so in an attempt to Christianize them. In explicating the Twelve Steps, in fact, he is less likely to cite Scripture than to quote from the AA Big Book and the "Twelve and Twelve." On the matter of the Steps' generic God language, Miller claims this is one reason for AA's remarkable success. Acknowledging that choosing one's conception of the divine can be frightening for Christians, Miller testifies that in his own experience the God who emerges during Step work is the God "revealed through the life, death, and resurrection of Jesus of Nazareth." In the end, Miller's appeal to fellow Christians is straightforward and personal: "I'm not saying that you have to do the Twelve Steps to be a good Christian," he writes. "I'm saying that if you are sick enough of being miserable and want to get over the pain and confusion of the Sin-disease, this is the best way I know to do it."[14]

No Christian writer has been more enthusiastic about the therapeutic value of the Twelve Steps than Tim Timmons. When his book *Anyone Anonymous* was published in 1990, Timmons was pastor of an Orange County, California, megachurch where he utilized the Steps extensively in pastoral counseling. According to Timmons, there is "no problem area out of [the Twelve Steps'] reach," including phobias, handicaps, abuse, divorce, bereavement, and bankruptcy. Timmons attributes his belief in the healing power of the Steps to the "positive, life-changing" results they have wrought in his own life. And since there has never been "a more productive system for personal problem solving," there is no need to revise the Steps (beyond changing "alcohol" to "our problem" in Step 1) or even confirm them with scriptural references. Finally, while Timmons believes Jesus is "the most adequate Higher Power," he does not press the issue; after all, he writes, Jesus was "down on religion."[15]

In 1993, Martin M. Davis, a professional counselor and bishop in the International Charismatic Church Network, published *The Gospel and the Twelve Steps: Developing a Closer Relationship with Jesus.* The book, which remains popular with Christian recovery groups and prison ministries in the US and appeared in a third edition in 2016, exudes Davis's confidence that the Twelve Steps are "firmly based on the *biblical* principles that form the foundation of authentic Christianity." For Davis, the act of turning our wills and lives over to God described in Step 3 is part of a lifelong process of sanctification, God's removal of our shortcomings in Step 7 is akin to justification, and Step 10 is an invitation to daily take up our cross and follow Jesus. The Steps are so aligned with the rhythms of Christian discipleship, in fact, that when we practice recovery principles in all our affairs, we engage in "true worship."[16]

Since all but one of these books first appeared between 1988 and 1993, they confirm the recovery revolution's impact on American evangelicalism during that period. Much more than other Christians, evangelical groups were keen to incorporate Twelve-Step recovery into their missions and ministries as it became a societal force. This can be explained partly as a function of evangelicals' desire to "engage the culture" and partly in terms of their familiarity and comfort with small group programs. Still, it is remarkable that representatives of a religious culture known for its skepticism toward secular ideologies so enthusiastically endorsed Twelve-Step recovery while expressing so little concern about its theological nonspecificity or spiritual eclecticism.

Mainline Embracers

Perhaps because they have long maintained a friendly posture toward AA and similar fellowships, in recent years nonevangelical Protestants have produced fewer published engagements with Twelve-Step recovery. Nevertheless, strong endorsements can be found in the stories of mainline Protestant leaders who have relied on it to save their lives and careers. One example is James B. Nelson's *Thirst: God and the Alcoholic Experience*, which we reviewed in an earlier chapter.

Another is *Help and Hope for the Alcoholic* by Alexander C. DeJong, a pastor in the Christian Reformed Church who after thirty years in the pulpit finds himself in an alcohol treatment facility. Forced to attend AA while in rehab, DeJong learns that the fellowship shares with his own faith tradition the paradoxical belief that "to become strong one must confess utter weakness; to be rescued, one must give up trying to save oneself." Following his discharge, DeJong discovers a pastoral calling among the "delightful, religiously complicated people" who attend his Twelve-Step meetings, people who, despite being injured by their church experience, listen respectfully as he witnesses to the healing power of Christ. DeJong believes that, regardless of whether they are aware of it, whenever "alcoholics have been set at liberty, it is by Christ's stripes that they are healed." Like other embracers, he does not believe the Steps need to be revised; nor does he support the formation of "Christian" recovery groups.[17]

Another mainline Protestant pastor whose ministry has been molded by Twelve-Step recovery is Episcopal priest John Z., author of *Grace in Addiction: The Good News of Alcoholics Anonymous for Everybody*. In the book's introduction, Z. relates his journey from "pothead teenager," to polysubstance abuser, to AA newcomer, and then, after four years of sobriety, to church visitor:

> At one of the initial services I attended, I remember reading for the first time in over ten years the words of confession from the *Book of Common Prayer*: "*We have erred and strayed from Thy ways like lost sheep. We have followed too much the devices and desires of our own hearts.*" I remembered the lines from my childhood. I remembered how abstract and irrelevant the whole religious endeavor had seemed to me in my youth. But now, in that low moment, I found in them a more complete understanding of myself than I had known in years.

This experience marks the beginning of a spiritual awakening that "connect[s] the dots between [Z.'s] life and Christianity" and eventually leads him to the Episcopal priesthood.[18]

Because Z. discovers in church "a deepening of the things I learned from the Twelve Steps about human nature and God," he perceives Christ secretly at work in AA. "Where there is redemption to be found, then there too is Christ," he writes. "Where there is healing, there is the presence of the Great Physician." But if Christ is accessible in AA, why should Christians in search of recovery remain in their churches? Z.'s answer points to a symbiotic relationship between Christianity and Twelve-Step recovery: When the church tells the right story—the story of bad people coping with their failure to be good through the grace of Christ—"the spiritual picture painted in Twelve Step recovery" comes into sharpened focus.[19]

Michele S. Matto's *The Twelve Steps in the Bible: A Path to Wholeness for Adult Children* reflects the insights of the recovery revolution, particularly for adults struggling with the consequences of growing up in dysfunctional families. At the time the book appeared, Matto was a United Churches of Christ pastor inspired by an ACA group she attended. She writes that although her fellow adult children tend to identify as atheists, it isn't the Christian God they reject but "some cosmic dysfunctional Parent in the sky who [is] judgmental, punitive, and very conditional and withholding of love." The God of grace whom she experiences and preaches, however, Matto finds alive and well in these meetings. This is because the Steps' spiritual wisdom, particularly as it applies to recovering adult children of alcoholics, is clearly reflected in Scripture.[20]

It is difficult to categorize a book such as John C. Mellon's *Mark as Recovery Story*, which interprets the New Testament book using the language and categories of Twelve-Step recovery. Mellon proposes that the community out of which Mark's Gospel emerged was part of a first-century Jewish recovery movement, a sobriety fellowship of "former drunkards turned water drinkers." Evidence for this hypothesis Mellon finds in Markan passages he believes correspond to "the transhistorical spirituality of today's Twelve-Step movement," passages that yield a fresh image of Jesus as "a humbled and ultimately anonymous recovering person." Mellon claims that viewing Jesus as alcoholic ratifies "the fullness of his humanity" without violating traditional views of his sinlessness and divine nature, thus making him "a more accessible model of God-reliant spirituality." In his choice of the Twelve Steps as a lens through which to view Christian origins, Mellon imagines a very different type of recovery Bible.[21]

CHAPTER 8

Roman Catholic Embracers

Organizations

There is considerable evidence that Twelve-Step recovery has been embraced by American Catholicism. In addition to a wide variety of diocesan recovery ministries, there are web-based resources such as "12-Step Review" (a site from which one can purchase "Our Lady of Recovery Prayer Cards" and a collection of books, lectures, and pamphlets by Fr. Emmerich Vogt, OP), the Venerable Matt Talbot Resource Center (dedicated to advancing the legacy of an Irish layman who maintained sobriety after taking an abstinence pledge in the 1880s), and the Ignatian Spirituality Project, which explores the intersection between Twelve-Step recovery and "the guiding principles" of that tradition. There are also book-length studies relating the Twelve Steps to the Catholic Church's sacraments and spiritual practices.[22]

The oldest American Catholic recovery organization is the Calix Society, which was founded in Minneapolis in 1947 and today operates chapters in about twenty US states, the UK, and Ireland. This dues-supported network of recovering alcoholics, their friends, and family members insists that it is not "Catholic A.A." since it regards the Twelve-Step program as "the best therapy for those afflicted with the disease of alcoholism." But to AA members who find themselves yearning for a faith they have neglected or abandoned, Calix says, "Come back home. You must maintain your sobriety through your affiliation with Alcoholics Anonymous, but let us help you to regain the spiritual life without which you may not succeed in the never-ending fight against your addiction." The group's inimitable motto is "substituting the cup that sanctifies for the cup that stupefies."[23]

Richard Rohr

Among the many publications by Richard Rohr—Franciscan friar and founder of the Center for Action and Contemplation, whose mission is to introduce seekers to the "contemplative Christian path of transformation"—is *Breathing under Water: Spirituality and the Twelve Steps* (2011). Rohr introduces this popular book with a statement that epitomizes Christian embrace of Twelve-Step recovery: "The Gospel message of Jesus and the Twelve Step message of Bill Wilson," he writes, not only share "a common inspiration from the Holy Spirit and the same collective unconscious" but on a practical level "are largely the same message, even in some detail."[24]

Rohr points to several ways in which these "two teachings" say "the same thing but with different vocabulary." For instance, each communicates the paradoxical truth that "we suffer to get well. We surrender to win. We die to live. We give it away to keep it." Rohr finds further links between Twelve-Step recovery and the church's faith in connections between sin and addiction, enlightenment and recovery, grace and ego-deflation, the kingdom of God and "vital spiritual experience," and awareness of the "log in [one's] own eye" and the condition of powerlessness. According to Rohr, these symmetries demonstrate that Christian faith and the Twelve Steps are each fed by "the very rich and nutritious 'marrow of the Gospel.'"[25]

Another parallel noted by Rohr is that both "programs" must be "worked" in order to be effective. Just as the Twelve Steps can be a path to "mere sobriety" as opposed to spiritual transformation, well-intentioned Christians— including clergy, Rohr notes—often fail to allow their faith to heal them at the unconscious level where issues of ego, control, and security operate. According to Rohr, freedom from self- and cultural-deception can be gained only through a "form of alternative consciousness" he describes as mystical or nondualistic. Twelve-Step recovery is an ideal path for spiritual healing, Rohr notes, because the Steps offer just this sort of alternative consciousness, teaching us to displace the "imperial ego" through surrender and a recognition of powerlessness.[26]

Like Christian adapters, Rohr connects each Step with passages in the Old and New Testaments. But he does so not as an adapter who believes the Bible is necessary for a proper understanding of the Steps but as an embracer who believes the Steps can clarify and repristinate Christianity. If the Twelve Steps appear to be "thoroughly biblical," Rohr argues, it is not because they were derived from Scripture. Rather, it is because, along with the Bible, they reflect a perennial wisdom that is sadly obscured in our religious institutions but that emerges into awareness as spiritual consciousness evolves. Just as Jesus is "a teacher of commonsense spiritual wisdom" who cannot be encompassed by a single religion, so the Steps are both fully Christian and universally relevant.[27]

Thomas Keating

Another prominent Roman Catholic figure who has explored the nexus between Twelve-Step recovery and Christian spirituality is Thomas Keating, Cistercian monk and teacher of a form of contemplation known as centering prayer. His thoughts on the Steps are set out in *Divine Therapy and Addiction: Centering Prayer and the Twelve Steps*, a book of interviews conducted by recovering alcoholic Tom S. and published in 2009. Before his death in 2018, Keating taught centering prayer through Contemplative Outreach, a spiritual network of individuals and faith communities "committed to living the contemplative dimension of the Gospel." In 2001 Contemplative Outreach launched 12 Step Outreach to promote centering prayer as a Step 11 prayer/meditation practice through workshops, retreats, and local prayer and meditation-themed recovery groups.[28]

Like other Christian advocates of the Steps, Keating argues for their applicability to problems far beyond alcoholism. He claims, in fact, that because they contain a remedy for humans' "basic affliction," described by Christians in terms like "fall" or "original sin," the Twelve Steps are universally applicable. The flawed character of human existence leads us to search for happiness apart from the divine presence, Keating observes, and addiction is one of the psyche's ways of medicating the pain caused by the resulting lack of intimacy with our Creator. Keating views working the Steps as a "transformative practice" that addresses this lost intimacy by facilitating an "ever-deepening relationship with God."[29] For instance, the admission of powerlessness at the heart of Step 1 is "the best disposition for beginning a spiritual journey," while Steps 4 and 5 resonate with the Christian ascetical tradition, "in which the revelation of one's faults and the discovery of one's interior motivation" are essential. Step 11 calls for a nonconceptual meditation practice in which "God has a chance to introduce God as God actually is"; and since it invites God into our lives as a mysterious presence, meditation works as well for atheists as for believers. Finally, Keating calls the spiritual awakening promised in Step 12 "a transformation of consciousness that penetrates and encompasses the whole of our lives."[30]

Because contemplation is a demanding spiritual practice, Keating devotes a good deal of space in *Divine Therapy and Addiction* to clarifying what it is and is not. As a decision to be in God's presence, contemplation is a "movement from concentration to receptivity, from conversation to communion," in which God does not so much talk to as embrace us. And since it involves making ourselves "vulnerable to the Ultimate Reality that we know loves us," contemplation does not entail forming and articulating thoughts. In fact, its main component is silence, which Keating refers to as God's first language. Most crucially, the "divine therapy" that takes place during meditation operates on an unconscious level where we are invested "in worldly objectives such as security, affection, esteem and approval, power and control."[31]

Not surprisingly, Keating is unconcerned with clarifying AA's God-language for a Christian audience. Throughout *Divine Therapy and Addiction*, in fact, he refers to God as "the Higher Power," since he views any further identifiers as inadequate and even misleading. For Keating, there is no need to improve on the Twelve Steps or adapt them for Christian purposes. They not only represent classical spiritual wisdom but "summarize the essence of the Christian contemplative tradition" in a succinct, straightforward, and non-sectarian form.[32]

Sister Molly Monahan

In an earlier chapter, we reviewed *Seeds of Grace: Reflections on the Spirituality of Alcoholics Anonymous* by Sister Molly Monahan, a nun who after undergoing inpatient treatment for alcoholism discovers both sobriety and a renewed commitment to her faith. In that context, we noted the ways AA catalyzed Monahan's vocational renewal after alcoholism left her spiritually depleted. We return to Monahan as an exemplar of Roman Catholic embrace of Twelve-Step recovery, based on her willingness to allow it to structure and guide her practice as a nun.[33]

Naturally, Monahan views the Steps through the prism of her own tradition, particularly the contemplative life's "purgative," "illuminative," and "unitive" stages. But her goal is neither to affix an ecclesiastical imprimatur to the Steps nor to force them into a Catholic or Ignatian theological frame. She simply observes that people "come to know and love God in A.A." because it offers

> a powerful God, who desires our well-being, who can and will help us if we ask, who has in fact helped us and helps us still. By virtue of our own experience and the stories we hear from others, then, this God cannot be the stern lawgiver, the punishing God that many say they were taught to believe in. This God has to be a loving God, whose love for us invites love in return.[34]

Monahan regards the Steps' references to "a Power greater than ourselves" and "God, as we understood Him" as "strokes of genius—or divine inspiration" on the part of AA's founders. The Steps' theological nonspecificity is necessary, she argues, given the theological divisions within Christianity, not to mention the wars, inquisitions, pogroms, and persecutions to which they have given rise. In contrast to a dogmatic faith, the Steps represent a broad path "to the recovery or the beginnings of faith" for those who are alienated from the religion of their youth, are unsure of their faith, or are without faith at all. In Monahan's view, "the mysteries of the Catholic faith" do not contradict AA's unelaborated view of a Higher Power, but "strengthen it and give it fuller expression."[35]

Conclusion

In this and the two previous chapters, we have utilized the typology of *rejecters*, *adapters*, and *embracers* to classify Christian approaches to Twelve-Step recovery and highlight each model's assumptions and implications. As we have seen, *rejecters* deny the possibility that Twelve-Step recovery can usefully inform Christian responses to addiction (assuming they believe in addiction), while *adapters* are open to Twelve-Step principles and practices but are wary of endorsing recovery without introducing adaptations designed to convince believers that it is biblical and Christ-centered. *Embracers* are distinguished by their nearly unqualified commendation of the Twelve Steps. Representing a variety of ecclesiastical traditions, they share the conviction that Twelve-Step recovery does not need to be adapted for Christians—or anyone else.

Many Christian embracers, particularly mainline Protestants and Roman Catholics, view the Twelve Steps as part of a universal wisdom that resonates with religious traditions from around the world. While this view is also shared by many non-Christian interpreters of Twelve-Step spirituality, Christian embracers perceive in the Steps, not only a perennial philosophy to which all religions point, but a lost dimension of Christianity that calls the church back to its origins. What sorts of efforts are those who hear this call making to recover church? To that question we turn.[36]

How Are Christians Reclaiming
What the Church Gave AA?

(let us count the ways)

In an important sense, this book was born in 2015 when I came across an announcement for a weekend conference on the church and recovery to be held at a retreat center in the Texas hill country. As the conference coincided with my spring break, I registered and convinced a friend in recovery to join me. In many ways, the weekend was a revelation. I learned not only that Christians from a variety of denominations had found recovery in Twelve-Step fellowships, but that there was at least one organization dedicated to bringing us together.

The conference represented the beginning of my quest to explore the various paths Christians are forging toward the goal of recovering church. This chapter explores what I've learned since that time from interviewing, worshiping with, and participating in retreats alongside Christians who are engaged in efforts to reclaim what the church gave AA. I will describe some of their efforts under the headings *gathering, prayer, meditation, worship, training, support,* and *duplication.*

Gathering

The retreat I attended in 2015 was sponsored by The National Association for Christian Recovery (NACR), which came into being under the leadership of Fuller Theological Seminary's Dale Ryan in 1989. As Ryan recalls, this was a time when church-based recovery ministries "were mostly small, disconnected, marginalized, and confronted by resistance from elements within the Christian community." In 2010 the NACR was reorganized under the leadership of Baptist pastor Teresa McBean and since then has held regional and national conferences that convene Christians involved in recovery and recovery ministry.[1]

The NACR does not endorse a particular strategy for recovery ministry, but provides resources and consulting help for Christians involved in, or interested in starting, programs that arise out of local contexts. In the process, the NACR casts a wide net that crosses ecclesiastical fault lines and attracts representatives from a wide variety of denominations, counseling centers, parachurch organizations, prison ministries, and street missions. At a time when Christians are often segregated by labels such as mainline and evangelical, the NACR emphasizes the commitments to sobriety and to Christ that unite its members.[2]

Another organizational effort to gather Christians with an interest in addiction and recovery began in 2018, when the Fellowship of Recovering Lutheran Clergy and Recovery Ministries of the Episcopal Church began jointly sponsoring an annual conference on Addiction & Faith. I attended the second conference in Minneapolis in 2019, which brought together nearly two hundred participants from the worlds of addiction treatment and the church, the latter represented by ordained clergy, denominational staff, youth leaders, and laypersons from fifteen Christian denominations. Although it is a programmatic effort of mainline Christian organizations, the Addiction & Faith conferences make space for a wide variety of approaches to recovery. At the 2019 conference these included yoga, spiritual direction, journaling, praying with the body, and spiritual drumming.

Out of the annual Addiction & Faith conferences was born the Center of Addiction & Faith, an online resource hub that sponsors virtual Twelve-Step meetings, some specifically for clergy. It remains unclear whether the main purpose of the Addiction & Faith movement is to raise awareness of the ways "the church and people of faith" can address addiction in their midst or to bring together Christians in recovery for mutual support (the latter goal is suggested by the on-site Twelve-Step meetings at Addiction & Faith conferences). In any case, like NACR, the Center of Addiction & Faith and the Addiction & Faith conferences provide spaces where one can find support for organizational efforts to recover church, as well as the interpersonal connections that are crucial to sustaining recovery.

Like many jurisdictions within the Episcopal Church, the Diocese of Texas (encompassing the eastern part of that state) has an active Recovery Commission whose mission is to "educate and empower the communities of the diocese to redeem the brokenness of addiction through wellness and God's love." In 2017 I participated in the commission's annual recovery weekend at Camp Allen in the piney woods northwest of Houston, whose theme was "Integrating Spirituality and the Twelve Steps." The thirty or so retreat participants hailed from a variety of Episcopal parishes in Houston, Austin, and the smaller towns in between.[3]

At the opening session, which had the format of a Twelve-Step meeting, participants introduced themselves and shared their stories. One man who identified as a recovering alcoholic said he was currently serving five years of probation related to a DWI conviction. His wife described her involvement in Al-Anon, and both agreed that Twelve-Step recovery, in addition to saving their marriage, had profoundly affected their experience of God. Another man said his most recent DWI arrest had precipitated his wife's decision to divorce him, as well as the prospect of a five-year prison sentence. Participants continued to share in this vein, speaking openly of slips, relapses, arrests, time spent "out there," and other consequences of their or their loved ones' addictions. As a result of this kind of honest sharing, before its first meal together the group achieved a level of transparency that set the tone for the weekend.

In later sessions, retreat participants spoke of their desire to negotiate a dual identity in the space between their churches and Twelve-Step fellowships. Several persons described eventually joining the congregations that hosted their Twelve-Step home groups. One young man, who had drunk his way through divinity school, said he found sobriety in AA but lost God along the way. When he made his way back to church, he told us, he found that his spiritual sensibilities had been profoundly shaped by Twelve-Step recovery. An older gentleman spoke of his discomfort moving back and forth between his church's sanctuary and its basement (where his AA home group met) until he concluded that he was encountering "the same God in both places." Whether shared by priests, seminarians, laypersons, or visitors, such stories bespoke a common struggle to relate recovery and faith.

As an outsider at the retreat, I was struck by how many participants had found their way to the Episcopal Church from other religious traditions. One woman shared that she had been a Roman Catholic for fifty years before following her husband to the Episcopal church where he had found sobriety. It was the first time in her life she had felt close to God, she said. Another woman, a former Southern Baptist, said she had reclaimed her faith through a Chapter 9 group (an AA affiliate also known as Couples in Recovery Anonymous), where she and her husband were in the process of rebuilding their marriage. A third woman, raised in a devout evangelical family, described taking a decade or so off from organized religion before reencountering God in Overeaters Anonymous and finding a home in an Episcopal parish.

For a few of those in attendance, including a priest who was among the retreat leaders, Twelve-Step recovery had actually been the vehicle for their introduction to Christianity. But most talked of returning to church after a spiritual awakening facilitated by one or another Twelve-Step fellowship. Many of these credited the Episcopal Church's undogmatic theological posture and openness to diverse expressions of spirituality for making it a congenial place to get to know the God they had encountered in AA or Al-Anon. Strikingly un-Episcopalian, however, was participants' frequent use of the word *miracle* to describe their experiences in Twelve-Step recovery. I could not remember hearing the term used so freely in any group of mainline Protestants.

Prayer

In some of my conversations at the recovery weekend sponsored by the Episcopal Diocese of Texas, I heard repeated references to "quiet time" and "two-way prayer," phrases I associated with the spiritual disciplines of the Oxford Group. After some inquiry, I discovered that this language reflected the influence of Rev. Bill Wigmore, former head of the diocese's recovery commission, who had recently started a group called Friends of Dr. Bob. When the retreat ended, I made the two-hour drive to Austin to meet Wigmore and learn more about his new endeavor.

Before a Sunday evening meeting of Friends of Dr. Bob in a nondescript storefront space on the outskirts of Austin, I spoke with Wigmore about how the group had come into being. He told me that after becoming a Jesuit in the early 1970s, he had served in the Peace Corps, joined the Catholic Worker Movement, and lived on a kibbutz in Israel. Somewhere along this path, he said, he came to the humbling realization that he was an alcoholic and began attending AA. In an autobiographical piece titled "Finding Jesus in the Basement," Wigmore describes how he ended up in an AA meeting that, unsurprisingly, met in a church basement. Though his first impulse was to seek help upstairs among the good church folk, he writes, he found that the alcoholics downstairs could "read [him] like a book."[4]

Wigmore eventually left the Jesuits and followed a call into the field of addiction treatment. But he struggled to connect his recovery with his faith until he was introduced to the world of "early AA" (that is, the fellowship of the late 1930s before the publication of the Big Book). Wigmore learned that by modeling their life on Oxford Group principles, AA's pioneers had achieved a 75 percent recovery rate even in the absence of frequent meetings. The key to their success, he concluded, was that these men were less concerned with doctrine than with "finding a personal and living relationship with Christ."

Through Wigmore's discovery of Oxford Group spirituality, his recovery and his faith came together via "direct experience of the power and presence of God" nurtured by the OG disciplines of "quiet time" and "two-way prayer." Wigmore delved deeply into these early "11th Step practices," shared them with friends and sponsees, and eventually came to regard them as indispensable tools for ministry with addicts. Impressed by the role of Episcopal priest Sam Shoemaker in transmitting Oxford Group ideals to AA's pioneers, Wigmore sought ordination to the Episcopal priesthood.[5]

The Friends of Dr. Bob meeting I attended consisted of two parts: a communion service open to anyone in Twelve-Step recovery, and an Eleventh-Step meeting based on the discipline of two-way prayer as practiced by Dr. Bob and other AA pioneers. Donning vestments, Wigmore welcomed a half-dozen of us to the initial service, which he described as "church for people who don't go to church." He then led us through a worship liturgy that integrated recovery themes. We confessed our sins, recited a psalm, listened to readings from the New Testament and the Big Book, offered up prayers of the people, listened to a homily that referenced addiction and recovery, and shared the Eucharist.

After a brief time socializing, four of us reconvened for the Eleventh-Step portion of the meeting. We were told that Friends of Dr. Bob is a fellowship of men and women seeking to follow the original program of Alcoholics Anonymous, including the Oxford Group's Four Absolutes: Absolute Honesty (no lying, no cheating, no stealing); Absolute Purity (purity of mind, purity of body, purity of the emotions, purity of heart, sexual purity); Absolute Unselfishness (seeking what is right and true ahead of what I want in every situation); and Absolute Love (loving God with all one's heart, soul, mind, and strength and loving one's neighbor as oneself).

We were introduced to two-way prayer as a method for making contact with God and receiving divine guidance. During morning quiet time, Wigmore explained, one sits quietly, reads from a sacred text of some kind, clears away tension with a few cleansing breaths, and uses a prayer notebook to record a question directed to God, such as "I've tried getting clean and sober before—please tell me what I need to do that's different this time." Then, with pen and notebook in hand, one listens for God's voice and records whatever comes to mind, without reflection or editing. If a message is not forthcoming, one asks, "If God were to speak to me, what would God, or Love, or Divine Wisdom say?" One stops writing when the process "becomes strained."[6]

Individuals who practice two-way prayer, we were told, meet weekly with a prayer partner to share messages and record reactions to each other's messages. This cosharing is an important aspect of the discipline, Wigmore explained, because messages are to be regarded as containing divine guidance only if others confirm their consistency with the Four Absolutes. Meeting participants who testified to their own experience with two-way prayer indicated that, more than guidance on specific matters, what they gained from the practice was a feeling of intimacy with God referred to in Step 11 as "conscious contact."[7]

Over dinner, Wigmore and I discussed his vision for Friends of Dr. Bob. He emphasized that introducing people to his practices of quiet time and two-way prayer were only means toward the ultimate goal of founding an Episcopal religious order based on these practices. I later learned that in 2018 Wigmore's dream was realized when the Sam Shoemaker Community was officially organized as a Christian community (as defined by the canons of the Episcopal Church). According to its website, the group includes five members "in various stages of formation" and is dedicated to "finding Christ in us and in those we serve by living a monastic Rule of Life grounded in prayer, study, fellowship, and service." Community members, who undergo a multiyear formation process, commit to introducing the lost practice of two-way prayer to "today's spiritual seekers" and finding innovative ways to "bring the Good News of the gospel to those in 12-Step Fellowships."[8]

As we talked in 2017, it became evident why Wigmore was no longer involved in diocesan recovery ministry. He had come to regard as futile all efforts to make the church "recovery friendly," he explained, because churches and Twelve-Step fellowships speak different languages and perform different functions. More importantly, he said, recovery groups can reach people who will never knowingly set foot in a church building. The meeting I had just attended seemed to prove as much, as two of the newcomers said they had not darkened the door of a church since their teenage years. As Wigmore put it, "while others are called to bring recovery to the church, I'm called to bring the church—to bring God—to recovery." Thus, his goal is not to Christianize or "churchify" Twelve-Step fellowships as much as to help them recover the spiritual tools utilized so successfully by AA's pioneers.[9]

The Diocese of Texas is a revealing microcosm of the often complex cross-pollination between the American church and Twelve-Step recovery. Through providing a diversity of spaces for people in recovery to gather, a single jurisdiction within one Christian denomination encourages two different conceptions of recovery ministry to flourish side by side. One seeks to *open the church to recovery* by sponsoring retreats and supporting programming in local congregations, while the other tries to *open recovery to the church* by introducing those who are alienated from organized religion to Christian spiritual disciplines that do not presuppose church membership.

Meditation

In exploring the interface between recovery and the church, I kept stumbling across the phenomenon of so-called Eleventh-Step groups designed to help people in recovery "improve [their] conscious contact with God." Based on my interest in the Christian contemplative tradition, I decided to learn more about an organization called 12-Step Outreach (12SO). The group's origins reach back to the 1970s, when Catholic monks were trying to revive the contemplative dimension of Christian faith and compete with the Eastern meditation practices that were attracting Catholic laypeople. Led by Abbot Fr. Thomas Keating, monks at Saint Joseph's Abbey in Massachusetts established a meditation discipline known as centering prayer (CP) that involves sitting quietly, consenting to God's presence, using a sacred word to nudge one's wandering thoughts back to this place of consent, and trusting in the healing power of God's indwelling presence.

12SO grew out of Contemplative Outreach, Ltd., an organization that was founded by Father Keating in 1986 to teach and spread the practice of centering prayer, and that continues to do so despite his death in 2018. The mission of 12-Step Outreach is to "pass on the gift of Centering Prayer and related spiritual practices . . . wherever there is a desire for deeper healing from anyone in 12-Step recovery." When used as a "daily supplement" to Twelve Step practice, the group contends, centering prayer has the capacity to deepen one's relationship with one's Higher Power. Reflecting the nonsectarian spirit of Twelve-Step recovery, 12SO downplays CP's Christian roots, describing it as a way to support the program of "human transformation" made possible by AA.[10]

My introduction to the work of 12SO came at a weekend retreat sponsored by 12-Step Outreach of Saint Louis and led by group members who had undergone rigorous training in centering prayer. The Saint Louis group is one of 12SO's more active chapters, hosting regular Eleventh-Step meditation meetings and centering prayer groups in the Saint Louis area, in addition to an annual centering prayer retreat. I attended the 2017 retreat along with about fifty others, mostly white baby boomers and millennials who identified as members of AA or Al-Anon. Although about half were first-time retreat attendees, most had at least some experience with centering prayer.

At the orientation session on Friday evening, retreat participants learned that the weekend's instruction would proceed along two tracks. Anyone who was not already "sitting" (practicing CP) twice daily was encouraged to participate in track 1, while more experienced practitioners were welcomed to join track 2. My own experience of centering prayer as an Eleventh-Step practice began early on Saturday morning in two twenty-minute sessions separated by a meditative walk around the chapel. Breakfast (which was taken in silence) was followed by a presentation on "the human condition." After a silent lunch there was "open time," during which participants were invited to "walk and talk" with retreat leaders to discuss their CP practice.

At dinner, the first meal to include "conversation," I sat down with one of the retreat leaders to learn more about 12SO in Saint Louis. I was told the group's founding figure was Donald Masters, a Vietnam veteran who began practicing centering prayer to deal with his post-traumatic stress disorder and eventually brought the practice to local Twelve-Step groups. In 2000, several of those whom Masters had introduced to CP traveled to Snowmass, Colorado, for a retreat with Fr. Keating and came back determined to develop a vibrant centering prayer program that would support Twelve-Step recovery in the Saint Louis area.

During the weekend I noted retreat leaders' frequent and earnest testimonies to the benefits of CP. The practice facilitates the movement from self-centeredness to God-centeredness, we were told, and enhances one's ability to realize the promises of recovery. We were taught that CP is an ideal method for dismantling what Keating calls "the false-self system," and that by helping identify character defects and repressed unconscious material, it is a valuable tool for working through Steps 6 and 7. ("We were entirely ready to have God remove all these defects of character," and "We humbly asked Him to remove our shortcomings.") We were informed that people often discover CP when their recovery has stalled or plateaued, and that couples who practice CP together report increased marital intimacy. And we were encouraged with the reminder that if "sitting" twice per day seems an overwhelming commitment, we should recall our initial reaction to being asked to attend "all those recovery meetings."

What was not said, but I sensed was true based on my conversations with leaders and retreatants, is that people in recovery are drawn to CP because it promises intimacy with a Higher Power whose qualities of gentleness and unconditional love were absent from their previous religious training. The message that God loves us and desires our healing is certainly welcome news for recovering addicts who may carry wounds inflicted by organized religion, as is the claim that in the process of transformation "God does all the work." Similarly, conceiving of centering prayer as a relationship with God that develops in silence is attractive to those from religious traditions where ritual prayers are the rule. (Significantly, many retreatants I spoke with said they had "grown up Catholic.")

Still, no one attending a CP workshop would get the impression that the practice of centering prayer is an easy path to intimacy with God. Again and again, we were reminded that the keys to success with CP are commitment and fidelity. These requirements were easy to fulfill during the retreat. But I wondered how many of us would continue our practice after returning home. The allure of CP is that it seems deceptively undemanding (*"just* keep your butt in the chair"); the challenge is maintaining consistency ("just *keep* your butt in the chair"). If people are willing to practice CP in the midst of their busy lives, it is in the hope of realizing its spiritual benefits, which one retreat leader described this way: "One sit per day is devotional; two sits per day is transformational." In order to achieve this transformational level of centering prayer practice, newcomers like myself were encouraged to try "thirty in thirty" (that is, thirty days of continuous CP practice).

12SO helps people in recovery realize the promise expressed in *Twelve Steps and Twelve Traditions* that "every A.A. who has a religious connection which emphasizes meditation will return to the practice of that devotion as never before." For church folk unfamiliar with meditation, centering prayer can be embraced as an ancient form of Christian devotion. For the nonreligious, meanwhile, it can be viewed as a nonsectarian spiritual practice that contributes to the goal of "mindfulness." 12SO tends in this latter direction. No attempt is made to hide CP's Catholic monastic origins (and Father Thomas is treated with a respect that borders on veneration). Yet references to Christ are not to be found in the group's literature and were conspicuously absent from retreat presentations. In other words, 12SO presents centering prayer as a way to enhance one's Step-11 practice, regardless of one's relationship to the Christian tradition.[11]

Worship

Thrive Church

Bill Wigmore's storefront service for "people who don't go to church" represents one way of allowing recovery to shape the experience of Christian worship. But there are many others, and each reflects the style and culture of the hosts, not to mention the people they hope to attract. One example is Thrive, which describes itself as a healing ministry of The Orchard, a United Methodist congregation with branches across north Mississippi. According to its website, Thrive is a group of junkies and ex-cons, teachers and construction workers, on drug court and getting out of treatment. . . . We are recovering atheists, agnostics, and religious fundamentalists. If you haven't figured it out yet, we are learning how to be okay with being not okay. And yet, by the grace of God, we are moving out of denial and into reality, out of resentment and into forgiveness, out of our dis-ease and into awakening![12]

These references to *treatment, recovering, denial, resentment,* and *awakening* suggest that Thrive is fluent in the language of recovery, and the service I visited bears this out. Thursday night worship at Thrive is preceded by dinner and followed by small group meetings for people struggling with substance abuse, codependency, sexual integrity, divorce, or grief. On the night of my visit, there were around fifty people in attendance, most of them between the ages of twenty and forty. Many were young parents taking advantage of Thrive's "prerecovery" care for children under twelve.

Thrive's worship space is dominated by a large screen behind a stage on which speakers and musicians take turns leading the service. There is no pulpit, no baptismal font, and no communion table, fixtures around which worship is organized in most Protestant churches. On the night I attended, the sermon was delivered by Colby Cuevas, care and recovery pastor at The Orchard, Tupelo. Dressed in a T-shirt and sandals, Cuevas spoke openly of his inpatient treatment for drug addiction and signaled his ability to relate to younger members of the congregation with informal questions like "do you feel me?" The basis for his sermon was the biblical story of Job, retold with references to "using," recovery, sponsorship, and the Serenity Prayer. Job was able to "surrender," Cuevas told the congregation, because he could "trust the process."

At Thrive, Twelve-Step recovery is incorporated into, but not adapted for, church use. There is no Christianized revision of the Twelve Steps and no recitation of Step-Scripture parallels. In fact, AA's Steps in their original version seem to be regarded as a product something close to divine inspiration. "I've met people who say AA didn't work for them," one speaker told the congregation, "but I've never met anyone who says the Steps didn't work for them." In place of a benediction, the service concludes with hand-holding and a group rendition of the Serenity Prayer, introduced by the words, "who makes us thrive . . . ?" In its language and rhythms, worship at Thrive feels considerably more like a Twelve-Step meeting than a Methodist worship service.

Thrive advertises itself as both a "ministry of The Orchard" and a "recovery community of people seeking healing and wholeness in Christ." This left me to wonder whether Thrive is best understood as a church program (like Celebrate

Recovery) or a church within a larger congregation (like Recovery Church). To be sure, its sponsorship of activities such as Eleventh-Step meditation meetings suggests that Thrive functions independently from its host congregation. Yet it must do so within the social and theological contexts of The Orchard and the United Methodist Church. For instance, Thrive's commitment to radical hospitality toward "anyone and everyone no matter what you've been through or what you're going through" would seem to place it at odds with the conservative resurgence within its denomination. This may explain why soon after my visit The Orchard announced it was leaving the Mississippi Conference of the United Methodist Church in order to steer clear of contentious arguments around sexuality.[13]

Recovery at Powell

Recovery at Powell, a weeknight service at Powell United Methodist Church outside Knoxville, Tennessee, where I visited in 2018, began as a Celebrate Recovery group. But Recovery at Powell shed the association with CR to pattern itself after a recovery service pioneered by a local multicampus congregation, Cokesbury United Methodist.

While neither church utilizes CR materials, both have preserved the group's program template. Meetings begin with a communal meal, continue with a worship service featuring praise music and a Twelve-Step themed message, and conclude in a series of open share groups governed by anonymity and confidentiality. At Powell, one can choose between groups for grief/loss support, chemical dependence, conquering codependency, and family support. There are also meetings for newcomers, as well as for friends and family members of those battling opioid addiction.[14]

But although Recovery at Powell is reminiscent of Celebrate Recovery in both structure and appeal (it brands itself as "a ministry for all those of us who are hurting from life"), I was struck by frequent references to the AA Big Book and the "Twelve and Twelve," by speakers who openly identified as recovering addicts rather than as struggling believers, and by repeated admonitions for Christians in recovery to keep attending Twelve-Step meetings. These efforts to keep Recovery at Powell from becoming overly churchified have made it possible for the church to build a solid bridge to the local recovery community. As director of recovery ministries Brooke Hartman explained, about a third of those who attend Recovery at Powell are active in local Twelve-Step recovery groups but are not church members.

Recovery House of Worship Brooklyn

Recovery House of Worship Brooklyn (RHOWB), just off Flatbush Avenue in Brooklyn, New York, is the flagship congregation of an urban church-planting movement with outposts in Staten Island, the Bronx, New Jersey, Pennsylvania, and California. The vision for Recovery House of Worship came to cofounder Edwin Colon, who is also pastor at RHOWB, when he converted to Christianity after years of spiritual exploration in Twelve-Step recovery.

RHOWB inhabits Baptist Temple, an 1894 brownstone structure in the Romanesque Revival style that was recently placed on the National Register of Historic Places. But when I visited on a Sunday morning in 2019, I found that the building's ornate and stately exterior housed a spare and intimate worship space. In the renovated basement, metal chairs were lined up before a crowded stage on which worship leaders jockeyed for space with members of a five-piece praise band. After thirty minutes of group singing that evoked mounting expressions of charismatic response, Pastor Colon took the stage.

While Colon's sermon included several references to recovery, they were less direct than the church's name had led me to expect. Recovery-coded terms such as *relapse, clean time,* and *acting out* were subtly inserted between references to Jonathan Edwards, Blaise Pascal, and early Christian debates over judaizing. There were allusions to recovery elsewhere in the service, including a reminder that participating in community service "will increase your clean time." But I found it odd that the daily Twelve-Step meetings at RHOWB were mentioned neither in the worship bulletin nor on the church's website. Overall, worship at Recovery House of Worship Brooklyn lacked the explicit references to addiction, treatment, and Step-work I had come to associate with recovery-friendly churches.

After reading some interviews with the church's pastor, I began to understand why. According to Colon, RHOWB is an attempt to demonstrate what can be accomplished through relationships and discipleship—along with a critical mass of recovering addicts in the congregation—"without much of an official recovery program." In Colon's view, RHOWB is not so much a church for people in recovery as a multipurpose "idol-killing machine." It directly serves addicts and recovering addicts in the community, for instance by partnering with a Christian residential recovery center. But RHOWB wants to be known as more than a "recovery church."[15]

Training

One indication of American Christianity's growing openness to Twelve-Step recovery is the number of training options available to current and future church professionals. The first graduate school to introduce coursework in support of addiction and recovery ministry was Fuller Theological Seminary in California, which offers a Certificate in Recovery Ministries that is built around courses such as Spiritual Formation and the Twelve Steps, Family Dynamics of Addiction, and Recovery Ministry in the Local Church. Other theological schools where one can study addiction and recovery are General Seminary of the Episcopal Church in New York City, where recovery-themed courses are taught by Rev. Stuart Hoke, adjunct professor of pastoral and ascetical theology, and Methodist Theological School of Ohio, where professor of theology Linda Mercadante teaches a class called Gender, Sin, and Addiction.

Lay training for congregation-based recovery ministries was pioneered by Faith Partners, Inc., which mobilizes local faith communities to address alcohol and drug abuse. A pilot program in Austin, Texas, in the 1990s laid the groundwork for this ministry that recruits and trains church members to collaborate with ecumenical organizations, hospitals, state agencies, and private foundations. Today Faith Partners operates nationally, training congregational teams to provide drug awareness, education, and recovery services through what it calls a ministry of presence. Since its inception, Faith Partners has trained 350 ministry teams in twenty-one states, representing nineteen faith traditions.[16]

In the mid-2000s, the Recovery Ministry Leadership Community (RMLC) began encouraging "church-based recovery" among congregations on the more conservative end of the ecclesiastical spectrum. The RMLC was a project of Leadership Network, an evangelical-leaning Dallas-based nonprofit that promotes innovation among church leaders. Dominated by Southern Baptist, Disciples of Christ, Church of Christ, and nondenominational community and Bible churches, the RMLC championed Twelve-Step recovery as a guide to church outreach. While the group embraced the Twelve-Step tradition, it tended to cast it in explicitly Christian terms, defining recovery as "the process of redeeming lives, learning to live in light of what Jesus has done for us."[17]

While Faith Partners and the Recovery Ministry Leadership Community both emerged to support team-based church recovery ministries, they arose from different concerns. RMLC was modeled on a Christ-centered "theology of recovery" in which the Bible is "the authoritative rule and guide" for the "intensive discipleship" that is Christian recovery. Meanwhile, Faith Partners sought to identify and marshal local church resources to address addiction in a multifaith, multiagency environment. Accordingly, the group's website avoids terms like *Christ-centered recovery*, while highlighting ministries that facilitate the integration of body, mind, and spirit.[18]

Support

Most Christian denominations offer resources to support addiction and recovery ministry at the local level. Among the most active in this regard is the Episcopal Church, whose involvement with Twelve-Step recovery reaches back to Rev. Sam Shoemaker, an early advocate of AA in New York. The dual mission of Recovery Ministries of the Episcopal Church (RMOEC) is to welcome unchurched members of AA and other Twelve-Step programs into Episcopal faith communities while raising awareness within these comunities about "the disease of addiction and the redemption and grace found in recovery." In addition to sponsoring a biannual national recovery "Gathering," RMOEC hosts a recovery-themed blog called *Through the Red Door* and publishes pamphlets with titles such as "Prayers in Recovery," "How to Start a New Diocesan Recovery Ministry," "Hosting a Twelve-Step Meeting in Your Church," and "Intervention."[19]

The United Methodist Church (UMC) also supports church-based recovery ministry in a variety of ways. These include helping congregations develop their own recovery programs or start chapters of Celebrate Recovery or Brianna's Hope (a Christ-centered recovery fellowship with chapters in Indiana and Ohio). One of the more distinctive recovery-friendly churches in the Methodist orbit can be found at Central Park United Methodist Church in Saint Paul, Minnesota (aka The Recovery Church), which, in addition to hosting Twelve-Step meetings six days a week in rooms with names like "Steps," "Bill Wilson," and Dr. Bob," offers "sober social events" and a recovery-based worship service designed to help participants "develop a stronger relationship with God, as they understand God."[20]

Other examples of self-styled recovery ministries within the UMC include The Way at Saint John's United Methodist Church in Memphis, the Open Door Community in Hattiesburg, Mississippi, and the FREE spiritual community in suburban Denver. Brainchild of the late UMC clergyman and celebrated songwriter and musician John Kilzer, The Way is a weekly Twelve Step–themed worship service that "fully embraces recovery in every sense of the word." Open Door, led by UMC clergyman and Pine Grove Behavioral Health Spiritual Director David Sellers, hosts Twelve-Step meetings and weekly Recovery Worship services. FREE is described by founders Ryan and Tami Canaday as a community "for addicts, loved ones of addicts, and spiritual refugees" that is "breaking the silence of addiction while creating space for healing, recovery, & spiritual connection."[21]

Virtually every Christian denomination—from Unitarian Universalists to Seventh Day Adventists—claims to offer institutional support to help churches respond to addiction. But these efforts are often poorly funded and organizationally opaque. For instance, the Presbyterian Church (USA)'s Presbyterian Addiction Action (PAA) program advertises resources for worship, teaching, and even launching PAA network affiliates. But the program is embedded within the Presbyterian Health, Education and Welfare Association, which itself falls under the denomination's Compassion, Peace and Justice Ministry program unit. Buried in denominational bureaucracy and short on resources, Presbyterian Addiction Action remains largely invisible at the local level.[22]

Within some denominations, recovering clergy have banded together to form their own associations. A leading example is the Fellowship of Recovering Lutheran Clergy, launched in 1990 by pastors from the Evangelical Lutheran Church in America (ELCA) and the Lutheran Church—Missouri Synod (LC-MS) to promote mutual support and encouragement among clergy in recovery from alcoholism. Similar work has been undertaken by interdenominational nonprofits such as the Clergy Recovery Network, which mentors ministry professionals through confidential online support groups and peer mentoring. The network is dedicated to guiding churches and ministers toward spiritual and organizational health "before, during and after [a] leadership crisis."[23]

Duplication

As we have seen, Celebrate Recovery is the dominant feature on the landscape of Christian attempts to accommodate Twelve-Step recovery. Three decades after its inception, the group has spread to virtually every American city and to many smaller towns. How does a ministry duplicate itself thirty-five thousand times in thirty years? To better understand the group's remarkable growth, in 2018 I attended Celebrate Recovery's Summit West at Saddleback Church in Lake Forest, California, where the movement was born.

As I walked the Saddleback campus—part megachurch, part Christian theme park—the sheer scale of the place lent insight into CR's stellar growth. As with the evangelical megachurch more generally, in CR size matters. Accordingly, three thousand people were expected at the summit, making it more than ten times larger than any other church-based recovery event I had attended. Something else I noticed as I waited to check in for the summit was how many participants wore clothing identifying their local CR chapter or an affinity group like "Broken Chains JC" (men and women who embrace the Christian biker lifestyle). I had to remind myself that people in Twelve-Step recovery do not wear T-shirts advertising this fact or identifying their home groups. As I would learn, disregard for the anonymity that is a hallmark of Twelve-Step culture is just one of the ways CR has churcified recovery.

On the first morning of the summit, I noticed another of CR's striking departures from Twelve-Step practice. In recovery fellowships, partly as a hedge against the grandiosity and self-importance that are believed to fuel addiction, leadership is understood as humble service that confers neither power nor prestige. At the summit, however, those occupying positions of leadership in Celebrate Recovery were repeatedly recognized and honored. As I learned over the course of the week, CR's leadership hierarchy is pyramid-shaped, with national leaders at the top, regional and state leaders beneath them, and local leaders near the pyramid's base. To indicate their place in this hierarchy, at the summit many CR leaders wore T-shirts designating their positions.

Speaking of T-shirts, another feature of CR culture that stood out at the summit was the group's relentless commitment to building its brand. After wading through a sea of merchandise on my way into and out of the meeting hall, I went online to gauge the extent of CR's marketing efforts. Naturally, a successful ministry with thirty-five thousand chapters is going to provide a lot of programming support. So it did not surprise me to find books, sermon series, curriculum kits, meeting guides for participants and leaders, outreach packs, booklets, downloadable PowerPoints, DVDs with recorded "testimonies to go," sobriety chips, and coins. These materials are analogous to those available from the service organizations of AA and other Twelve-Step fellowships.

But perusing these materials did not prepare me for the vast quantity of other merchandise I found advertised on CR's website, which included journals, prayer journals, devotionals, backpacks, tote bags, messenger bags, hydro bottles, keychains, cell phone holders, decals, aprons, license tag frames, motorcycle and car flags, tumblers, note cards, coffee mugs (travel and ceramic), yard signs, lanyards, patches, banners, hope boxes, hope stones, milestone markers, bumper stickers, and pens. In addition, there was a line of CR "gear" featuring "Hope Hoodies," "Jeremiah 29:11" and "Isaiah 43" shirts, jogging tights, polos, beanies, and baseball caps, not to mention a line of "I heart CR" stickers, wallets, and wristbands. And I haven't mentioned accessories related to Celebration Place (for children) or The Landing (for teenagers).

Having browsed through several hundred items of apparel and accessory items bearing the CR brand, I was less surprised by the emphasis summit speakers placed on numbers—of participating churches, of attendees at local groups, of programs under the CR umbrella, of bikers belonging to the movement, of prisons hosting CR programs, of countries where CR is active, of languages into which CR resources have been translated, and so on. This focus on numerical growth was also reflected in endorsements of CR's expanding array of specialized groups—CR Inside (prisons), Welcome Home (veterans), and CR Alone (for those without spouses) are among the newer ones—as well as in the manufacturing metaphors favored by summit speakers ("CR is a testimony factory," "CR is a leadership factory," etc.).

Although they seem natural enough in the world of the evangelical megachurch, each of these features of CR—its glorification of leadership, its relentless marketing, and its heavy emphasis on promotion and growth—directly conflicts with elements of Twelve-Step culture that are codified in AA's Twelve Traditions. For instance, Tradition 2 ("our leaders are but trusted servants; they do not govern") clarifies the way leadership is understood in Twelve-Step fellowships, while Tradition 11 ("our public relations policy is based on attraction not promotion") bars AA from commercial marketing and other forms of self-promotion, and Tradition 12 ("anonymity remains [our] spiritual foundation") stresses not only privacy but humility. Developed by men who learned that sobriety required them to restrain their instincts as "irrepressible promoter[s]," the Twelve Traditions have much to teach Celebrate Recovery.[24]

Yet it is the elements of CR that contrast most sharply with the ethos of Twelve-Step recovery that seem most responsible for the organization's remarkable growth. Given this, I left the summit wondering whether CR's outsize influence on the church's efforts to embrace recovery is, on balance, a good thing. On the one hand, CR has effected a revolution in the way Christians interact with one another. For several days I had the extraordinary experience of being among Christians who introduce themselves by naming their struggles and faults. Even if many choose to keep things vague ("I'm Jan, and I struggle with life issues" was one introduction I heard at a break-out session), something powerful happens when people lead with their flaws, as it were. Instead of projecting a curated image one hopes others will find acceptable, the convention in CR is to publicly identify with one's defects and intractable problems. "I'm Steve, a believer who struggles" is not as revealing, perhaps, as "I'm Steve, and I'm an alcoholic," but it's a good deal more transparent than "I'm Steve, and I'm just fine." In encouraging a paradigm shift in the way Christians self-identify, CR models the vulnerability and transparency that have long made AA an object of Christian envy.

It is also true that CR has imported the language of recovery into churches like no other organization. And by emphasizing that recovery is a process—"a Crock-Pot, not a microwave" is the way one speaker at the summit put it—the organization has helped displace the view that addiction is a problem one overcomes through willpower or fervent prayer. There is also an emphasis on quality control in CR that keeps local groups from departing too far from the organizational template. Each CR group, in fact, is expected to remain "DNA compliant," which means recognizing Jesus Christ as "the one and only Higher Power"; using only the Bible and CR curricula; offering single-gender small groups that follow CR guidelines; holding only face-to-face meetings (although this expectation was suspended during the recent pandemic); being accountable to Christ, the local church, and CR; and adhering to local church policies. As a result, there is enough consistency among CR groups that, as is generally the case with Twelve-Step fellowships, visitors know what to expect.

On the other hand, I worry that by adapting Twelve-Step recovery to church culture, CR has diluted or displaced aspects of the Twelve-Step ethos that Christians have long admired and say they want to retrieve. CR's efforts to churchify recovery—for instance, by claiming that the Steps derive from Jesus's Beatitudes, by emphasizing trained leadership and scripted teaching, and by prohibiting offensive language—make it difficult to avoid the conclusion that Celebrate Recovery has not made church more like AA as much as it has tried to make AA more like church.

Conclusion

How are Christians reclaiming what they gave AA? As this chapter suggests, they are doing so with earnestness, energy, and a great deal of imagination. In scale, their efforts range from the five-member Sam Shoemaker Community to Celebrate Recovery's thousands of chapters. They include ecumenical groups dedicated to bringing Christians together across theological fault lines and denominational programs designed to help local churches address addiction in their midst. Some train individuals to pray or meditate in ways that sustain recovery; others prepare congregational teams to deliver addiction and recovery services. Some are housed within a single congregation; some represent a diocese, conference, or denomination; some have an interdenominational focus.

Despite their differences, each of these efforts to recover church has succeeded in reclaiming at least some of what Christians admire about AA and other Twelve-Step fellowships. In the case of Celebrate Recovery, it is the habit of acknowledging and connecting through brokenness. Friends of Dr. Bob and the Sam Shoemaker Community retrieve the Oxford Group–inspired practices believed to underlie AA's early success at helping alcoholics achieve sobriety and spiritual renewal. Experiments in recovery-themed worship—whether they are allied with a suburban consortium like Recovery Church, are part of an urban church-planting movement like Recovery House of Worship, or arise to meet the needs of a single congregation—allow corporate Christian life to be shaped by a commitment to recovery. 12-Step Outreach introduces recovering persons to a meditation practice rooted in an ancient Christian tradition. Seminary courses and programs train future church leaders to understand and employ the lessons of Twelve-Step recovery.

As impressive as these efforts are, however, none has sought to provide a coherent theological framework for thinking about addiction and recovery. To that challenge we now turn.

What Does the Church Bring to Recovery?

(in a word, theology)

At the time I started recovery, I was involved in individual, couples, and group psychotherapy at a counseling center that is best described as spiritual but not religious. Every program in which I participated there integrated therapeutic work with an eclectic combination of spiritual practices that included Tai Chi, yoga, equine therapy, holotropic breathing (accelerated respiration designed to induce an altered state of consciousness), body work (massage aimed at releasing trauma), smudging and saging (sacred cleansing with burnt herbs), meditation (sitting, walking, and lying down), acupuncture, psychodrama, and Reiki (a form of alternative medicine also known as energy healing). Although these practices took me out of my comfort zone, I eventually came to appreciate many of them. Others, however, consistently triggered what I call my bullshit detector.

Reiki is the spiritual practice that never fails to set off this internal alarm. And the warning has sounded frequently over the years, because every therapeutic intensive in which I've participated has included at least one Reiki session in which a group of sweet, older women offer their services as spiritual healers. As clients lie on massage tables in a darkened room bathed in the calming sounds of New Age music, these palm healers spend twenty minutes or so moving their hands a few inches above our bodies. Although people I respect tout Reiki's therapeutic effects, I have never felt anything other than drowsiness.

I'm sure Reiki practitioners would say this is because I'm too left-brained, too intellectually rigid, too unwilling to suspend disbelief. I would say it's because I don't accept the premise that "universal energy" can be read and manipulated by Reiki practitioners. But my primary complaint about Reiki is not that it's unsupported by science; it's that when its advocates describe it as a method of manipulating "life force energy" that "comes from God," they do not acknowledge that they are doing theology. It may be poor theology lacking discipline and self-awareness, but it's theology nonetheless.[1]

What does the church bring to recovery? At the very least, it should bring the habit of theological reflection, not as a method of gatekeeping designed to exclude the unfamiliar, but as a discipline of critical reflection on experience illuminated by the Christian tradition. The church has the responsibility to marshal the resources of that tradition in thinking about God, God's creation, how the vitiation of that creation is expressed in sin and addiction, and how redemption applies to every facet of human experience. This chapter examines some of the concepts Christians have recruited to make sense of addiction, before turning to the matter of how Christian theology might elucidate the phenomenon of recovery.

Models of Addiction

Despite being a persistent feature of human experience throughout recorded history, addiction has largely eluded attempts to understand, let alone treat, it. At present, there are at least a dozen common ways of conceptualizing addiction, including theories that focus on its cognitive, educational, developmental, sociocultural, and public health dimensions. If there is anything on which these approaches agree, it is that addiction is a multifaceted phenomenon with biological, psychological, sociological, and spiritual components. This broad consensus that spirituality has a role to play in understanding and treating addiction represents an invitation for Christians to say something about it. What do they have to say?

Sin or Sickness?

Applying Christian theology to the problem of addiction inevitably raises questions about the role played by sin, and this pulls theology into an age-old debate over whether addiction should be conceived in moral or medical terms. As we have seen, the moral model, which regards addiction as persistent sinful behavior, has been under sustained attack since the emergence of the alcoholism movement and the rapid spread of AA in the 1940s. Since that time, Christians who treat alcoholism have offered scientific and practical reasons for rejecting the moral model and viewing addiction as "sickness, not sin." From a scientific perspective, they argue, the moral view ignores evidence of alcoholism's psychological and physiological dimensions. More practically, a moral perspective on alcoholism tends to increase the feelings of shame that fuel desire for alcohol's "blessed oblivion."[2]

143

The disease model's role in reducing this sense of shame, first noted by Howard Clinebell, was reinforced by studies of alcoholism among religious professionals in the 1980s and 90s. In *The Rehabilitation of Clergy Alcoholics* (1982), for instance, Joseph Fichter noted that 92 percent of respondents in a survey of recovering clergy alcoholics reported that viewing their condition as an illness helped relieve their feelings of guilt, shame, and humiliation to some degree, with half reporting that these feelings had been removed "completely." Similarly, in a 1995 study focusing on members of Catholic religious orders, Eleace King and Jim Castelli found that 89 percent of respondents said the characterization of alcoholism as a disease reduced their feelings of shame, guilt, and humiliation either completely or partially.[3]

More recently, the Christian case for adopting a disease model of addiction has been expanded to include its role in supporting church recovery ministries. Thus, in *The Recovery-Minded Church: Loving and Ministering to People with Addiction* (2016), Jonathan Benz places the notion that "addiction is a sin" at the top of a list of myths that impede the church's efforts in this area. Nevertheless, despite practical reasons for emphasizing the physical dimensions of addictive behavior, the medical and moral views of addiction are not mutually exclusive, and a responsible view must take into account its sinful effects at both the individual and societal levels. Thus, a theological analysis of addiction must move beyond the moral/medical dichotomy and consider the complex relationship between sin and disease.[4]

Since the middle of the twentieth century, theologians have tried to clarify this relationship by using the concept of addiction to explicate sin's meaning in the modern world. In *The Nature and Destiny of Man*, for instance, Reinhold Niebuhr explained that "drunkenness is merely a vivid form of the logic of sin every heart reveals: Anxiety tempts the self to sin; the sin increases the insecurity which it was intended to alleviate until some escape from the whole tension of life is sought." In other words, as an effort to relieve the anxiety of existential insecurity, habitual intoxication is a symbol of and a paradigmatic response to the human condition. In the 1980s, theologians William Lenters and Patrick McCormick capitalized on addiction's prominence in the wider culture to seek to reestablish some relevance for the Christian concept of sin. Lenters claimed that addiction had come to function the way sin had traditionally, inasmuch as it had come to be understood as constitutive of the human experience. McCormick pursued the connection from the other direction, as it were, describing "sin as addiction."[5]

During the last twenty-five years, Christian theologians have continued to investigate the connections between sin and addiction. In *Not the Way It's*

Supposed to Be: A Breviary of Sin (1996), Cornelius Plantinga observes that in individual cases, the relationship of the medical and moral components of addiction can be hopelessly opaque: Are addicts people with a bad habit of making sinful choices? Victims of biological and social forces they can resist but not overcome? Persons who awaken those forces by habitually making bad choices? Individuals who addicted themselves by misbehaving at a time when they still had the power to choose well? Because these questions are unanswerable in any individual case, Plantinga concludes that we are compelled to view addicts as "in some intricate combinations, both weak and willful, both foolish and guilty." They are, he writes, "a dramatic portrait" of sin's main dynamics, its "warped longings, split wills, encumbered liberties, and perverse attacks on one's own well-being."[6]

Writing in a similar vein, in *Victims and Sinners: Spiritual Roots of Addiction and Recovery* (1996) Linda A. Mercadante points to some surprising continuities between the medically informed "addiction-recovery model" of human behavior and the way sin has been understood in the Christian tradition. Adopting Niebuhr's view of sin as a "tragic but faulty response" to the anxiety that plagues finite but free human beings, Mercadante regards addiction as a misguided attempt to minimize existential dis-ease. When addiction functions in this way, Mercandante argues, sinful behavior is self-perpetuating and addicts become both victims *and* sinners in this sense. Their plight is well-described by the classical Christian idea of sin as a "voluntary necessity," which Mercandante notes is precisely the view set out in the program of AA, in which "original sin" is uncoupled from "original guilt."[7]

In *Addiction and Virtue* (2011), Kent Dunnington follows Plantinga and Mercandante in arguing that modern conceptions of addiction are actually quite compatible with the classical Christian view of sin as a condition that both precedes and implicates human beings. Although Dunnington agrees that addiction has come to function as sin once did—as a shorthand description of the universal human predicament—he believes the Christian doctrine of sin offers modern addiction discourse much-needed "explanatory and descriptive insight." For instance, he points out that the paradox of necessity and responsibility in AA's conception of alcoholism was well articulated by Augustine, who taught that while we are unable not to sin, our sinning remains in some sense voluntary.[8]

Standing in essential agreement with these writers, Christian ethicist and recovering alcoholic James B. Nelson claims that rendering an accurate description of the alcoholic experience requires the languages of sin *and* sickness, and that alcoholics do not have a problem with the concept of sin as such, only with sin-talk that is "shallow, moralistic, judgmental . . . [and] focuses on willful rule breaking." As indications of the sinfulness underlying his own alcoholic behavior, Nelson identifies selfishness, perfectionism (the belief that "if I were good enough or if I achieved enough others would accept me, maybe even admire and love me"), control ("the primal sin of humanity"), and attachment (a tendency toward idolatry). Nelson further notes that whenever someone in an AA meeting testifies to "profound estrangement," it is sin they are describing. "Every drunkalogue I have ever heard—or ever given," he writes, amounted to a confession of sin.[9]

Furthermore, Nelson views the concept of original sin as useful for capturing the way alcoholism is experienced as a physical ailment beyond one's control. In referring to "a fallenness that somehow exists prior to our own fall," the Christian idea of original sin affirms that something prior to our own choices has contributed to our predicament, just as alcoholism precedes the behaviors by which it is defined. In this sense, Nelson writes, alcoholism "is not just *like* original sin. It *is* original sin in one manifestation." Using another classical theological concept to describe the pervasive and insidious nature of the alcoholic experience, Nelson invokes what the sixteenth-century Reformers called "total depravity," identifying vivid expressions of the phenomenon in alcoholism's impact on his reasoning, prayer life, and relationships.[10]

Sin and Sickness?

It would appear, then, that a Christian theological assessment of addiction will frustrate any attempt to assume a strict dichotomy between the moral and medical models. Another argument against such a dichotomy is that it is rejected by most Americans. Opinion polls suggest, in fact, that while Americans give lip service to addiction's status as a disease—that is, a chronic and perhaps hereditable medical problem analogous to cancer or diabetes—they are unable to disassociate it from moral failure.

For instance, a 1982 Gallup poll found that 80 percent of Americans agreed with the statement "alcoholism is a disease," a proportion that was virtually unchanged when Gallup asked the question again in 2006. Yet in 1985 a survey of American Presbyterians revealed that 55 percent of church members and elders believed "moral weakness in individuals" was a factor in the increasing use of alcohol. This view remained stubbornly persistent among members of the American public in 2014, when a Johns Hopkins Bloomberg School of

Public Health study found that drug addicts were "much more likely" than victims of mental illness to face the stigma associated with "moral failing."[11]

These numbers suggest that, despite widespread cultural acceptance of the disease model, Americans continue to think about addiction interchangeably, even simultaneously, the way Christian theologians have tended to do—as both physical malady and moral weakness. Not surprisingly, the same is true of those who struggle with addiction, particularly if they have been socialized in the church. Evidence for this dual consciousness can be found in the words of two Christian alcoholics writing fifty years apart. In 1958, Catholic priest Father Ralph Pfau, believed to have been the first Catholic priest to join AA, confessed:

> I had full confidence in the A.A. program, but there was one fact which I still couldn't accept completely. That was the theory that alcoholism is a disease. From time immemorial, alcoholism had seldom been distinguished from drunkenness, and I had grown up committed to this idea. I was ashamed of my own moral weakness, and even after two years in A.A., I still suspected that it was moral weakness which had caused me to drink. . . . I told alcoholics every day that they were sick, but I had my fingers crossed when I said it. I didn't—couldn't—believe that it was true.[12]

In 2004 James B. Nelson acknowledged a similar difficulty in thinking about his alcoholism as anything other than a moral weakness. Despite his familiarity with evidence that alcoholism was a disease, Nelson struggled to relate this evidence to his own case because he was convinced that being an alcoholic made him "defective down to [his] core."[13]

To clarify the complicated relationship of sin and disease in alcoholism, Nelson adapts a typology developed by Howard Clinebell in which distinct views of the interaction between sin and disease are plotted along a spectrum. On one end of this spectrum is the *purely sin* position, which regards addiction as "caused by personal failings that become habituated in a stubborn sinful pattern." On the other end is the *purely disease* position, which assumes that a certain percentage of those who drink are "biologically programmed to develop the disease of alcoholism." In between these poles are three mediating positions: The *begins as sin and becomes disease* position holds that "clinical addiction begins as personal sin, then gradually develops into an obsessive-compulsive disease process"; the *sin and disease mixed together* position posits that "moral failures contribute to the mental obsession with drinking and purely biological factors result in abnormal physical responses to alcohol";

and the *disease resulting from sin* position views addicts as victims of "sinful social systems" beyond their control.[14]

For Nelson, this typology not only clarifies AA's distinctive conception of alcoholism as a result of *sin and disease mixed together*; it reveals how well this view lines up with classic Christian thinking. In fact, Nelson compares contemporary debates about the interplay of sin and disease in addiction to the fifth-century theological controversy between Augustine and Pelagius. Like contemporary advocates of the *purely sin* model, Nelson writes, Pelagius insisted that God would never command humans to do things of which they were incapable. He wanted, in other words, "to close the door to easy excuses for bad behavior." However, Augustine's view that "the will is so disabled by sin that it cannot choose the good except through the gift of divine grace enabling it to do so" represents the *sin and disease mixed together* understanding of addiction that is embedded in Twelve-Step programs and that resonates with Nelson's own experience of alcoholism. This conception of the problem not only presents a challenge to the supposed incompatibility of the moral and medical models but demonstrates the continuing relevance of Christian theology for illuminating a condition in which sickness and sin both play a role.[15]

Anxiety

Despite the theological necessity of acknowledging addiction's moral dimensions, many Christian thinkers are hesitant to employ the *language* of sin in describing the condition. One alternative approach has been to characterize addiction's soul-anesthetizing effects as an unproductive response to anxious feelings of estrangement from one's Creator. As we have seen, Reinhold Niebuhr famously interpreted "drunkenness" in this way—as a method for relieving the anxiety he believed was constitutive of the human condition. In a formulation that reflected AA's own view of the matter, Niebuhr called alcohol abuse "sinful ego-assertion" that "unduly compensates for [one's] sense of inferiority and insecurity."[16]

Niebuhr's view of addiction's dynamics continued to prove influential among Christian authors in the 1950s and '60s. For instance, Howard Clinebell argued that addicts try to soothe the discomfort of existential anguish through the "anxiety-deadening effect" of drugs and alcohol, while Joseph E. Keller referred to alcohol as a vehicle for anesthetizing the "anxiety of estrangement," and Wayne E. Oates claimed that alcoholics are in search of "redemption from the burden of [their] humanity, the power of [their] guilt, the threat of [their] insecurity."[17]

More recent writers, less likely to employ explicitly Niebuhrian language, have construed addiction as a self-defeating response to the human predicament, a desperate reaction to the spiritual "dis-ease" whose chief symptom is a free-floating sense of "longing, frustrated desire, and deep dissatisfaction." Shais Taub commends this theological explanation of addiction to Jewish readers, writing that addicts are "profoundly disturbed and unsettled with their own existence as an entity apart from God" and use their drug of choice to "briefly simulate relief from this condition."[18]

Idolatry and False Worship

Addiction has been linked to idol worship since at least the 1980s, when M. Scott Peck opined that "all addictions are forms of idolatry." Peck was followed in this assessment by psychiatrist Gerald May, who in *Addiction and Grace* (1988) wrote that addiction makes all human beings idolaters to their objects of attachment, "prisoners of [their] own impulses and slaves to [their] own selfish idols." More recently, scholars from a variety of fields have endorsed the explanation of compulsive behavior as practical idolatry. For instance, philosopher Francis Seeburger refers to addiction as a "perversely clever copy of that transcendent peace of God"; psychologist Wayne E. Oates defines it as a "habitual or compulsive devotion" to anything or anyone other than Jesus Christ; and theologian Cornelius Plantinga opines that, because it reflects a longing for transcendence, "addiction is finally about idolatry." Summing up this tradition, Richard Rohr calls addiction "a god who cannot save."[19]

Some Christian authors construe the idolatry of addiction in terms of false or disordered worship. Sharon Hersh, for instance, portrays the addict as bowing at the altar of a substance or activity that "takes away stress, pain and loneliness for a while and gives him or her a sense of control." For Edward Welch, addiction tempts human beings to worship themselves and their own desires rather than the true God. Kent Dunnington perceives in addiction a sort of "counterfeit worship," a pursuit of ecstasy that can be found only in right relationship with God. From a less overtly theological perspective, David Foster Wallace observes that

> in the day-to-day trenches of adult life, there is actually no such thing as atheism. There is no such thing as not worshipping. Everybody worships.

The only choice we get is what to worship. And the compelling reason for maybe choosing some sort of god or spiritual-type thing to worship—be it JC or Allah, be it YHWH or the Wiccan Mother Goddess, or the Four Noble Truths, or some inviolable set of ethical principles—is that pretty much anything else you worship will eat you alive.[20]

While those comparing addiction with idolatry tend to have substance abuse in mind, the analogy can be applied to process addictions as well. "The idolatry we see in codependency is a distortion of creation," write Nancy Van Dyke Platt and Chilton R. Knudsen, one that makes the addict "the sole focus of the codependent's life." Idol worship is also a common theme in theological interpretations of compulsive sexuality, which is often portrayed as a "symptom of the disease of sinful idolatry."[21]

Divided Self

In addition to sin and idolatry, another biblical theme that lends itself to contemporary discussions of addiction is the divided self. The image is prominent in Paul's Letter to the Romans, where the apostle famously laments, "I do not understand my own actions. For I do not do what I want, but I do the very thing I hate" (Rom. 7:15). As Paul explains his dilemma, although he wills to do the good demanded by the law, his "flesh" prevents him from following through. Those who struggle with addiction have long beheld in this passage a mirror of their own misery and of Paul's hope that Christ will rescue them from their "body of death."[22]

In *Confessions*, Augustine uses similar terms to describe the state of his soul just prior to conversion: "The new will which had come to life in me and made me wish to serve you freely and enjoy you," he confesses to God, "was not yet strong enough to overcome the old, hardened as it was by the passage of time." Augustine describes these two wills as being at war within him in a contest that, as he puts it, "tore my soul apart." As Christopher C. H. Cook has noted in describing this Pauline-Augustinian conception of compulsive behavior, addiction and the struggle to overcome it reflect a division of the self "between openness to the grace and power of God in Christ, on one hand, and openness to the power of sin, on the other hand."[23]

If a divided-will explanation of addiction is favored by many lay Christians, it is because it has support in both Scripture and the theological tradition. But it is also endorsed by mental health professionals, including psychiatrist

Gerald May, who characterizes addiction as a will-splitting force. On May's reading, addiction should be ascribed not to humans' failure to make good choices but to sin's power to divide and burden the soul.[24]

Misplaced Desire for God

Bill W. famously said that alcoholics try "to find God in a bottle." In claiming that the thirst for alcohol springs from spiritual longing, Bill was paraphrasing William James, who in *The Varieties of Religious Experience* wrote that alcohol's sway over mankind is due to its "power to stimulate the mystical faculties of human nature, usually crushed to the earth by the cold facts and dry criticisms of the sober hour." Along with James and Bill W., the conviction that intoxication reflects a longing for union with the divine was held by Carl Jung, who suggested to AA forerunner Rowland H. that a cure for his alcoholism might lie in "a spiritual or religious experience—in short, a genuine conversion."[25]

The conviction that alcoholism expresses a misplaced desire for God was common in therapeutic circles in the 1950s and '60s. Howard Clinebell claimed that "for the alcoholic, religion and alcohol often are functionally interchangeable," and Wayne E. Oates opined that the alcoholic, "seek[ing] his redemption in a bottle," yearns to transcend himself "through the temporary senses of omnipotence which alcohol gives him." More recently, James B. Nelson has written that in the throes of his own alcoholism, his "thirst for the Spirit became confused with [his] thirst for spirits." Based on this experience, Nelson avers that all addiction can be boiled down to a "misdirected search for God."[26]

Support for this view of addiction's roots may also be found in the work of German theologian Dietrich Bonhoeffer, who understands the longing after God that is part and parcel of the human condition as a legacy of our first parents. In *Creation and Fall*, Bonhoeffer writes that after the fall, Adam's "indescribable thirst for life" leads inevitably to despair, since he lives out of his own resources, is imprisoned within himself, and has become his own god. His solitary decision to exist in and of himself, Bonhoeffer observes, "plunges Adam into . . . a desperate, an unquenchable, an eternal thirst . . . for life." But because he has become his own god, the more passionately Adam seeks after life, the more completely he is ensnared by death.[27]

The references above to Bill W., William James, and Carl Jung confirm that the view that addiction is an expression of misplaced yearning for the divine has found purchase well beyond the church. Other authors who endorse this perspective are philosopher Seeburger, who portrays addiction as "the illusion of having found God himself—or the way to do without God altogether." Similarly, Ernest Kurtz and Katherine Ketcham write that turning to the "magic" of chemicals signifies a doomed attempt to fill a spiritual void, as the addict wagers that something wrong on the inside can be fixed by something from outside. Finally, Rami Shapiro notes the irony that in addiction "we thirst for what we already have. . . . We thirst for God."[28]

Message and Gift

Another theological assessment of addiction would give it revelatory significance by interpreting it as a divine message regarding the human condition and our need for God. Kent Dunnington, for instance, argues that because addiction represents the privileging of immanence over transcendence, addicts are "forceful and eloquent" contemporary prophets who point to "the peril that a denial of the transcendent brings." For Anderson Spickard, recovering addicts sound a note of grace in the world by teaching us "to value each day for itself, to breathe deeply, and practice simplicity." And Jonathan Benz perceives in the addict a prophetic invitation to seek the prodigal God "who greets long-lost children with great big bear hugs and throws lavish parties to welcome them home." "In the face and story of the addict" who has returned home, Benz writes, Christians recognize their own brokenness and need for grace. In all these renderings, addiction is considered a cracked mirror that invites us to recognize our own share in human brokenness.[29]

Similarly, Gerald May argues in *Addiction and Grace* that addiction should be considered "a sacred disease" whose only cure is grace. God creates us for love, May writes, but our attachments distort our desire and separate us from our divine source. When addiction convinces us we are not God, however, grace comes to our rescue to transform desire. According to May, because addiction can lead us back to God, every effort to combat it is consecrated. In this sense, addiction represents not only the deepest human dis-ease but "a most precious gift from God." More than an indication that something is wrong, addiction is a sign of "something more profoundly right than we could ever dream of," of "God's song of love in our soul."[30]

Like May, Sharon Hersh believes addiction conveys a gift in the form of an emphatic message that we are not gods. In this way, the experience of addiction is a cure for what Hersh calls "the last addiction"—the idea that I can save myself with myself. Similarly, Francis Seeburger perceives a holy dimension in addiction that sharpens one's spiritual perception. "Once addicts live the addictive process through to its natural end," he observes, they are freed from the illusion that there can be any substitutes for God. "Viewed from that perspective," Seeburger concludes, "addiction is the cure for idolatry."[31]

Resources for a Theology of Recovery

Each of these perspectives on addiction draws attention to its theological dimensions while confirming its relevance for all who share in the human condition. Who, after all, cannot relate to being entangled in sin, experiencing a divided will, feeling the gnaw of existential anxiety, being tempted by idolatry, or misdirecting their longing for God? But if addiction can be theologized as an emblem of the human predicament in a fallen world, then recovery should be understood, in part, as the journey toward reconciliation with our Creator. What follow are some preliminary attempts to imagine recovery through the lens of Christian theology.[32]

Recovery and Sanctification

In an effort to make theological sense of recovery, Christians often identify it with the process of sanctification (through which believers pursue the goal of moral perfection with aid from the Holy Spirit). Although this theologically laden term is rarely invoked, it underlies many attempts to commend recovery for Christians. For instance, Thomas Hamilton Cairns defines recovery as the life-long process through which people affected by addiction "grow toward becoming all that God intends for them to be." Liz Swanson and Teresa Mc-Bean, meanwhile, call recovery "the process of . . . learning to live in light of what Jesus has done for us." And William Struthers characterizes recovery as "spiritual formation" in which a brain that has been habituated to viewing pornography is "rewired" to desire holiness.[33]

An obvious parallel between recovery and sanctification is the assumption that each must find visible expression in one's life. According to New Testament usage, sanctification involves efforts to live a holy life in response to the gift of salvation—for instance, by abstaining from fornication, controlling one's body, and fairly treating one's brothers and sisters. Likewise, according to the "promises" of AA, the fruits of recovery affect one's "whole attitude and outlook upon life" and include "los[ing] interest in selfish things and gain[ing] interest in our fellows." Additionally, some Twelve-Step groups identify their

own "signs of recovery," which may include learning to love oneself, accepting one's imperfections and mistakes, becoming honest and vulnerable, and
developing true intimacy with others.[34]

Sanctification and recovery, then, each entail putting into practice a way
of life one claims to have embraced. And since it is possible for a member of a
church or recovery fellowship to avoid experiencing real transformation, the
one who is technically Christian has much in common with the technically
abstinent. In the religious realm, these people are referred to as nominal Christians; in recovery fellowships, they are "merely sober" or, worse, "dry." Richard
Rohr observes that the religious equivalent of "mere sobriety" for which many
Christians settle is faith absent the "vital spiritual experience" that brings "a
real transformation of the self."[35]

Recovery and Divine Humility

The search for a communal space where it is fine *not* to be fine is a theme
one encounters again and again in the literature of Christian AA envy. Regardless of whether the salient feature of Twelve-Step recovery is understood
to be transparency, honesty, or vulnerability, the point is the same: Twelve-
Step fellowships allow and encourage men and women to be present in their
brokenness, to offer glimpses of their true selves, to testify to powerlessness,
unmanageability, and the limits of self-propulsion—all without fear of being
shamed or judged.

Ernest Kurtz's succinct description of this feature of AA (and, by extension,
of other Twelve-Step fellowships) is "the shared honesty of mutual vulnerability openly acknowledged." According to Kurtz, mutual vulnerability's transformative role in recovery confirms the ancient religious insight that strength
arises from weakness. From a Christian perspective, vulnerability is modeled
for us in divine humility, a theme expressed in the concepts of *kenōsis* (Christ's
self-emptying described in Phil. 2:7), *paschal mystery* (the suffering, dying,
and rising that comprise the drama of the gospel and the rhythm of Christian
life), and *divine descent*, which assumes that Christian existence will mirror
the story of Christ, "who descended from the glory of heaven and experienced
death and the utter depths of our humanity."[36]

Among the Christian theologians who have explored the concept of divine
humility is Dietrich Bonhoeffer, who spoke often of the "suffering God." Writing to Eberhard Bethge from prison on July 16, 1944, Bonhoeffer distinguished
"human religiosity," which directs people in need to the power of God, from

the Bible, which "directs people toward the powerlessness and the suffering of God." This difference is paramount, Bonhoeffer wrote, because "only the suffering God can help." In Christology lectures he delivered several years earlier, Bonhoeffer sounded a similar theme, noting Jesus's "particular way of existing as the Humiliated One." In Christ's humiliation, Bonhoeffer observed, he is "no longer recognizable visibly as the God-human," but appears "incognito, as a beggar among beggars, an outcast among outcasts."[37]

Echoing Bonhoeffer, Richard Rohr invokes the notion of a suffering God to describe the healing power of recovery: "Suffering people can love and trust a suffering God. Only a suffering God can 'save' suffering people. Those who have passed across this chasm can and will save one another." One way for Christians to remember that they are a suffering people is to remind each other that they worship a suffering God. But it is difficult for a church to model this truth if its members feel they must deny their own suffering or find alternative spaces where it can be safely acknowledged.[38]

A robust theology of divine humility helps recover church because it invites Christians to hear in addicts' stories of hitting bottom reflections of God's own story of suffering, humiliation, and surrender. In fact, viewing recovery through the lens of divine humility reminds us that whether our bottom is high ("I was unable to function without alcohol") or low ("I was sentenced to prison time after my third DUI"), we are comforted by a God who knows the depths of human degradation and hopelessness. To be in recovery, after all, is to receive regular reminders that our project of self-management has failed and we stand in need of God's grace. Such reminders will be welcome in a community that is shaped by the divine self-emptying that gives a paschal shape to Christian discipleship.[39]

Recovery and Messiness

The adage that recovery is about "progress, not perfection" can be read as an acknowledgment that it is bound to be messy. To be sure, the path of recovery leads in the direction of sobriety and serenity; but it is full of pitfalls, including slips, full-fledged relapses, reversions to old behavior, moments of euphoric recall, storms of "stinking thinking," encounters with long-deferred consequences, and sabotage by coaddicts who are invested in preserving a dysfunctional system.

These temporary setbacks are a natural part of recovery in the same way doubt is a natural part of faith, although Christians are hardly known for their openness to the darker side of the spiritual journey. A recovering church may or may not have to deal with active addiction or serial relapse, but it should expect and welcome the sorts of messiness implied by a culture of transparency, vulnerability, rigorous honesty, fearless self-scrutiny, and bold amends-making. As Richard Rohr reminds us, *"you cannot heal what you do not acknowledge,* and what you do not consciously acknowledge will remain in control of you from within, festering and destroying you and those around you." The Twelve-Step version of this truth is "we're only as sick as our secrets."[40]

An aspect of Twelve-Step recovery that will *feel* messy to many Christians is the informality reflected in its lax language and dress codes, its insistence on nonprofessional leadership, and its commitment to maintaining "the least possible organization." Churches may be tempted to eschew these forms of messiness, particularly in the area of leadership, where it is often difficult "to place principles before personalities" (as AA's Twelfth Tradition puts it). In many churches, in fact, personality is often allowed to trump principle through an ingrained habit of deference to pastoral leadership. Thus, while any church effort to embrace recovery will require the support of clergy, in order to ensure that the Twelve-Step ethos flourishes, clergy who oversee these efforts should be working a program of recovery themselves.[41]

Recovery and Testimony

Many have commented on the crucial importance of storytelling in Twelve-Step recovery. Dan P. McAdams observes that AA encourages alcoholics to "re-story" their lives as redemptive tales, creating novel self-narrations that achieve "coherence and authenticity." Similarly, James B. Nelson notes that both storytelling and story hearing are crucial to the healing process in AA. The "little stories" of each person in a recovery fellowship, he writes, become part of a group's "big story" that recovery is possible.[42]

To the extent that churches provide reliable meeting spaces for Twelve-Step fellowships, they endorse this sort of redemptive testimony. But when stories of redemption are relegated to the church basement, they cannot bring hope and healing to sanctuaries, classrooms, and fellowship halls. For that to happen, churches must find ways to honor the sort of storytelling that takes place in Twelve-Step newcomer meetings, where "old timers" give voice to the community's values by "disclos[ing] in a general way what [they] used to be like, what happened, and what [they] are like now." While it may run the risk of repelling visitors, practicing a similar type of storytelling ritual would make clear that churches are fellowships not of the righteous but of the redeemed.[43]

One way to incorporate storytelling in worship settings is to solicit vocal requests for accountability and support. Among the most spiritually poignant moments I have experienced in recovery came at a Friday night worship service at a local church. In preparation for his closing prayer, the pastor asked whether anyone "felt their sobriety threatened" (a phrase heard in many Twelve-Step meetings). Most of those present must have been as shocked as I was, because there followed several seconds of utter silence. Finally, a man spoke up to say that although he had been encouraged by the service, he was terrified that as soon as he left the church he would "go back out" and drink.

As I reflected on the minister's question and this brave man's response, I realized that I had witnessed an invitation to public confession. Ostensibly at least, confession is a standard part of most Christian worship services. But in my experience, acts of personal confession are confined to "a moment of silence." In fact, most churches offer few opportunities for people to share their sins and struggles with another person, whether inside or outside formal services. What if churches were to take seriously the biblical mandate to "confess your sins to one another and pray for one another that you may be healed" (James 5:16)? What if worship leaders were to ask whether anyone feels their sobriety (emotional or otherwise) threatened? What if they were to wait patiently for a response?

Recovery and In-Reach

As was noted earlier, millions of Americans are in recovery from substance or process addictions and millions more *need* recovery from one or both. So, whether a church's focus is on those who are in recovery or those who should be, the potential for outward-facing recovery ministry seems virtually unlimited.

But in a recovering church, recovery ministry must involve in-reach as well as outreach. That is, it must challenge members to embody traits of the Twelve-Step movement that have long aroused envy in Christians. This means letting recovering people set the tone for church life by modeling what it means to live in humility and gratitude, by refusing to project an outside that does not match their inside, by preferring honesty and vulnerability to sanctimony and religious posturing, and by calling out church leaders who are not sober or are merely abstinent. In all these ways a church's recovering members can become its teachers and guides.

Conclusion

The process of recovering church will involve more than making recovering addicts feel welcome among the "normies." It will include efforts to create a community of faith where recovering people humbly set the spiritual emphasis. In such a community, church members, no matter what addictions or dysfunctions they do or do not claim, will be encouraged to embrace the way of life encoded in the Steps. As they do so, the church will become more like AA.

Does Twelve-Step Recovery Work?

(define *work*)

Every other year or so, I teach an undergraduate course called Addiction, Recovery, and Spirituality. It's an elective class, so the students are self-selecting. Many enroll in the course, in fact, because they want to understand why their mom or dad or sister or brother or aunt or uncle or cousin can't get and stay sober. Often the family addict has been to rehab more than once and has tried and failed at Twelve-Step recovery. In these students' view, if the Steps haven't worked for the parent, sibling, or other relative whose addiction has thrown their family into chaos, then they don't work at all.

Does Twelve-Step recovery work? While this would seem to be a question for the beginning of a book like this, I've placed it at the end for two reasons. First, trying to determine the effectiveness of Twelve-Step recovery can be quite confusing. Passionate voices on both sides of the question cite research, spout statistics, and relate anecdotes, with the loudest voices belonging to Twelve-Step advocates who swear the program saved their lives and critics who believe it is the modern equivalent of snake oil. But even if we filter out these polarizing views, we are left with what appear to be cogent arguments on both sides of the debate.

The second reason for deferring this matter is that the criteria for determining the effectiveness of Twelve-Step recovery are different for the church than they are for researchers, therapists, and those who design treatment programs. For these professionals, the effectiveness of AA, for instance, can be quantitatively assessed using categories like "percent days abstinent" or "drinks per drinking day." But in addition to wanting to know whether Twelve-Step fellowships keep addicts sober, the church has a qualitative concern: Do Twelve-Step programs deliver on their claim to effect spiritual transformation in those who adopt them? Or, to put it another way, are the promises outlined in the AA Big Book to be trusted?

We are going to know a new freedom and a new happiness. We will not regret the past nor wish to shut the door on it. We will comprehend the word serenity and we will know peace. No matter how far down the scale we have gone, we will see how our experience can benefit others. That feeling of uselessness and self-pity will disappear. We will lose interest in selfish things and gain interest in our fellows. Self-seeking will slip away. Our whole attitude and outlook upon life will change. Fear of people and of economic insecurity will leave us. We will intuitively know how to handle situations which used to baffle us. We will suddenly realize that God is doing for us what we could not do for ourselves.

These promises are recited each day in Twelve-Step meetings around the globe by millions of people who struggle with alcoholism or other addictions, compulsions, and dysfunctions. When the person leading the meeting asks rhetorically whether these are "extravagant promises," group members reply in unison, "we think not." Then the leader continues: "They are being fulfilled among us, sometimes quickly, sometimes slowly. They will always materialize if we work for them."[1]

Do these promises *really* materialize for those who work for them? The answer to this question is important. Before we commit ourselves to the profound changes required to make church more like AA, it would be nice to have some assurance that doing so will result in more freedom, happiness, serenity, and peace, not to mention less self-pity, self-seeking, and fear. If there is evidence that these promises can be realized in a recovering church, then recovery would seem to work in ways that justify Christian envy.

Spiritual Awakening

One thing is clear: spiritual awakening is not a fortunate but unintended consequence of working the Steps; it is the key to the Twelve-Step program's "spiritual solution" to addiction. In fact, sobriety is only one effect of what the AA Big Book calls a "deep and effective" spiritual experience that revolutionizes one's "whole attitude toward life, toward our fellows and toward God's universe." For his part, Bill W. referred to this experience using phrases like "personality change," "transformation," "a new state of consciousness and being," "a profound alteration in one's reaction to life," and "a mysterious process of conversion."[2]

Perhaps Bill W.'s claims for the program he coauthored should be taken with a grain of salt. But alcohol researchers have repeatedly confirmed what *Twelve*

Steps and Twelve Traditions refers to as the "radical change in . . . outlook" that results from working the Steps. Among the first was Gregory Bateson, who in the 1970s described the cognitive and affective shifts that occur in recovery as "a revisioning of self-in-relation-with-others and self-in-world" that changes one's entire frame of reference for living. Building on this research, in the 1980s Stephanie Brown determined that the Twelve-Step program can transform addicts' very identities, "dramatically alter[ing] their attitudes, beliefs, and values, and thus their interpretations of themselves and others."[3]

Such fundamental shifts in the way reality is perceived are described by William R. Miller and Janet C'de Baca as "quantum changes" that involve a re-structuring of one's value system, with the biggest gains appearing in qualities such as forgiveness, generosity, honesty, humility, and personal peace. While Twelve-Step recovery is not the only path to quantum change, it is not an uncommon one. Here is how one of Miller and C'de Baca's subjects describes their experience in AA:

> In all my years of searching for solutions I had studied lots of different faiths and religions, philosophies of the world, and dabbled in the occult. I realized that [AA] was essential truth that pulled together all the truths of all the great religions and philosophies. . . . Now I have that sense of unity above it all and what the world is really about. . . . Now I use my faith in God to guide me for everything. I'm practicing, learning more and more to pray every day about everything. . . . I'm learning to trust in God's guidance.[4]

Whatever we think of this person's claim to have grasped an essential truth combining "all the great religions and philosophies," Christians cannot help but admire a program that can so profoundly impact one's faith, prayer life, and trust in God. Yet it is fair to ask how common this sort of transformation is among those who work Twelve-Step programs.

Spiritual Awakening and Sobriety

Evidence of a correlation between recovery and spiritual growth is not hard to find. For instance, in *If You Work It, It Works! The Science behind Twelve Step Recovery*, clinical psychologist Joseph Nowinski describes several studies that bear out the connection. One study of active AA members cited by Nowinski found that more than half reported praying or meditating twice daily and reading some form of spiritual literature three times per week. Another study found that active AA members with an average of sixteen years of sustained sobriety displayed levels of spirituality comparable to that of a control group of Christian clergy.[5]

Another recent book, *What Is Alcoholics Anonymous?* by Marc Galanter, explores the spiritual lives of physicians who are active in AA. Over 80 percent of those studied by Galanter reported having had a "spiritual awakening" in the fellowship. Although most of these awakenings were gradual in nature, Galanter notes that they were positively correlated with stable abstinence and the absence of alcohol cravings, and thus could be regarded as crucial to the physicians' long-term sobriety. Nor were these fleeting experiences. Galanter observes, in fact, that the majority of physicians who reported having undergone a spiritual awakening in AA continued to feel "God's presence in their lives on a daily basis."[6]

In *Blessed Are the Addicts*, therapist John A. Martin develops his own portrait of recovery's spiritual blessings based on years of counseling with recovering addicts. According to Martin, the spiritual fruits yielded by recovery include creativity, lovingness, humility, service, and reconnection with self and others, not to mention a decline in fear, bias, and rigidity. Like Galanter, Martin emphasizes the durable and expansive nature of these changes. He argues, in fact, that because it represents the inverse of addiction's "bottomless pit," recovery is a condition "without ceiling" that defies "constriction, limitation, and a priori dimensions of any kind." Thus, it is not surprising that, for many, recovery initiates a season of creativity, insight, excitement, vocational discovery, and increased religious involvement.[7]

The correlation between recovery and spiritual growth has been shown to apply even among religious professionals. According to a study conducted by Joseph Fichter, 95 percent of recovering clergy alcoholics who were AA members said their recovery involved a spiritual awakening (compared with 65 percent of nonmembers). In addition, clergy in AA were much more likely to report greater dependence on God's grace, more and better prayer, and a deeper sense of humility. Crucially, Fichter describes the spiritual transformation experienced by clergy in AA not as a substitute for their previous beliefs and commitments but as a "reawakening, revival, or renewal of the religious faith they already possessed." He adds that whether clergy reported having had a "reawakening" through AA was key to predicting their level of spirituality in the years afterward.[8]

In another study of AA's impact on the spiritual lives of religious professionals, Eleace King and Jim Castelli studied members of Catholic religious orders who identified as alcoholics. They found that although 97 percent of recovering religious were involved in AA to some degree, on virtually every measure of well-being, *regular* AA attenders were "happier, healthier, more positive, and less likely to engage in addictive behaviors than those in other groups." As the authors enumerate, AA involvement among members of Catholic religious orders is associated with better self-understanding, deeper humility, stronger theological beliefs, greater dependence on God's grace, improved quality of ministry, better prayer, and better availability to people. Confirming Fichter's findings, King and Castelli conclude that, rather than alienating these men and women from their religious communities, AA involvement results in closer ties.[9]

A Home for the Spiritually Awakened?

Twelve-Step programs teach that ongoing sobriety requires that one maintain a "fit spiritual condition," that one be engaged in an ongoing effort to "perfect and enlarge" one's spiritual life by improving one's "conscious contact with God." Naturally, such a sustained emphasis on spiritual development is likely to lead recovering people to seek the company and support of others who are embarked on a similar path. In fact, there is evidence that a spiritual rebirth initiated through the Steps often leads people in recovery back to religious communities from which they have become estranged, rekindling their interest in a dormant faith.[10]

For instance, Dennis Meacham writes that for people in recovery, faith communities offer "a logical extension" of the spiritual groundwork laid by a Twelve-Step fellowship. Marc Galanter cites recovering clients, many of them physicians, who report that their search for a Higher Power in AA led them back to the God of their youth. Christina Grof remarks that some who enter recovery, "having experienced a profound surrender . . . find deep meaning in reconnecting with the tradition of their roots." And John Z. writes that because AA is "fundamentally Christian," it is often only a matter of time before many in the fellowship find that their faith "makes sense in a way that it never did before."[11]

These prodigal sons and daughters are in search of things not offered in their recovery communities, including communal worship, administration of the sacraments, and Christian formation. But they also bring a spiritual dynamism that can exert a powerful force within congregations. In the words of Jonathan Benz, recovering addicts are "some of the brightest, most spiritually attuned people I have ever met . . . and when they wake up spiritually they are on fire."

Richard Rohr concurs, noting that people in recovery often have "a unique and very acute spiritual sense; more than most people." Kent Dunnington goes so far as to observe that while "churches often wonder what they can do to help addicted persons," the more important question is how a church can "learn from its addicted members what real spiritual community looks like."[12]

If there is any truth to these claims, churches would do well to embrace disaffected Christians who find recovery, from whom they can expect an infusion of spiritual energy, not to mention help in creating the Twelve-Step ethos that makes a religious community feel more like AA. In return, churches can offer these wayward children a faith community shaped by the disciplines of worship, prayer, confession, and fellowship. But if they are discouraged from practicing the honesty and transparency to which they have become accustomed in Twelve-Step fellowships, they are not likely to stick around long enough to appreciate the benefits of church membership.

When Recovery Doesn't Work in Church

Recovery may work in effecting the sort of awakenings that send people in search of a community to nurture their newfound spiritual sensibilities. But these sensibilities will not always be a good fit for the communal disciplines that shape a Christian congregation. In fact, it is an open question whether someone whose understanding of God and the spiritual life has been forged exclusively in recovery will feel at home in a community bounded by faith commitments. The answer will depend to a large extent on whether their recovery reflects the spiritual values AA inherited from the Oxford Group. Below are a few areas in which conflict may occur.

Selves That Are Redemptive

As we have seen, in the wake of the recovery revolution, many expressions of recovery ignored or dissented from central aspects of the Twelve-Step model. Perhaps the chief defection from Twelve-Step philosophy concerned exaltation of the self, its needs, and its purported divinity. Assessing America's culture of recovery at the end of the 1990s, sociologist Robert Wuthnow described "a beguiling mixture of therapeutic, recovery and religious advice" shaped by a "spirituality of the inner self." He warned of what he regarded as a fateful shift in recovery culture from fearless inventory-taking to unconditional acceptance of one's "perfect" self, and he observed that many in recovery had chosen as their Higher Power a force within themselves.[13]

It was probably inevitable that the discourse of the self would find a home in recovery culture. As psychologist Dan P. McAdams explains, the cultural narrative he refers to as "the message of the redemptive self" has long been a prominent feature in American intellectual history. McAdams notes that Americans have always told redemptive stories about themselves—in Puritan religious journals, slave narratives, Horatio Alger stories, and self-help books by authors such as Norman Vincent Peale, Napoleon Hill, Wayne Dyer, Scott Peck, Stephen Covey, Melody Beattie, Rick Warren, and Oprah Winfrey. In its own way, McAdams writes, each of these stories gives expression to the American myth of the redemptive self—that "good, true, and innocent" inner core that is redeemed through "actualization."[14]

As we have seen, the feminist, post-Twelve-Step, and codependency movements have all been vehicles for recovery's infiltration by the myth of the redemptive self. Whatever we think of these movements, there is no doubt that the authors, texts, and groups associated with them have been critical to the recovery of many people, particularly women and others whose life experiences differ markedly from those of the middle-class men who pioneered AA. When the women's alcoholism movement portrayed problem drinking among women less as a disease than as a by-product of low self-esteem rooted in an internalization of patriarchal values, affirmations of the self moved to the center of the recovery process, and AA's "critique of self-will and self-centeredness" was effectively inverted.[15]

Designed to address the special needs of recovering women, Women for Sobriety (WFS) reflects this very process. According to WFS, because "guilt, depression, and low (or no) self-esteem" are problems for which women commonly turn to mind-numbing substances, recovery necessitates a focus on increasing "self-value, self-worth, and self-efficacy." To help women "learn awareness of self and fulfillment of self," WFS recommends a series of acceptance statements that include "I am a competent woman, and I have much to give life" and *"I am in charge of my mind, my thoughts, and my life."* Similarly, Charlotte Kasl's "16 Steps for Discovery and Empowerment" affirm women's "intelligence, strengths and creativity," their confidence to "see what [they] see . . . know what [they] know and . . . feel what [they] feel," and their determination to "seek out situations, jobs, and people who affirm [their] intelligence, perceptions and self-worth."[16]

Correspondingly, codependency theorists of the 1980s argued that the addictive patterns afflicting many women are based in low self-esteem, the solution to which is nurturance of the inner child and efforts to increase individuation and autonomy. As John Steadman Rice argues, however, despite the codependency movement's outsized role in mainstreaming recovery, it actually fostered a revision of the Twelve-Step model in which adult addictive behavior came to be understood as a symptom of unresolved childhood trauma. In other words, the codependency movement taught that because the self is fundamentally good, harm done to others should be charged to diseased family systems. Rejecting AA's contention that addiction resulted from "self-propulsion," the movement pointed instead to betrayal of the self through other-directedness.[17]

If McAdams is correct about the redemptive self's deep roots in the American mind, versions of recovery such as these that tout the self's goodness, power, and sacred character will continue to thrive. And it may be argued that they have an important role in mediating recovery to those who do not share the privileged cultural position from which AA's male pioneers decried the "bondage of self." But churches that want to make recovery work must remain sensitive to the ways efforts to heal and heed the sacred self conflict with a Christian theological anthropology that stresses the effects of sin and the need for divine grace.[18]

Gods That Are Less than Personal

Another barrier to making recovery work in church lies in what AA calls the "method of substitution," according to which those who struggle with the concept of God in Step 2 are encouraged to "make A.A. itself [their] 'higher power.'" In this spirit, Twelve-Step fellowships have long encouraged the non-religious to identify Nature, the Universe, their home group, or even an inanimate object as their Higher Power, at least on an interim basis. Predictably, Christian critics have expressed concern about this tendency, complaining that in Twelve-Step fellowships "any god will do."[19]

To be honest, there is a sense in which "any god *will* do" in Twelve-Step recovery, at least as one is making a beginning. This very low entry bar can be traced to "Bill's Story" (chapter 1 of the AA Big Book), which reveals that while Bill W. had no trouble believing in "Creative Intelligence, Universal Mind or Spirit of Nature," he balked at the idea of "a God personal to me." Even after witnessing "a miracle directly across the kitchen table" (a sober Ebby T.), the being Bill thought of as "Czar of the Heavens" continued to arouse his antipathy. The breakthrough came when Ebby suggested that Bill "choose [his] own conception of God." He did so, although all he could muster at that moment was the willingness "to believe in a power greater than myself."[20]

In Twelve-Step meetings to this day, one hears invocations of Higher Powers that are vague, impersonal, and, it should be said, not very high. But this does not mean that the Twelve-Step program requires that God be thought of in impersonal terms. In fact, even as it is careful to depict God in ways that will not repel unbelievers, AA's program literature keeps the divine "who" firmly in view, depicting a God who acts in the lives of recovering alcoholics, of whose presence one becomes conscious, and with whom one is invited into relationship. These promises of intimacy reveal that the Being at the center of the AA program is more loving Father than energy field, more Self-discloser than First Cause.[21]

To be sure, AA's "Power greater than ourselves" is not the God of Abraham, Isaac, and Jacob; still, it is an intensely personal deity who is "concerned with us humans," a "new-found Friend" who removes sins and breaks the stranglehold of alcohol dependence. "The central fact of our lives today," we read in the Big Book, is "the absolute certainty that our Creator has entered into our hearts and lives in a way which is indeed miraculous." Even chapter 4, "We Agnostics," emphasizes that alcoholism's spiritual solution involves a God "with whom we may form a relationship." Those who doubt this possibility are assured that although some early AAs had even less confidence in the divine order than Bill W., they received power and direction when they could admit the possibility of "a Spirit of the Universe underlying the totality of things."[22]

More evidence for the claim that belief in a personal deity is normative in Twelve-Step recovery can be found in *Twelve Steps and Twelve Traditions.* The word *Providence* in the "Twelve and Twelve" may evoke for some readers a benign deistic force unconcerned with the needs of individual men and women. But the same providential power that rules the universe is described as "performing [a] miracle" of deliverance in the lives of alcoholics. The suffering alcoholic is, in fact, enjoined to find "God's will for [them]," to choose "reliance" on God, and to prepare for "the grace of God to enter" their lives. Significantly, the "Twelve and Twelve" affirms the immanent as well as the transcendent side of God—"the hound of heaven" as well as the universal overseer—the former reflected in the possibility of discerning "God's intention for us." "If the Creator gave us our lives in the first place," we read, "then He must know in every detail where we have since gone wrong."[23]

If there is a point in the "Twelve and Twelve" where we might expect the concept of a personal God to be soft-pedaled, it is in the discussion of Step 11 ("sought through prayer and meditation to improve our conscious contact with God"), where accidents, sickness, cruelty, and injustice are conceded as evidence for atheism. Yet this passage is actually one of the places AA's commitment to traditional theism stands out most clearly. "Some of us," the book relates, could find no evidence of "a God who knew or cared about human beings." But the unexpected results of the author's tentative experiments in prayer are cited as convincing evidence of God's loving concern. The chapter concludes with the confident assertion that because God lovingly watches over us, "we know that when we turn to Him, all will be well with us, here and hereafter."[24]

Gods That Are Excessively Nice

Given the role that shame and judgment can play in compounding addiction, it is natural that perceptions of the divine forged in the crucible of recovery tend to emphasize love, grace, and acceptance. In 1992, Wendy Kaminer identified this phenomenon, noting that in recovery literature God is invariably portrayed as the ideal parent whose love one can reject but never exhaust. "There is no revenge in recovery, and little Old Testament justice," Kaminer wrote, adding that the God relied upon by many in recovery could be counted on to issue "cloying positive messages" that remind them of their lovability. Writing about the same time, Robert Wuthnow observed that the deity reigning in the small groups he studied was "a God of love, comfort, order and security" who lacked any trace of "judgment, wrath, justice, mystery, and punishment."[25]

Indeed, an exclusive emphasis on divine love and acceptance is a distinctive feature of post-Twelve-Step recovery. Karen Casey's popular devotional *Each Day a New Beginning*, for instance, portrays God as a "collaborative, nonthreatening, nonjudgmental force," while Charlotte Kasl's "16-Steps for Discovery and Empowerment" invoke a "God/Goddess/Universe/Great Spirit/ Higher Power" that awakens the healing wisdom within us without demanding confession or surrender. One path of entry for this nonjudgmental and undemanding God into the world of Twelve-Step recovery is Emotional Health Anonymous (EHA). *The Twelve Steps for Everyone Who Really Wants Them*, a book for use in EHA groups, describes a Higher Power that is strikingly undemanding: "Hier [a gender-inclusive neologism] does not expect us to pray or go to church . . . or engage in any form of rite, ritual, or worship whatsoever," because Hesh [another gender-inclusive neologism] is "within each and every living being and non-living thing in the Universe including our own hearts, or guts, or heads."[26]

Recovery's emphasis on an unfailingly accepting God reflects what sociologists Christian Smith and Melinda Lundquist Denton call "moralistic therapeutic deism." In *Soul Searching: The Religious and Spiritual Lives of American Teenagers* (2005), Smith and Denton coined this phrase to describe a worldview whose main premises are that God exists; that God wants people to be nice, happy, and feel good about themselves; and that God is available when one is experiencing a problem. Consequently, "moralistic therapeutic deism" ignores such traditional religious values as repentance, living as a servant of a sovereign divine, or building character through suffering. According to Smith and Denton, in this amateur theology God is regarded as "something like a combination Divine Butler and Cosmic Therapist," a being who helps us feel better about ourselves without becoming "too personally involved in the process."[27]

Obviously, deistic images of Divine Butlers and Cosmic Therapists are part of the cultural air we breathe. But a church that wants to become more like AA should remember that while God's faithful lovingkindness is a biblical concept, so are God's justice, righteousness, and judgment. It should go without saying that these attributes cannot be divorced from the divine character on therapeutic grounds.

Theology That Is Too Permissive

Twelve-Step recovery's association with conceptions of God that are impersonal, benign, and grandfatherly are often seen as a natural result of the Steps' "theological permissiveness," a term used to refer to the lack of content in phrases like "Power greater than ourselves" and "God as we understood Him." Thus, Tim Stafford believes the Steps cater to those who prefer to define God rather than allowing God to define them, and Linda Mercadante reminds those in recovery that "God is the one who confronts us and creates us, rather than the other way around." Yet other Christian writers regard the Steps' theological permissiveness as a gift to be appreciated rather than as a problem to be overcome.[28]

AA has always been keen to convince alcoholics that since the "realm of Spirit is broad, roomy, and all-inclusive," when it comes to God "the hoop" through which one has to jump is much wider than it appears. This "pragmatic pluralism" helps ensure that all who suffer from addiction can find healing, "regardless of their belief or lack of belief." In fact, according to the Big Book, the theological latitude implied in the Steps ensures that any conception of a Higher Power, however inadequate, is "sufficient to make the approach and to effect a contact" with God. But it is important to note that this latitude was intended, not only to ensure that agnostic and atheist alcoholics could "get the program," but to allow all who work the Steps to experience a gradual awakening to God.[29] This emphasis on growth in the alcoholic's spiritual development is particularly clear in *Twelve Steps and Twelve Traditions*, which reminds those at work on Step 2 that "you don't have to swallow [it] all right now . . . all you really need is a truly open mind." In fact, readers are informed, it is not until Step 5 that many an agnostic or atheist has "first actually felt the presence of God." Step 7's emphasis on humility, furthermore, is designed to shift alcoholics' attitudes further in God's direction, and Step 12 enables them to "awaken to the presence of a loving God in their lives." This spiritual path was so common that by the 1950s it was associated with a familiar type in AA: the doubter who begins the program unable to conceive of any power higher than his home group, but who eventually comes to "love God and call Him by name."[30]

Another standard type identified in the "Twelve and Twelve" is "the guy full of faith, but still reeking of alcohol" who must realize that recovery "has to do with the quality of faith rather that its quantity." Such people reveal a benefit of AA's theological permissiveness that has been noted over the years by Christians who work closely with alcoholics. In the 1950s pastoral counselor Howard Clinebell claimed that this feature of the fellowship's program allowed alcoholics' "religious formulations to grow as [their] experience changes." In his 1966 book on the church's ministry to alcoholics, Joseph Keller similarly endorsed the Steps' "watered down" God-language. "With a distorted concept of God that makes him unthinkable or out of reach," Keller wrote, the alcoholic often needs the Steps' theological nonspecificity to "at least keep his mind open."[31]

Attempts to help Christians appreciate the practical advantages of the Steps' theological permissiveness have only intensified over time. In *Dying for a Drink* (1985), physician Anderson Spickard observed that he had never known an alcoholic whose faith was damaged by the AA program, and that "most alcoholics deepen their faith commitment while working through the Twelve Steps." More recently, in their 2010 study of addiction in congregations, Nancy Van Dyke Platt and Chilton R. Knudsen reported that when dealing with impaired clergy, discussions of how God should be understood distract from the real issue, the abuse of alcohol. Platt and Knudsen even argued that calling on the name of Jesus in Twelve-Step meetings represents a "digression from sobriety" that "provides a point of argument for anxious newcomers." And in *Breathing under Water*, Richard Rohr referred to the phrase "God as we understood Him" as part and parcel of AA's spiritual genius. While it appears to confirm the notion that in AA "any god will do," according to Rohr this language expresses the fellowship's confidence that "anyone in need of mercy as much as addicts are would surely need and meet a merciful God."[32]

The advantages of Twelve-Step recovery's theological permissiveness are borne out in several of the recovery memoirs that were reviewed in an earlier chapter. As we saw there, it is not unusual for seasoned Christians who work the Steps to "come to understand" the God of Scripture in a new light. In fact, this phenomenon is visible in many stories of Christians who find recovery. In *God, Help Me Stop!*, for instance, author Claire W. relates that she is surprised in recovery "to discover the God [she] wanted in the Bible." Similarly, Terry Webb tells the story of a monk who leaves his community in disgrace for in-patient alcoholism treatment, only to realize that Jesus Christ is the Higher Power he needed to keep him sober. As these anecdotes suggest, Twelve-Step recovery's theological permissiveness may actually help Christians discover a connection with God that has eluded them in church.[33]

This is not to say that the journey of recovery leads inevitably to the God revealed in Christ. From a Christian perspective, it is probably safer to say that the Steps' theological nonspecificity represents both invitation and temptation; that is, the Steps invite us to trust "the God of our understanding" while tempting us to fashion a god in our image. It is easy to understand why someone who struggles with feelings of shame and unworthiness may need to begin recovery with a Higher Power that is familiar and nondemanding. But if recovery doesn't draw them into the presence of the God who commands as well as loves, they will never know their Creator.

Recovery That Points Inward

One of the persistent charges lodged against Twelve-Step recovery is that the self-scrutiny it entails encourages people to ignore problems beyond their own lives, including systemic determinants of addiction such as trauma and poverty. This is how David Rieff framed the complaint in *Harper's* in 1991:

> Instead of political action, AA followed its spiritual progenitor, the early-twentieth-century Oxford Group, in preaching a species of personalized moral rearmament that would accomplish what political action had failed

CHAPTER 11

to do—They'd do away with booze. In the process, a "social problem" was transformed into a "disease" over which alcoholics insisted they had no control.[34]

Rieff noted that the 1980s had witnessed a reiteration and deepening of recovery's inward focus that was detectable in the codependency movement's retreat from social realities into the most private self, the "inner child."

This critique of recovery as socially disengaged navel-gazing was echoed by Wendy Kaminer in *I'm Dysfunctional, You're Dysfunctional: The Recovery Movement and Other Self-Help Fashions* (1992), which blamed recovery culture's "cult of victimization" for collective resignation in the face of pressing social problems. Such resignation is enabled, Kaminer argued, by recovery groups that construe emotional trauma as "child abuse" and in the process deny any meaningful hierarchy of suffering. When the comfortable middle-class baby boomer thinks of his or her inner child as metaphorically homeless, Kaminer reasoned, solving real homelessness doesn't appear so urgent.[35]

Similar charges have been leveled at the Twelve-Step model by those concerned with addiction in indigenous and ethnic communities, with some viewing the Steps' focus on individual dysfunction as a mismatch for groups that view liberation in collective terms. These are real concerns that must be addressed when determining whether recovery will work in church. In fact, the criticism that recovery privileges personal well-being to the exclusion of the broader good should serve as a warning to the Christian community. It would be ironic if in its desire to address the societal scourge of addiction, the church abandoned its prophetic mission. Thankfully, as a community concerned with social as well as personal shalom, the church provides a natural counterweight to recovery's tendency toward self-focus.[36]

Recovery That Is Domesticated

A final consideration that may be relevant for determining whether Twelve-Step recovery works in church is the tendency of some Christians to promote recovery as a wellness regime designed to help church folk live their best lives. If the Twelve-Step paradigm is our guide, any program of "recovery" should involve an acknowledgment of powerlessness, a turning of one's will and life over to God, an identification and removal of character defects, and a humble making of amends. But the more the Steps are applied to problems beyond alcoholism, the more difficult it has been to maintain the focus on these essential

172

features of the Twelve-Step model. By the 1950s, AA was already acknowledging that nonalcoholics had applied the Twelve Steps to "other difficulties of life," employing them as a guide to "happy and effective living." In the 1970s this process began to accelerate in response to growing awareness of the addictive power of drugs, food, sex, and gambling, not to mention the effects of trauma and family dysfunction on adult behavior. Given the Twelve Steps' continual application to problems never imagined by its founders, one wonders if there are any limits to the process of adaptation.[37]

Perhaps the limit has been reached when Twelve-Step recovery becomes a plan for healthy living. This is precisely what we find in books like Joe Klaas's *The Twelve Steps to Happiness* (1982), which prescribes the Steps for every problem, and every goal, one can imagine. Would you like to be happy or successful? According to Klaas, the Steps are "a surefire way" to achieve both, a "miraculous nonreligious path to happiness and success" that has led "millions of hopeless humans, alcoholic or not, to lead joyous productive lives." For Klaas the Steps are a "magic formula" for solving human problems, as useful for people with terminal cancer and AIDS as for alcoholics.[38]

If few Christians share Klaas's trust in the Steps' miraculous efficacy, some have echoed his confidence in their relevance for all of life. Among them is Vernon J. Bittner, a Christian psychotherapist who in *Twelve Steps for Christian Living* (1987) argued that the Twelve Steps are of use to anyone seeking to live "a more healthy lifestyle." This approach to expanding recovery's relevance has found programmatic expression in Celebrate Recovery, which applies the Steps to all the "hurts, habits and hang-ups" one is likely to find in a congregation. But if Twelve-Step recovery is domesticated to the point that it becomes a church-endorsed scheme for successful living, it will not help the church become more like AA.[39]

Conclusion

How can we increase the likelihood that Twelve-Step recovery will work in church? While remaining wary of redemptive selves, impersonal or undemanding gods, permissive theology, inwardly directed people, and domesticated programs, we should be on the lookout for signs that the promises of recovery are "being fulfilled among us, sometimes quickly sometimes slowly." Such signs include people experiencing freedom, happiness, and serenity; learning from past mistakes in ways that benefit others; shedding feelings of uselessness and self-pity; outgrowing their natural selfishness; losing fear of others and of economic insecurity; and gaining a new outlook on life rooted in confidence that God is doing for them what they cannot do for ourselves. If these signs become apparent in a congregation's life, it may be that recovery is working in church—that the process of recovering church is underway.[40]

What about Sex Addiction?

(is that even a thing?)

Meet John, a college sophomore living alone in an off-campus apartment. Lately he's been missing a lot of morning classes. While he doesn't want to admit it, the problem is the hours he spends at night streaming pornography on his laptop. Despite mounting evidence that his porn habit is beginning to affect his grades and relationships, John can't seem to stop. It all began in eighth grade when his parents bought him a smart phone. They didn't realize they were giving him a pocket pornography portal that would allow him to self-soothe any time he became bored or anxious. His porn habit escalated in high school, although fear of getting caught helped keep it in check. The freedom of college life diminished that fear, however, and porn now has him in its grasp.[1]

Although she has no moral objections to pornography, John's girlfriend wants him to stop. She sees his porn use as a betrayal of their relationship, not to mention evidence that she is unable to meet his physical needs. So John has stopped talking with her about it. He's afraid she'll figure out that his mind is flooded with pornographic images when they are together sexually and that he can't get aroused without summoning them. With all this on his mind, lately John's begun to experience performance problems. He blames it on school stress, and his girlfriend is very understanding. But he worries it might be more than that. He's heard of young guys getting so into porn that they become unable to perform with real women. Is it happening to him? At nineteen? He needs to talk with someone, but who?

Over Christmas break, John meets up with a high school friend who confides in him that he's been having similar problems. The friend explains that the free time and privacy that come along with living in his parents' garage apartment have caused his porn use to spin out of control. John listens intently, finally summoning the courage to share about his own pornography problem. Relieved to learn he is not alone, John's friend invites him to a meeting where, he says, other guys their age are talking about this stuff. John agrees to go, but when he walks into the room, it's not what he's envisioned. There are plenty of young men there, but also some his dad's age, including a few he recognizes.

John takes a seat, closes his eyes, and tries to listen. Someone is reading about "guilt, self-hatred, remorse, emptiness, and pain," about being "driven ever inward, away from reality, away from love, lost inside ourselves." "Our habit made true intimacy impossible," the reader continues. "We could never know real union with another because we were addicted to the unreal. . . . Fantasy corrupted the real; lust killed love." John sits in stunned silence. It's as if someone has been reading his thoughts and taking careful notes. Is it really possible that others know how he feels? He settles into his chair as men take turns telling their stories for the "newcomer." When one of the voices sounds familiar, he realizes that the speaker is a pastor at the church where John's family attends.[2]

After the meeting, the man approaches John, shares his phone number, and even offers to be his temporary sponsor. But he asks John not to tell anyone he's seen him at this meeting. "It could cost me my job," he says. John agrees but is confused. Their church is theologically liberal, hosts several Twelve-Step groups, and prides itself on outreach to the homeless, many of whom struggle with addiction. He's even heard church elders speak openly about their recovery from alcoholism and drug abuse. Would knowledge of his struggles with sex really cause the church to fire this man?

"John" is made up, but as a composite of experiences shared with me by young men I know, his story is real. And it raises some pointed questions for the church. What are Christians doing to help those who struggle with sexual compulsivity, particularly in a world of ubiquitous, free, high-definition pornography? Why is sex treated differently than other forms of compulsivity for which people seek recovery? And is it true that in many churches it is safer for pastors to conceal their struggles with sex than to have it known they attend a Twelve-Step fellowship?

Sex Addiction and Church

The answer to the last question is, sadly, yes. In most churches, including liberal ones, sex addiction[3] is inseparable from the stigma it must bear in the culture at large, and fear of this stigma pushes Christians to seek support and healing elsewhere. Thankfully, many find recovery in a Twelve-Step "S-fellowship"—a collective designation for Sexaholics Anonymous (SA), Sex and Love Addicts Anonymous (SLAA), Sex Addicts Anonymous (SAA), and Sexual Compulsives Anonymous (SCA). But most of those who do are careful to conceal this fact from their church communities.[4]

Each of these S-fellowships was founded in the 1970s, before the term *sex addiction* had entered common parlance and before researchers had begun to describe the condition. Thus, unlike Twelve-Step groups for adult children of alcoholics and codependents, S-fellowships did not emerge in response to a therapeutic trend. Rather, they grew organically from the experiences of men and women, in many cases longtime AA members, who found relief from sexual compulsivity in the Steps. Like other Twelve-Step groups, S-fellowships tend to meet in churches. But the arrangement has always been complicated.

For instance, while the first SLAA meetings were held in private homes, the group eventually sought space in a local congregation known for hosting Twelve-Step fellowships. The pastor welcomed the group to use the church's facilities as long as it adopted a name that did not include the word *sex*. After some soul searching, SLAA acceded to the pastor's request by agreeing to be known publicly as the Augustine Fellowship. The name's pious associations pleased the pastor, but what had commended the name to SLAA's leaders were Augustine of Hippo's sexual struggles, which the church father describes with remarkable honesty in his *Confessions*. Indeed, based on an inability to control his "bodily desire" and an admission that he engaged in sex "within the walls of [God's] church during the celebration of [God's] mysteries," the SLAA leadership suspected that Augustine "was probably one of [them]." Thus, the name Augustine Fellowship seemed a fitting choice for a recovery group that sought to protect its members' anonymity while hinting that sexual compulsivity has long been a feature of human experience, even among the saints.[5]

In some ways, not much has changed since the Augustine Fellowship of Sex and Love Addicts Anonymous was incorporated in 1976. Brave men and women continue to seek spaces where they can safely discuss sexual compulsivity, and good church folk remain hesitant to provide those spaces. Part of the problem is a widespread belief that sex addiction is a scientific-sounding excuse for behavior that is at best selfish, at worst predatory. This view was on display in the late 1990s when it was suggested that the condition might explain Bill Clinton's serial infidelity. Skepticism toward the notion that sex could be addictive emerged again following revelations of Tiger Woods's sexual escapades in 2010. The prevailing attitude was summed up in a banner flown over the Masters golf tournament that year which read "Sex addict? Yeah. Right. Sure. Me too." Six and a half years later, public cynicism had diminished little, as Anthony Weiner's stint in "sex rehab" was portrayed as a desperate effort to avoid the consequences of his actions.[6]

But church resistance to serious discussions of sexual compulsivity is based in more than persistent cultural stereotypes. In an age when clergy sexual misconduct grabs headlines, Christians want to keep at arm's length any suggestion that sexual compulsivity may be a problem in their midst. Furthermore, in recent decades mainline Protestants have begun to view sex less as a matter of personal morality than of social justice, shifting their focus away from individual choices toward systemic issues such as human trafficking and labor conditions in the sex trade. Finally, mainliners are keen to avoid any hint of the repression, shame, and body denial that Christians have long projected onto human sexuality. Aware of the ways people of faith have contributed to sexual repression, many contemporary Christians desperately want to be perceived as sex-positive. All this has left them ill-equipped to offer clear ethical guidance in a world of ubiquitous sexual content.

Can Sex Be Addictive?

The argument that sexual behavior can be addictive is based in part on an analogy with so-called process addictions involving food, gambling, gaming, and exercise, in part on similarities between sexual compulsion and substance dependency. For instance, researcher Stefanie Carnes notes that sex addiction develops and manifests "in the same basic ways, with the same basic consequences" as alcoholism or drug addiction. Psychologist William Struthers adds that the tolerance, withdrawal, and progression observed in some pornography users fit the American Psychiatric Association's criteria for diagnosing substance abuse and dependence. And therapist Paula Hall observes that the only significant difference between sex addiction and substance dependency is the absence of visible side effects, which only makes the condition more likely to be denied and ignored. As Hall notes, you can't drink alone for eight hours every night without those around you noticing that something is wrong. The same is not true, however, if that time is spent streaming porn.[7]

Sex addiction was first addressed by clinicians in the 1980s. The trailblazer in the field was Patrick Carnes, whose groundbreaking *Out of the Shadows: Understanding Sex Addiction* was published in 1983. Carnes defined sex addiction as a pathological relationship with mood-altering chemicals, in this case dopamine and other neurotransmitters associated with sexual arousal. As with other forms of dependence, Carnes noted, in sex addiction a behavior that begins as a way of feeling pleasure becomes a futile attempt to relieve pain. *Sexaholics Anonymous*, the basic text of SA, describes this paradox:

> Over time, the sense of pleasure begins to diminish; we feel less relief. The habit starts producing pain, and the hangover symptoms begin appearing when the pleasure is outweighed by the pain: tension, depression, rage, guilt, and even physical distress. To relieve this pain, we resort to our habit again. As we constantly call on our addictive act for instant relief, our emotional control declines. We can go into impulsive behavior and mood swings, of which we are often unaware. Intimate and social relationships deteriorate.[8]

Furthermore, according to Carnes, sex addiction resembles other addictive processes in the role played by denial (living a "double life" is typical), as well as the presence of a pattern of preoccupation, ritualization, compulsivity, and despair. Finally, Carnes observes, those in relationship with sex addicts display the same coaddictive patterns found in the families of alcoholics and other addicts.[9]

In Carnes's view, sex addiction is related to a delusional thought process driven by faulty core beliefs, such as "I am basically a bad, unworthy person," "no one would love me as I am," "my needs are never going to be met if I have to depend upon others," and "my most important need is sex." He suggests that children are set up for addiction later in life when sex is confused with nurturance and sexual release becomes a self-comforting routine linked to secrecy and shame. According to Carnes, this need for comfort is the engine that drives the adult sex addict: "The sexual experience is the source of nurturing, focus of energy, and origin of excitement," he writes. "It is the remedy for pain and anxiety, the reward for success, and the means for maintaining emotional balance."[10]

Carnes emphasizes that sex should not be deemed compulsive based solely on its frequency or type, but on whether it is secret, is abusive to self or others, is used to avoid or is a source of painful feelings, and is empty of caring. Under these conditions, he writes, sex contributes to an addictive cycle "in which what someone does to relieve pain makes him or her hurt even more." Because this cycle leads to feelings of powerlessness and unmanageability, Carnes views Twelve-Step programs as crucial to long-term recovery. Although several S-fellowships were already flourishing when *Out of the Shadows* appeared, the work of Carnes and others confirmed that, whatever society's attitudes toward sexual compulsivity, it could be arrested using the Twelve Steps forged by AA.[11]

Yet despite these promising theoretical and practical efforts, the concept of sex addiction has continued to come under fire. As has been mentioned, some claim it is nothing more than a way of excusing unacceptable and even criminal behavior by identifying it as part of a disease process (although it should be said that neither sex addiction therapists nor S-groups endorse such thinking). Others conflate sex addicts with sex offenders, even though most sex addicts do not act criminally, and most sex offenders do not fit the criteria for addiction. Finally, sex therapists and sexologists cast suspicion on the training and motivation of those who work in the field of sex addiction, claiming that they pathologize normal human behavior with treatments that are shame-based and sex-negative.

As a scholar, I find such turf battles petty and tiresome; but as a pastor and a person in recovery, I regard the vilification of sex addiction and the researchers, therapists, and support groups that have grown up to treat it as insensitive and dangerous. In this sense, I agree with Paula Hall that *sex addiction* should be the term of choice for describing out-of-control sexuality because "that's how people who actually struggle with it say that it feels." In fact, many who claim to be "addicted" to sex do so on the basis of solid experience, having logged years of sobriety in AA or some other Twelve-Step fellowship, only to conclude that all along their "primary addiction" was to sex. Such people often half-jokingly refer to S-fellowships as "AA's graduate programs."[12]

In any case, it is conservatively estimated that sex addiction affects 3–6 percent of American adults, a number that represents up to twenty million tortured souls, about 30 percent of them women. Many times that number, of course, are in some sort of relationship with a sex addict. Based on these statistics, it is not surprising that options for sex addiction treatment and recovery continue to grow. And yet many who are affected by the condition suffer silently in church pews—not to mention pulpits—where they are trapped in isolation and shame. And because these are the very conditions in which it thrives, sex addiction is perpetuated by Christians' resistance to acknowledging it.

The Cybersex Revolution

Today most sexual compulsivity involves the internet in some way—through hookup apps, chat rooms, webcams, sexting, and streaming videos. But it is not just an increase in the variety of outlets for erotic expression that has fueled the rise of sex addiction. According to clinical psychologist Al Cooper, cybersex is so alluring because it combines accessibility, affordability, and anonymity in a novel combination. Psychiatrist David Greenfield further illumines the addictive power of online sex by noting that because it offers a high degree of unpredictability and novelty, the internet operates on a "variable ratio reinforcement schedule" (VRRS) that is particularly resistant to extinction. Thus virtual "hits" appeal to human brains precisely because they are unpredictable, intermittent, and vary widely in attractiveness. When the internet's VRRS is combined with mood-enhancing sexual content, Greenberg observes, the addictive potential of this content is enhanced.[13]

Based on the internet's intoxicating properties and its ever-expanding offerings of sexual content, researchers have come to regard cybersex as a qualitatively new threat to sexual health. Some call it the "crack cocaine" of sex addiction, although the analogy is misleading inasmuch as online sexual content is largely free, is much easier to find than illegal substances, and can be discovered accidentally through intermediate gateways. The essential role played by the internet in most sex addiction is indicated by Carnes's observation that the condition's twin pillars are the "absence of a relationship and the desire for heightened excitement." Add the assumption that one can engage in cybersex without real-world consequences, and it is easy to understand why sex addiction thrives in virtual environments.[14]

A dominant feature of the cybersex revolution is the ubiquity of pornographic streaming sites. As of 2016, there were more than 4.2 million of these sites in the US alone, attracting, at any given moment, thirty million unique users—that is, more than Netflix, Twitter, and Amazon combined. According to Pornhub, one of the largest and most popular online aggregators of pornographic videos, in 2019 there were forty-two billion visits to its site, about 115 million per day, and users uploaded nearly seven million of their own videos. The average age of Pornhub users was thirty-six, with twenty-five- to thirty-four-year-olds making up the largest single demographic, and 60 percent of users identifying as millennials or postmillennials. (These statistics are skewed, of course, by Pornhub's refusal to acknowledge use of its site by anyone under eighteen.)[15]

When distinctively Christian responses to sex addiction began to appear in the late 1990s, they came mainly from evangelical authors who were responding to alarming reports on the frequency of internet pornography use among Christians. Attempting to gauge the scope of the problem, a 2001 study undertaken by *Christianity Today* asked pastors whether they ever viewed pornography on the internet (at the time, only 89 percent of respondents were online). Fifty-seven percent answered "never," 21 percent "a few times a year," and 6 percent "a couple of times a month or more." The author of the article reporting these findings took solace in the fact that, although the percentage of pastors who had been exposed to porn was about equal to that of other internet users, the frequency of their visits was notably less.[16]

By 2014, however, those who researched porn use among Christians were finding little reason for solace. A study commissioned by Proven Men Ministries and conducted by Barna Group found that among self-identified Christian adult men ages eighteen to thirty, 77 percent viewed pornography at least monthly, and 36 percent did so on a daily basis. Furthermore, 32 percent claimed they were "addicted" to porn. Among Christian men ages thirty-one to forty-nine, 64 percent reported viewing porn at least monthly, with 18 percent reporting they were "addicted." Most disturbing, perhaps, was the finding that 77 percent of interviewees in the older age group said they had viewed pornography while at work during the previous three months.[17]

The picture of porn use among Christians became even clearer in a 2016 study by Josh McDowell Ministries that surveyed a nationally representative sample of over three thousand teens, young adults, and Christian pastors. The study's results as reported in "The Porn Phenomenon" were attention-grabbing, if overstated by an impassioned McDowell, who announced the need for "a Bonhoeffer or a Wilberforce to stand up to pornography the way they did to Nazism and slavery." Among the study's findings: 71 percent of young adults and half of teens reported coming across what they consider to be pornography at least once a month; one-third of women under twenty-five reported seeking out porn at least monthly; and 14 percent of pastors and 21 percent of youth pastors said they struggled with porn use, with 12 percent and 5 percent of these groups, respectively, saying they were "addicted."[18]

These studies gained little attention outside evangelical circles, unless mainline Protestants were framing them as the latest chapter in the long story of Christians' discomfort with sex. In an article for Religion News Service, Jonathan Merritt wrote that, more than anything, the "The Porn Phenomenon" reflected the narrative of cultural declension favored by evangelicals, according to which America is in moral decline and "pornography is a single wave in a larger tsunami of social change." A more nuanced perspective on the evangelical encounter with pornography is offered by Samuel Perry's *Addicted to Lust: Pornography in the Lives of Conservative Protestants* (2019), which places recent Christian responses to porn in the context of evangelical assessments of its social costs going back to the 1970s.[19]

Perry notes that conservative Protestants' "sexual exceptionalism" predisposes them to view porn use not only as worse than other habitual sins, but as uniquely reflective of one's spiritual condition. Other features of evangelical culture that explain its robust response to the cybersex revolution, according to Perry, are a concern with personal purity, a tendency to associate pornography with homosexuality and the morally dubious practice of masturbation, and a "pietistic idealism" that locates the roots of sexual sin in lustful thoughts. All of this, Perry notes, contributes to a mentality of "moral incongruence" that helps explain why conservative Protestants are more likely to use porn more compulsively, more likely to report their porn use, and more likely to describe themselves as "addicted." To indicate the outsize role pornography has come to play in the evangelical mind, Perry reports that Protestants who affirm the Bible's authority are more likely to say that their church condemns watching porn than that it condemns extramarital sex.[20]

But if we focus exclusively on the ways evangelical alarm over pornography use reflects the peculiarities of conservative Protestant culture, we risk framing the debate over porn's effects as a culture war between "sexually repressed, mindless religious fanatics and progressive, orgasmic, freed sexual liberals." For the truth is that conservative Protestants are far from the only ones expressing concern about America's "pornification" (a word that now appears in the *Oxford English Dictionary*). In fact, what clinicians refer to as problematic pornography use (PPU) has been linked by researchers to impairment in sexual function, social avoidance, decreased productivity, and psychopathology. Pornography has also caught the attention of those concerned with its effects on public health.[21]

Among the latter is Jennifer Johnson, a Virginia Commonwealth University sociologist who identifies as feminist and progressive. In early 2017, Johnson told National Public Radio that the explicit, violent, and misogynistic sexual images young people are encountering earlier and earlier in their sexual development suggest that pornography's impact is something we can neither "fully see [nor] fully understand at this moment." In an attempt to gauge this impact by measuring how porn affects heterosexual males' interactions with women, Johnson and a team of researchers surveyed nearly five hundred college men, ages eighteen to twenty-nine, and compared their sexual preferences with their rate of pornography use.[22]

Johnson's team found that 51 percent of college men in their study masturbated to pornography several times per week, 19 percent used it several times per month, and 13.5 percent were daily users. More disturbingly, the men who watched more pornography "deliberately conjured up pornographic images to maintain arousal during sex and preferred pornography over real-life sexual encounters." Based on this and other evidence, Johnson expressed concern with porn's role in "defining masculinity as embodied through violence, hostile attitudes towards women, and gender inequality." Furthermore, she noted, because the pornography that is cheapest and easiest to access contains high rates of violence, it provides "the dominant sexual framework to which boys are socialized and to which girls, as sexual partners, must respond."[23]

If Johnson is mainly concerned with the effects of porn on women who must deal with the expectations it creates, other researchers have focused on the problems specific to pornography's consumers. These include its effects on the arousal templates of developing boys (whose first exposure is generally between ages nine and thirteen), its ability to alter their sexual tastes toward the increasingly extreme or deviant, the phenomenon of tolerance and escalation, its role in sexual dysfunction—including porn-induced erectile dysfunction (PIED)—and the way repeated exposure to pornographic images "rewires" the brain. Research has also illuminated the interpersonal consequences of porn consumption, including the feelings of betrayal felt by partners of secret porn users, which are often as intense as those experienced by victims of in-the-flesh sexual infidelity.[24]

Pornography and the Protestant Mainline

While Roman Catholics have recently begun to wake up to the menace of internet pornography, one looks in vain through the catalogs of mainline Protestant publishers for resources on the subject. When liberal Protestants speak of pornography at all, they are likely to focus on its implication in human oppression—that is, its presentation of women as sex objects, its aesthetic messages related to the female body, its ties to the global sex trade, and its role in the exploitation of children. While these are without doubt important considerations for Christians, they seem inevitably to displace attention from the growing evidence of porn's consequences for those who regularly consume it, particularly young people.[25]

In the case of my own church, the Presbyterian Church (USA), the most recent denominational response to pornography I can find was adopted by the denomination's General Assembly in 1988. Written before the advent of the internet era, *Pornography: Far from the Song of Songs* does not address the reality we know today—free porn delivered in privacy to devices with high-definition screens and the capacity to connect with millions of other devices across the world. But although this two-hundred-page Presbyterian Church (USA) policy statement was written when pornography was distributed via video cassettes, subscription cable television, and "dial-a-porn" phone services, in many ways it continues to represent mainline thinking about pornography's role in American culture.[26]

Careful to distinguish themselves from the antismut crusaders who were so vocal in the 1980s, *Pornography*'s authors emphasize that, as far as the church is concerned, the central issue raised by porn is not the purported disturbance of "traditional norms of sexual morality" but the "gross distortion of power revealed in its graphic sexual images." "Whatever else it may tell us," they write, "pornography offers irrefutable evidence that this culture is patriarchal. Not only the materials themselves, but the industry that supplies them and the market that consumes them, are built on an inequality of power between men and women." In other words, pornography is not about sex but power; its salient feature is not titillation but dehumanization.[27]

Accordingly, *Pornography* carefully avoids any suggestion that sex is in itself "dirty, obscene or sinful" or that sexually explicit materials, even those designed solely for sexual arousal, are in themselves evil. The authors stress that such a "morality view" of pornography, rooted in efforts to shore up "traditional family values" through a nostalgic emphasis on the patriarchal family and traditional gender roles, will not help the church step out of the long shadow cast by Christianity's demonization of sex and sensuality. Instead, the document commends a "feminist view" (perhaps more accurately described as "liberationist"), which understands sin as manifest primarily in systemic oppression rather than personal immorality.

The question of "harm"—that is, of pornography's purportedly negative influence on those who consume it—is answered by the authors of *Pornography* through their denial of a causal relationship between pornography and criminal or antisocial behavior, particularly sexual violence. Since the document's position is that pornography is more a manifestation than a source of sexual violence, what primarily concerns its authors is the harm suffered by women who participate in the making of pornography, and those who become victims of the sexual violence it normalizes.

The problem with *viewing* pornography, according to the document, lies in consumers themselves, for whom porn serves as an "outlet for emotional frustration or a cure for loneliness," its use a futile attempt to fill "a void left by lack of self-esteem, the failure of relationships, or a sense of meaninglessness." Thus, *Pornography* leaves readers to infer that, apart from its connection with "a historical pattern of dominance and submission in human relationships," there is no danger associated with habitual pornography use beyond what it indicates about the pitiful lives of those who consume it.[28]

Despite how much pornography itself has evolved over the past three decades, Nadia Bolz-Weber's recent writing on Christians and sex adopts a perspective very similar to that articulated in *Pornography: Far from the Song of Songs*. Bolz-Weber claims that if Christians can be assured porn has been "ethically sourced," that is, produced without injustice or exploitation, they have no reason to shun it. With regard to the harm of pornography consumption, she argues it could be reduced by diminishing the shame connected with viewing erotic imagery, which only increases sexual compulsivity. As with earlier assessments of pornography by liberal Protestants, Bolz-Weber's determination to avoid viewing porn through a moral lens leads her to discount the possibility that it might be harmful *per se*.[29]

The Presbyterians who authored *Pornography: Far from the Song of Songs* can be excused for failing to take seriously porn's effects on habitual users, given that in 1988 it was, as they noted, "quite easy for middle-class suburban families to insulate themselves from pornographic images." Today such a claim can only appear quaint. In the internet age, Christians who could once insulate themselves from pornography must now reckon with the reality of unlimited free access to pornographic videos that can be streamed on any web-connected device, not to mention the ready availability of erotic content depicting abusive, nonconsensual and even criminal acts.[30]

This latter feature of the online pornography landscape came into sharp perspective in late 2020 in a *New York Times* investigative piece by Nicholas Kristof. In "The Children of Pornhub," Kristof revealed that the pornographic videos dominating the online environment include thousands that have been made and used without the consent of the people appearing in them, who are often underage girls. As Kristof put it, by streaming (and allowing users to download) these depictions of assault and exploitation, Pornhub monetizes "child rapes, revenge pornography, spy cam videos of women showering . . . and footage of women being asphyxiated in plastic bags." Kristof found that while Pornhub makes nominal efforts to moderate such content, it has a considerable financial interest in ensuring that it remains available and searchable.[31]

Even in erotic content that is professionally produced, alarmingly frequent portrayals of misogynistic violence cause one to wonder whether "ethical sourcing" counts for much in the adult film industry. But the issue with which Kristof is concerned is Pornhub's failure to monitor, remove, or block the re-uploading of videos that depict acts in which consent is likely absent, not to mention those that are clearly nonconsensual since they involve children or feature the rape of unconscious women and girls. Kristof's disclosure of how easily such acts, many of them criminal, can be found on Pornhub revealed that, whatever might be said of ethical standards in the adult film industry, the pornography distribution network is dominated by companies with little interest in fighting exploitation or child abuse.

Significantly, neither Kristof nor the children of Pornhub whose heartbreaking stories he documents would describe themselves as antiporn. In his words, "it should be possible to be sex positive and Pornhub negative." But Kristof's investigation revealed that producers of adult content that require proof of age and consent make up a small and dwindling part of the pornography ecosystem, one that struggles to compete with largely free, loosely moderated distrubutors like Pornhub. It appears that until this situation changes, porn consumers who are opposed to abuse and exploitation will have to rely on advertisers, credit card companies, and government agencies to convince porn-streaming sites to remove content for which there is considerable popular demand.[32]

What about Shame?

Let's say that, despite the systemic obstacles, one is able to curate porn in such a way as to ensure that it has been produced by consenting adults under nonexploitative conditions. This standard having been met, the promoters of porn-positivity would assert that any problems stemming from pornography consumption are attributable to the sexual shame it provokes in the viewer. Are they correct?

Samuel Perry's research on evangelicals' relationship with pornography would appear to support the contention that porn's ill effects are a function of the mindset with which one approaches it. As Perry notes, much of porn's negative impact on people's mental health and relationships stems from "the cultural meaning" it has for them. This means that, in the case of conservative Protestants, the "moral incongruence" that accompanies their porn use is a result of beliefs about sex and personal morality peculiar to that group. This would seem to indicate that the key to minimizing porn's deleterious effects lies in reducing the shame linked with sexual expression. Do the negative effects of porn consumption, then, stem mainly from the religious sensibilities that shape its users?

First, it is important to remember shame is not in itself a bad thing. In fact, while it may be an uncomfortable emotion, shame is integral to the functioning of human conscience. For instance, while we need not feel shame at receiving bodily pleasure, treating others' bodies as mere ends for our pleasure is shameful indeed. As Dietrich Bonhoeffer reminds us, because shame vis-à-vis other people forces human beings to "acknowledge their limit," it is a revelatory reminder of others' bodily integrity. Second, research reveals that consumers of pornography may experience its harmful effects quite apart from their moral convictions or state of mind. In fact, Perry cites a "vast and growing body of literature" suggesting that porn use can negatively impact romantic and family relationships, sexual functioning, mental health, and even interactions with strangers. Naturally, this impact is felt most by people in committed partnerships. Among men, for example, porn use is associated with lower quality and stability in romantic relationships; and, in part because women often view men's porn use as a form of betrayal, it is *never* associated with positive marital outcomes.[33]

Thus, at the risk of appearing judgmental, insufficiently progressive, or even puritanical, churches cannot ignore the mounting evidence of porn's potentially injurious effects on those who view it habitually, regardless of how they feel about doing so. In particular, churches must educate their members on the implications for young people of our culture's increasing pornification. Because intergenerational discussions of pornography can be awkward, it is tempting to accept the opinions of experts who reassure us that the vast majority of people can enjoy cybersex and internet porn without experiencing negative consequences, just as they enjoy alcohol and other drugs without becoming addicted. But where young people are concerned, the analogy with addictive substances is weak. Are boys and girls exposed to alcohol on average at age eleven? Is alcohol available at all times from sources that even attentive parents have difficulty monitoring? Does early exposure change kids' neurobiology in ways that make it difficult for them to enjoy alcohol responsibly later in life?[34]

The fact is that young people's relationship with pornography today is quite different from that of their parents and even their older siblings. "Porn has always been around," those of us over the age of thirty think. "We looked at it, even had our own stashes; but it didn't interfere with our sexual development." But such dismissive attitudes ignore the facts that today porn not only is much easier to access (even inadvertently) but is delivered in ways that place it at the cutting edge of the digital world in which young people are immersed. Indeed, in recent years, pornography has become a driver in tech development, spawning innovation and shaping the evolution of technological platforms. The porn-delivery revolution now underway involves virtual reality (VR), which is expected to become a billion-dollar-a-year business by 2025, while other near-future innovations include pornbots and haptic technology (which adds a sense of touch). And, of course, the more dynamic and lifelike pornography becomes, the greater its effects on developing brains.[35]

Based on its ubiquity and its capacity to drive and exploit tech innovation, pornography today defines sexual norms in ways it could not in the past. Thus, in a world in which 87 percent of men use pornography each month, sexual content that is violent, involves the degradation and humiliation of women, and is overwhelmingly focused on genitalia has a greater role than ever before in shaping people's views of "normal" sex. Surely Christians should be at least as concerned as sociologists with the sexual scripts internet porn is "inscribing on the sexual identities of younger people." Surely Christians should take porn's impact on intimate relationships at least as seriously as the brave celebrities at Fight the New Drug, whose motto is "porn kills love."[36]

Evangelicals and Sex Addiction: Reinventing the Recovery Wheel

If mainline Protestants have generally ignored or downplayed sex addiction, in the evangelical world concern with the phenomenon has given rise to a cottage industry of books, programs, curricula, and ministries aimed at helping Christians fight a perpetual battle with addictive sex, particularly habitual porn use. Unlike an earlier cohort of evangelicals who assailed pornography's effects on the nation's crime rate, moral identity and "traditional values," those leading the charge today are focused on the struggle of individual Christians (usually men) to resist the allure of internet porn. The dozens of books by evangelical publishing houses that deal explicitly with pornography traffic in images of enslavement, spiritual warfare, and breaking free from, conquering, or overcoming sexual temptation, while they offer practical strategies to help Christians "win the war," "fight for purity," "break the bonds," "slay the dragon," or "close the window." Emphasizing the goal of sexual purity, these books present "heart transformation" and repentance as the only effective antidotes to habitual pornography use.[37]

These books are the public face of what Perry calls conservative Protestantism's "purity industrial complex," whose impact can also be seen in the recent proliferation of internet filters, accountability software, conferences, multimedia series, and specialized ministries. Among the latter are groups like Operation Integrity, Ultimate Escape, Belt of Truth Ministries, L.I.F.E. Recovery International, Awaken Recovery, Faithful and True, Route 1520, Be Broken Ministries, Blazing Grace, Pure Desire Ministries, Pure Life Ministries, XXXChurch, Dirty Girls Ministries, Freedom Begins Here, Stone Gate Resources, New Creation Ministries, Prodigals International, and Bethesda Healing Workshops. These ministries offer a wide array of resources, including counseling, consulting, inpatient treatment, on-site workshops, online courses, small group workbooks, radio shows and podcasts, and mobile apps.

What most of them do not offer is encouragement for Christians who struggle with sexual compulsivity to seek recovery in a Twelve-Step S-fellowship. This is particularly puzzling with regard to Sexaholics Anonymous (SA), given that SA's emphasis on the role of lust in sexual compulsivity resonates with conservative Protestants' "pietistic idealism," that is, their belief that God is more concerned with the heart than with outward behavior. Indeed, SA's definition of sexual sobriety—"no sex with self or with persons other than the spouse for those who are married, freedom from sex of any kind for the unmarried, and progressive victory over lust for everyone"—corresponds with evangelical conceptions of normative sexual behavior. Yet even though SA meetings are teeming with Christians who have entered recovery to address a pornography habit, one peruses evangelical books on sex addiction in vain for endorsements of SA or other S-fellowships.[38]

It is not as if the authors of these books are opposed to considering secular perspectives on their subject matter, as many of them cite research on the roots, types, and stages of sex addiction, include sex addiction assessment tools, and rely on studies that identify its direct and indirect impact on women. Furthermore, these authors draw on the results of research into the ways pornography "rewires" the human brain and generally embrace the "addiction paradigm" to describe sexual compulsivity. As Perry notes, one consequence of these evangelical authors' description of habitual pornography use as "addiction" (not to mention their employment of related terminology such as "sobriety," "detox," "triggers," and "relapse") is a tendency for conservative Protestant men to self-diagnose as porn addicts and to overreport sex addiction generally. In fact, it is common for evangelical men to describe themselves as "totally addicted" to porn, even if they do not fit the clinical profile for addiction.[39]

However, despite evangelical culture's adoption of the language of addiction to describe compulsive porn use, the perceived usefulness of the Twelve-Step model for addressing sex addiction is diminished by the influence of what Perry calls "biblical counseling." According to this approach, pornography use—compulsive or otherwise—is rooted in sinful thoughts and fantasies and is thus amenable to change through mental effort. In fact, because porn use stems from inordinate beliefs and desires, there will be no permanent change in behavior until one *believes* the truth about God and *values* God above all things. For this reason only techniques and strategies that are "gospel-centered" and focused on "heart transformation" are deemed to be effective.[40]

Thus, Twelve-Step recovery is strangely absent from the evangelical tool kit for treating a persistent behavior that is experienced as an enslaving addiction.

What has replaced this tried-and-true method of recovery are attempts to re-train the mind with recovery commandments, freedom covenants, and Bible verses collected in purity packs, as well as fellowship strategies that call for establishing accountability relationships, Christ-centered support groups, so-called defense perimeters, and fight clubs. Why reinvent the recovery wheel? Why not follow, or at least adapt, an established method for achieving sexual sobriety? The answer is not completely clear, but if sex and pornography addiction are the serious problems evangelical Christians claim, incorporating Twelve-Step S-fellowships into a congregation's ministry would seem a natural and effective way to address these problems while making the church more like AA.

Conclusion

While sex-positivity is an admirable goal, particularly for those who want to escape Christianity's long shadow of sexual shame and repression, the term hardly captures the promise and peril of human sexuality. Like every good divine gift, sex has the potential to enhance our intimacy with God and with one another. But if the Bible is clear about anything, it is that human beings, left to their own devices, will abuse and corrupt God's gifts. This lesson emerges in the first pages of Genesis, where what is arguably humankind's greatest endowment—free will—is misused with disastrous consequences. The lesson of this and many other Bible stories is that the more precious the gift, the more damage will result when it's perverted to selfish ends. Thus, to assume we can talk in exclusively positive terms about something that is as freighted with potential for splendor and debasement as sex is to ignore everything our tradition teaches us about human stewardship of God's gifts.

Yet talking about sex is precisely what churches should do. This is particularly true for a recovering church, since it will eventually have to acknowledge the reality of sex addiction. For once a community of faith becomes a safe place to discuss alcoholism and drug addiction, in time someone who is addicted to gambling or food will want to bring their whole selves to church as well. From there it is only a matter of time before someone finds the courage to reveal that he or she is a recovering sex addict. At that point, it will become startlingly clear whether that church has become anything like AA.

When Is Recovery Finished?

(when you are)

In a passage from the AA Big Book that is read in Twelve-Step meetings immediately following a recitation of the Steps, attendees are warned not to become discouraged, since "we claim spiritual progress rather than spiritual perfection." Like many in recovery, I find those words quite reassuring. But I try to keep in mind that the standard by which progress in recovery is measured is Step 12's pledge "to practice these principles in all our affairs." What does it mean to practice recovery principles in all one's affairs? For me, it goes beyond attending meetings, working with sponsees, staying in touch with my own sponsor, or carrying the message to others. It is a pledge to incorporate recovery into every part of my life.[1]

In the process of writing this book, I've been on the lookout for opportunities to allow recovery to help me integrate aspects of myself that have long remained separate. The first arrived when I had the chance to develop a new course called Addiction, Recovery, and Spirituality at Rhodes College, where I teach. The class allowed me to be known not just as a professor and ethnographer of the recovery movement but as an addict, coaddict, sponsor, and sponsee. At first, exposing parts of myself that I generally keep out of the classroom felt transgressive; but eventually I became convinced that partially pulling back the curtain of professorial authority was a way of enhancing my connection with students. Since then I have felt a bit more integrated in the classroom, where I spend a good deal of my working life.

On the heels of that experience, a few months later I summoned the courage to "come out" to my congregation as a person in recovery as part of an adult forum in which I had been asked to speak about addiction. As I related a brief version of my own recovery story for the hundred or so people in attendance, I tried to read the reactions on people's faces. I wasn't sure what I saw there, and I was still a bit apprehensive when members of the audience lined up to talk with me afterward. So, I was relieved when many of them thanked me for signaling that it was safe to talk about addiction and recovery in our church. One man, whom I had known for many years, proudly showed me his business card, which read "Friend of Bill W." For a while afterward I felt exposed, but also more integrated.

Now that I had church members' attention, how could I model for them what recovering church looked and felt like? The answer came when one of the pastors asked my wife and me to lead a group on marriage recovery. Although we were used to talking about our struggles within the safe confines of an anonymous fellowship, doing so among church folk was a different matter. Churches have long been the site of choice for weddings and, more recently, have developed divorce recovery programs where the newly single process their grief, reimagine family life, locate potential partners, and, eventually, recouple. But between wedding and divorce, we reasoned, there are a lot of places on the marital journey where the church could be of service.

My wife and I agreed, then, that the need for marriage recovery was real. But could we re-create in a church setting the support we had found in Recovering Couples Anonymous when our relationship was in trouble? We decided to give it a shot, planning a multiweek program based on Twelve-Step principles that addressed a variety of topics, including coupleship invaders, family of origin issues, attachment styles, healthy conflict, deepening intimacy, and agreements around things like household labor and sex. We began and ended meetings with RCA readings (which are adapted from AA materials) and modeled openness about our past failures and current struggles.

In this experiment in recovering church, we were joined by seven brave couples—some straight, others gay, some married, others partnered, some together many years, others newlyweds, some in traditional families, others blended, some known to us, others virtual strangers. The group's success, and the clamor to repeat it, proved to us and to the church's leadership that couples in our congregation—even those that appear to be strong—crave the kind of transparency and mutual support offered in Twelve-Step fellowships. Without a lot of effort or fanfare, we had created a space that was informal, rigorously honest, and open enough to brokenness for people to feel seen and known, the sort of space that makes one believe church *can* be like AA.

The next frontier in my quest for personal integration was the colleagues among whom I work. It is one thing to disclose a stigmatized condition in a church community among people who have known you and your family for decades. It is quite another to do so in the professional environment where you make your living. But once I became willing, opportunities for self-disclosure began presenting themselves. When the college hired a new president, one of her first acts was to form an Ad Hoc Alcohol Task Force, on which I volunteered to serve. At the first meeting, as members went around the table introducing themselves, I identified as a recovering addict. Doing so generated opportunities to raise the profile of recovery on our campus and allowed me to feel just a bit more integrated.

But what of the larger academy? Did I have the courage to acknowledge my identity as a person in recovery in a professional guild where people carefully curate their images and jealously guard their reputations? As it turned out, I would soon have an opportunity to find out. The largest professional organizations in my discipline are the American Academy of Religion (AAR) and Society of Biblical Literature (SBL), which meet jointly each year the week before Thanksgiving, when ten thousand religion and Bible professors from around the world descend on the hotels and convention spaces of a major American city for five days of papers, parties, and posturing.

Since everyone in attendance shares an interest in the study of religion, from afar the AAR/SBL annual meeting appears to be a grand community of intellectual inquiry and collegial support. But on the ground, it feels more like an academic *Hunger Games* in which participants risk everything to compete for scarce commodities—particularly jobs, book contracts, and peer recognition. The potential rewards are great, but so are the pitfalls. For instance, competitors must negotiate an opaque academic caste system with its intricate hierarchies of rank, institutional prestige, and name recognition. Clearly, *community* is not the best word to describe the context in which this competition takes place.

For me and many others, the emotional aftermath of the AAR/SBL annual meeting is predictable. No matter how much positive affirmation I receive, no matter how lively the discussion provoked by the paper I presented, no matter how many people congratulate me on my latest book, I leave feeling depressed and spiritually empty. And over the past decade, my postmeeting depressions have been more pronounced as I become accustomed to the genuine community on offer "in the rooms." No one in the recovery meetings I attend has read my books, and most don't know or care what I do for a living. My sponsor, who does know, understands about as much about my job as a college professor as I do about his as a manager of commercial real estate. Yet he knows me better, more authentically, than any of the ten thousand "colleagues" with whom I attend AAR/SBL meetings.

So, imagine my surprise in 2016 as I glanced through the conference program book and noticed something about an "Academy Anonymous Recovery Meeting." The published description referred to these gatherings (there was one scheduled each day of the conference) as "daily open discussion meetings for those seeking some serenity and support amid the craziness of the conference." The meetings, it went on, were open to members of any Twelve-Step group or anyone suffering from a substance or process addiction. I've since learned that a number of academic professional societies support their recovering members in this way, but at that moment I was utterly gobsmacked to learn that the official program of the AAR/SBL included on-site recovery meetings.

I caught the last Academy Anonymous meeting of the conference with about ten other men and women, scholars representing every rung on the academic ladder, from graduate student to senior professor. Most identified alcohol as their presenting problem, while a few mentioned food or sex. But all agreed that they struggled to remain sober at these conferences because they trigger the very feelings of restlessness, irritability, and discontentment that fuel their addictions. Indeed, this has long been a struggle for me. In addition to feeling spiritually and emotionally depleted by these gatherings, I often leave carrying the shame of having "used." Somehow, I had never connected the two things—the loneliness, isolation, and resentment the meetings provoke in me and the desire to numb these emotions through self-medication.

Needless to say, I now attend Academy Anonymous meetings regularly—religiously, one might say. For me they are oases of spiritual connection in a sprawling desert of isolation. What's it like to attend a recovery meeting full of religion professors? Not as strange as you might expect. Even though everyone present has been socialized to speak carefully about the divine, once in that room participants suspend caution and refer to God freely, without irony or quotation marks. They've learned the hard way that being a religion expert will not keep them sober, and that, in fact, the grandiosity behind such titles is part of what drives their addictions.

While the makeup of the group changes each day, those who attend these Academy Anonymous meetings become part of my tribe in a way that is hard to explain. As different as we may appear, we share something that binds us spiritually: the decision to risk being known for who we are in an environment that makes such knowing very, very difficult. We wager that taking this risk will help keep us and others sober—emotionally and otherwise.

So, it's progress, not perfection. I'll keep trying to practice recovery principles in all my affairs, although I know my journey of recovery won't be finished until I am. In the meantime, I'll keep integrating the disparate parts of myself, revealing them when to do so seems safe and appropriate. Whether my church will become more like AA in the process is hard to predict. But I can control only what I can control, and I will let go of the rest. May God grant me the wisdom to know the difference.

Notes

Chapter 1

1. Martha Henriques, "Alcoholism Epidemic in the USA: More Than 1 in 8 Americans Are Now Alcoholics," *International Business Times*, August 11, 2017, http://www.ibtimes.co .uk/alcoholism-epidemic-more-1-8-americans-are-now-alcoholics-1634315; Austin Frakt and Aaron E. Carroll, "Alcoholics Anonymous vs. Other Approaches: The Evidence Is Now In," *New York Times*, March 10, 2020, https://www.nytimes.com/2020/03/11/upshot /alcoholics-anonymous-new-evidence.html.

2. Josh Katz, Abby Goodnough, and Margot Sanger-Katz, "In Shadow of Pandemic, U.S. Drug Overdose Deaths Resurge to Record," *New York Times*, July 15, 2020, https:// www.nytimes.com/interactive/2020/07/15/upshot/drug-overdose-deaths.html; "Problematic Pornography Use: A Brief Introduction," *Forensic Scholars Today* 5, no. 1 (July 2019), https://online.csp.edu/blog/problematic-pornography-use-a-brief-introduction/.

3. Gemma Mestre-Bach, Gretchen R. Blycker, and Marc N. Potenza, "Pornography Use in the Setting of the COVID-19 Pandemic," *Journal of Behavioral Addictions*, April 15, 2020, 1–3; James Murphy and Meaghan McDevitt Murphy, presentation at Idlewild Presbyterian Church, Memphis, June 21, 2020.

4. James Kimmel Jr., "What the Science of Addiction Tells Us about Trump," *Politico*, December 12, 2020, https://www.politico.com/news/magazine/2020/12/12/trump -grievance-addiction-444570.

5. John F. Kelly et al., "Prevalence and Pathways of Recovery from Drug and Alcohol Problems in the United States Population: Implications for Practice, Research, and Policy," *Drug and Alcohol Dependence* 181 (December 2017), https://www.sciencedirect.com /science/article/abs/pii/S0376871617305203. According to the Substance Abuse and Mental Health Services Administration, in 2018, 20.3 million people age twelve or older had a substance use disorder, of whom only 11.1 percent had received treatment at a specialty facility during the previous year. See *Key Substance Use and Mental Health Indicators in the United States: Results from the 2018 National Survey on Drug Use and Health*, https://www .samhsa.gov/data/sites/default/files/cbhsq-reports/NSDUHNationalFindingsReport2018 /NSDUHNationalFindingsReport2018.pdf.

6. Katie Witkiewitz et al., "What Is Recovery?," *Alcohol Research* 40, no. 3 (September 2020): 1–12.

7. Trysh Travis, *The Language of the Heart: A Cultural History of the Recovery Movement from Alcoholics Anonymous to Oprah Winfrey* (Chapel Hill: University of North Carolina Press, 2013), 12.

8. "List of Twelve-Step Groups," Wikipedia, https://en.wikipedia.org/wiki/List_of _twelve-step_groups.

9. Travis, *Language of the Heart*, 6, 58; "12 Essential Steps Toward Overcoming Your Addiction to White Privilege," Diedrariggs, January 24, 2018, http://www.deidrariggs .com/2018/01/24/12-essential-steps-toward-overcoming-your-white-privilege/; Robin Room, "Healing Ourselves and Our Planet: The Emphasis and Nature of a Generalized Twelve-Step Consciousness," *Contemporary Drug Problems* 19, no. 4 (Winter 1992): 717–40, https://www.celebraterecovery.com/?id=1:getting-started.

10. "The Promises of RCA," http://recovering-couples.org/webdocs/admin/The -Promises-of-RCA.pdf.

Chapter 2

1. Robert K. Nace, "Alcoholics Anonymous Speaks to the Church," *Journal of Clinical and Pastoral Work* 22 (1949): 124–32.

2. Jerome Ellison, *Report to the Creator: A Spiritual Biography of Our Era* (New York: Harper & Brothers, 1955), 172.

3. Samuel Shoemaker, "What the Church Has to Learn from Alcoholics Anonymous," http://www.a-1associates.com/aa/LETTERS%20ETC/WhatChurches.htm.

4. Frederick Buechner, *Whistling in the Dark: A Doubter's Dictionary* (San Francisco: HarperOne, 1988), 4–5. See also Seth Barnes, "AA Looks More Like Church Than a Lot of Churches," *Radical Living*, April 1, 2007, http://www.sethbarnes.com/post/aa-looks-more -like-church-than-a-lot-of-churches.

5. Terry Webb, *Tree of Renewed Life* (New York: Crossroad, 1992), 88, 149; Frances Jay, *Walking with God through the Twelve Steps: What I Learned about Honesty, Healing, Reconciliation and Wholeness* (Chicago: Liturgy Training, 1996), 24.

6. Linda Mercadante, *Victims and Sinners: The Spiritual Roots of Addiction and Recovery* (Louisville: Westminster John Knox, 1996), x, 4; Edward T. Welch, *Addictions: A Banquet in the Grave* (Phillipsburg, NJ: Presbyterian and Reformed, 2001), 118.

7. Richard Rohr, *Breathing under Water: Spirituality and the Twelve Steps* (Cincinnati: Franciscan Media, 2011), xvi, 65, 25, 71.

8. Rohr, *Breathing under Water*, 47, 42.

9. John Z., *Grace in Addiction: The Good News of Alcoholics Anonymous for Everybody* (Charlottesville, VA: Mockingbird Ministries, 2012), 20.

10. John Z., *Grace in Addiction*, 140, 149, 22; Ernest Kurtz, "Whatever Happened to Twelve-Step Programs?," 20, http://www.williamwhitepapers.com/pr/Dr.%20Ernie %20Kurtz%20on%20Twelve-Step%20Programs%2C%201996.pdf.

11. Rebekah Simon-Peter, "15 Things AA Can Teach the Church," Rebekah Simon-Peter, July 20, 2017, https://www.rebekahsimonpeter.com/aa-can-teach-the-church/.

12. R. Brad White, "Sinners Anonymous," Changing the Face of Christianity, September 2, 2012, http://www.changingthefaceofchristianity.com/opinions-and-editorials /sinners-anonymous/; Lee Wolfe Blum, "What the Church Can Learn from AA,"

Lee Wolfe Blum, September 26, 2013, http://leewolfeblum.com/what-the-church-can-learn-from-aa/. The phrase *sinners anonymous* is used by many writers to indicate how church could become more like AA; see, e.g., https://www.lasalette.org/reflections/378-sinners-anonymous.html; http://www.micahbales.com/sinners-anonymous/; https://www.dictionaryofchristianese.com/sinners-anonymous/; and http://www.bible.ca/ef/expository-1-corinthians-6-9-11.htm.

13. Scot McKnight, "What the Church Can Learn from AA," Jesus Creed, August 9, 2014, http://www.patheos.com/blogs/jesuscreed/2014/08/19/what-the-church-can-learn-from-aa-by-t/; James Tower, "Recovering Church: A Quaker's Thoughts on AA," Practicing Resurrection Together, March 21, 2013, https://practicingresurrectiontogether.wordpress.com/2013/03/21/recovering-church-a-quakers-thoughts-on-a-a/.

14. Michael Patton, "What the Church Can Learn from Alcoholics Anonymous," Credo House, January 7, 2016, http://credohouse.org/blog/what-the-church-can-learn-from-alcoholics-anonymous.

15. David Fitch, "The Church Gathering Should Be Like a Good AA Meeting," Missio Alliance, June 12, 2013, http://www.missioalliance.org/the-church-gathering-should-be-like-a-good-aa-meeting/.

16. Kathleen Hirsch, "Why Can't Church Be More Like AA?," Crux, October 1, 2015, https://cruxnow.com/faith/2015/10/why-cant-church-be-more-like-aa/.

17. Nicole Unice, "Leadership the AA Way," womenleaders.com, February 1, 2012, https://www.christianitytoday.com/women-leaders/2012/february/leadership-aa-way.html?paging=off.

18. Grant McDowell, "My Small Group, Anonymous," *Christianity Today*, January 21, 2014, https://www.christianitytoday.com/pastors/2014/january-online-only/my-small-group-anonymous.html.

19. Kent Dunnington, "Small Groups Anonymous," *Christianity Today*, April 22, 2019, https://www.christianitytoday.com/ct/2019/may/small-groups-anonymous.html?share=eZuLaCLzDjheOWoibxLjF8xafoEn31iF. See also "What IF . . . Church Was Like 12-Step Recovery," Facebook, May 12, 2017, https://m.facebook.com/notes/day-7/what-if-church-was-like-12-step-recovery/1368759239881743/.

20. Ron Halverson and Valerie Deilgat, *Living Free: A Guide to Forming and Conducting a Recovery Ministry* (San Diego: Recovery, 1992); *Twelve Steps and Twelve Traditions* (New York: Alcoholics Anonymous World Services, 1952), 75; Patton, "What the Church Can Learn from Alcoholics Anonymous."

21. James B. Nelson, *Thirst: God and the Alcoholic Experience* (Louisville: Westminster John Knox, 2004), 137.

22. *Twelve Steps and Twelve Traditions*, 149.

23. Dale Ryan, "Knowing Where You Are: Social Location and Recovery Spirituality," National Association for Christian Recovery, http://www.nacr.org/center-for-recovery-at-church/knowing-where-you-are.

24. Ernest Kurtz, *Not-God: A History of Alcoholics Anonymous* (Center City, MN: Hazelden, 1991), 187; James W. Fowler, "Alcoholics Anonymous and Faith Development," in *Research on Alcoholics Anonymous: Opportunities and Alternatives*, ed. Barbara S. McCrady and William R. Miller (New Brunswick, NJ: Rutgers Center of Alcohol Studies, 1993), 113–35, here 133; Elizabeth A. Swanson and Teresa A. McBean, *Bridges to Grace: Innovative Approaches to Recovery Ministry*, Leadership Network Innovation Series (Grand Rapids: Zondervan, 2011), 137.

25. Trysh Travis, *The Language of the Heart: A Cultural History of the Recovery Movement from Alcoholics Anonymous to Oprah Winfrey* (Chapel Hill: University of North Carolina Press, 2009), 73, 82; *Twelve Steps and Twelve Traditions*, 29, 37.

26. David Foster Wallace, *Infinite Jest* (New York: Back Bay Books, 1996), 279, 538.

27. *Twelve Steps and Twelve Traditions*, 62.

28. "The Recovery Family," in *Recovery Devotional Bible*, ed. Verne Becker (Grand Rapids: Zondervan, 1993), xxi; Nelson, *Thirst*, 189.

Chapter 3

1. J. Keith Miller, *A Hunger for Healing: The Twelve Steps as a Classic Model for Christian Spiritual Growth* (New York: HarperCollins, 1991), xii.

2. Miller, *Hunger for Healing*, 27, 33.

3. Miller, *Hunger for Healing*, 49, 51–52.

4. Miller, *Hunger for Healing*, xii, 52.

5. Nate Larkin, *Samson and the Pirate Monks: Calling Men to Authentic Brotherhood* (Nashville: Thomas Nelson, 2006), 10. Hereafter, page references to this book are given in parentheses in the text.

6. This narrative has been supplemented by comments Larkin made at the National Association for Christian Recovery Regional Conference in Nashville, March 31, 2017.

7. T. C. Ryan, *Ashamed No More: A Pastor's Journey through Sex Addiction* (Downers Grove, IL: InterVarsity, 2012), 99, 30.

8. Ryan, *Ashamed No More*, 129, 130.

9. Ryan, *Ashamed No More*, 105, 165. Ryan tries to soothe evangelical discomfort with Twelve-Step spirituality by making the dubious claim that Bill W. "had a personal and significant life encounter with Jesus Christ" (106).

10. Ryan, *Ashamed No More*, 107, 119, 103, 189.

11. James B. Nelson, *Thirst: God and the Alcoholic Experience* (Louisville: Westminster John Knox, 2004), 101. Hereafter, page references to this book are given in parentheses in the text.

12. Heather Kopp, *Sober Mercies: How Love Caught up with a Christian Drunk* (New York: Jericho Books, 2013), 22. Hereafter, page references to this book are given in parentheses in the text.

13. *Sober Mercies* reminds us that Twelve-Step recovery does not work for everyone and does not resolve every problem. Kopp reports that her father, who suffered from addiction and mental illness, committed suicide. And while her oldest son, Noah, finds recovery toward the book's end, two years after the publication of *Sober Mercies* he experienced a psychotic break that took him on a killing rampage in their hometown of Colorado Springs.

14. Sister Molly Monahan, *Seeds of Grace: Reflections on the Spirituality of Alcoholics Anonymous* (New York: Riverhead Books, 2001), 10, 25. Hereafter, page references to this book are given in parentheses in the text.

15. Fellowship of Recovering Lutheran Clergy, *Our Stories of Experience, Strength & Hope!* (Bloomington, IN: AuthorHouse, 2005), xi, 21–22, 28, 41, 43.

16. Fellowship of Recovering Lutheran Clergy, *Our Stories*, 53–54, 62, 77, 84–85.

17. Alexander C. DeJong, *Help and Hope for the Alcoholic* (Wheaton, IL: Tyndale House, 1982), 62.

18. Bill Morris, *The Complete Guide for Recovery Ministry in the Church: A Practical Guide to Establishing Recovery Support Groups within Your Church* (Nashville: Thomas Nelson, 1993), 27, 262.

19. In Terry Webb, *Tree of Renewed Life: Spiritual Renewal of the Church through the 12-Step Program* (New York: Crossroad, 1992), 75, 77, 84, 85, 88, 93.

20. *As Bill Sees It: The A.A. Way of Life; Selected Writings from A.A.'s Co-Founder* (New York: Alcoholics Anonymous World Service, 1967), 95.

21. Nelson, *Thirst*, 180.

Chapter 4

1. While rates differ by city and region, statistics for the Memphis metropolitan area are instructive. In 2017, 66 percent of Narcotics Anonymous meetings, 83 percent of Sex and Love Addicts Anonymous meetings, 80 percent of Al-Anon meetings, and 100 percent of Sexaholics Anonymous and Overeaters Anonymous meetings met in churches.

2. Trysh Travis, *The Language of the Heart: A Cultural History of the Recovery Movement from Alcoholics Anonymous to Oprah Winfrey* (Chapel Hill: University of North Carolina Press, 2009), 30.

3. Linda A. Mercadante, *Victims and Sinners: The Spiritual Roots of Addiction and Recovery* (Louisville: Westminster John Knox, 1996), 51, 57; Terry Webb, *Tree of Renewed Life: Spiritual Renewal of the Church through the Twelve-Step Program* (New York: Crossroad, 1992), 37.

4. Glen Chesnut, *Changed by Grace: V. C. Kitchen, the Oxford Group, and A.A.*, Houndsfoot Foundation Series on Spirituality and Theology (New York: iUniverse, 2006); Walter Houston Clark, *The Oxford Group: Its History and Significance* (New York: Bookman, 1951), 54, 125, 127–28.

5. William L. White, *Slaying the Dragon: The History of Addiction Treatment and Recovery in America*, 2nd ed. (Bloomington, IL: Chestnut Health Systems, 2014), 170.

6. Ernest Kurtz, *Not-God: A History of Alcoholics Anonymous* (Center City, MN: Hazelden, 1991), 10, 16; White, *Slaying the Dragon*, 171.

7. White, *Slaying the Dragon*, 172.

8. Kurtz, *Not-God*, 35.

9. White, *Slaying the Dragon*, 173–74. Kurtz notes that differing attitudes toward the Oxford Group in New York and Akron became evident in divergent interpretations of the name "Works Publishing, Inc.," AA's publishing arm. New Yorkers associated it with the adage "it works," while Akronites saw it as a reference to the book of James (*Not-God*, 68).

10. Mercadante, *Victims and Sinners*, 55; Kurtz, *Not-God*, 46, 47, 51, 102; White, *Slaying the Dragon*, 173–74; Chesnut, *Changed by Grace*, 81.

11. Travis, *Language of the Heart*, 116, 117, 114, 141–42; Kurtz, *Not-God*, 54; Chesnut, *Changed by Grace*, 33.

12. Travis, *Language of the Heart*, 136; White, *Slaying the Dragon*, 174, 176–77, 178.

13. Travis, *Language of the Heart*, 33, 71; *Alcoholics Anonymous: The Story of How Many Thousands of Men and Women Have Recovered from Alcoholism*, 4th ed. (New York: Alco-

holics Anonymous World Services, 2001), 11, 153. For other references to miracles or the miraculous, see pp. 12, 25, 50, 55, 57, 85, 133; and *Twelve Steps and Twelve Traditions* (New York: Alcoholics Anonymous World Services, 1952), 25, 62, 63, 97, 105, 110.

14. Clark, *Oxford Group*, 30, 108, 110; White, *Slaying the Dragon*, 200; Kurtz, *Not-God*, 48–50, 105; Travis, *Language of the Heart*, 122, 31, 33; Webb, *Tree of Renewed Life*, 74; *Alcoholics Anonymous: The Story*, 12.

15. Kurtz, *Not-God*, 182; Mercadante, *Victims and Sinners*, 77, 109, 78.

16. Charles Bufe, *Alcoholics Anonymous: Cult or Cure?*, 2nd ed. (Tucson: See Sharp, 1998), 59; Ron Halverson and Valerie Deilgat, *Living Free: A Guide to Forming and Conducting a Recovery Ministry* (San Diego: Recovery, 1992), 12–13; Kurtz, *Not-God*, 46–50; *Twelve Steps and Twelve Traditions*, 103; Clark, *Oxford Group*, 27, 28, 143; Linda Mercadante, "Sin and Addiction: Conceptual Enemies or Fellow Travelers," *Religions* 6 (2015): 614–25.

17. Clark, *Oxford Group*, 65, 25, 209, 250, 92.

18. Kurtz, *Not-God*, 79, 80; Pfau's story is told in Father Ralph Pfau and Al Hirshberg, *Prodigal Shepherd* (New York: J. B. Lippincott, 1958).

19. Kurtz, *Not-God*, 84–85; *Alcoholics Anonymous Comes of Age: A Brief History of A.A.* (New York: Alcoholics Anonymous World Services, 1957), 269.

20. Harry Emerson Fosdick, "1939 Book Review of *Alcoholics Anonymous*; Also a Quotation from His Autobiography," in *Alcoholics Anonymous Comes of Age*, 322–23; Kurtz, *Not-God*, 93.

21. Robert K. Nace, "Alcoholics Anonymous Speaks to the Church," *Journal of Clinical and Pastoral Work* 22 (1949): 124–32, 126, 128; White, *Slaying the Dragon*, 263, 269; Edward C. Sellner, *Christian Ministry and the Fifth Step*, Professional Education 8 (Center City, MN: Hazelden, 1981), 8. See also E. W. Belter, *God in a Bottle or Christ in the Cup: The Church's Ministry to Alcohol and Other Drug Abusers* (Racine, WI: Good Shepherd Health Systems, 1990), chapter 11, "Steps Four, Five, Six and Seven: A Part of the Pastor's Ministry"; and Gregory P. Gabriel, "How Do You Hear a Fifth Step?," *Journal of Ministry in Addiction and Recovery* 2, no. 2 (1995): 97–115.

22. Kurtz, *Not-God*, 71, 76, 232, 234.

23. Kurtz, *Not-God*, 232–33. See also online resources, including AA Agnostica (https://aaagnostica.org/), AA Beyond Belief (https://aabeyondbelief.org/), and Secular AA (https://secularaa.org/).

24. Ernest Kurtz and William L. White, "Recovery Spirituality," *Religions* 6 (2015): 59–81, 63, 70. See p. 64 for a list of publications that describe a secular spirituality for recovery from addiction.

25. *Alcoholics Anonymous*, xx; Joseph Nowinski, *If You Work It, It Works! The Science behind 12 Step Recovery* (Center City, MN: Hazelden, 2015), 138; Robert Weiss, *Sex Addiction 101: A Basic Guide to Healing from Sex, Porn and Love Addiction* (Deerfield Beach, FL: Health Communications, 2015), 222, 224.

26. Carol Glass, "Addiction and Recovery through Jewish Eyes," in *Addiction and Spirituality*, ed. Oliver J. Morgan and Merle Jordan (St. Louis: Chalice, 1999), 235–47, here 241–43.

27. Linda R., "The Courts, AA and Religion," AA Agnostica, May 27, 2012, http://aaagnostica.org/2012/05/27/the-courts-aa-and-religion/; Kurtz and White, "Recovery Spirituality," 71.

28. James Christopher, *How to Stay Sober: Recovery without Religion* (Amherst, NY: Prometheus, 1988), 31, 27, 29, 28, 57.

29. Kurtz and White, "Recovery Spirituality," 63, 70.

30. "Pastor John Baker's Testimony," http://www.celebraterecovery.co.uk/pastor
-john-bakers-testimony/.

31. Robert Kenneth Jones, "Sectarian Characteristics of Alcoholics Anonymous,"
Sociology 4, no. 2 (May 1970), 181–95; Arthur H. Cain, "Alcoholics Can Be Cured—Despite AA," *Saturday Evening Post*, September 19, 1964, https://silkworth.net/alcoholics
-anonymous/alcoholics-can-be-cured-despite-a-a-saturday-evening-post-september-19
-1964/; Arthur H. Cain, "Alcoholics Anonymous: Cult or Cure?," *Harper's*, February 1963,
https://silkworth.net/alcoholics-anonymous/alcoholics-anonymous-cult-or-cure-harpers
-magazine-february-1963/; Kurtz, *Not-God*, 144.

32. Francesca Alexander and Michelle Rollins, "Alcoholics Anonymous: The Unseen
Cult," *California Sociologist* 7 (1984): 33–48; Travis, *Language of the Heart*, 61, 62; Christopher, *How to Stay Sober*, 65, 6; Bufe, *Alcoholics Anonymous*, especially chapter 10. Bufe's
assessment is summarized in Charlotte Davis Kasl, *Many Roads, One Journey: Moving beyond the Twelve Steps* (New York: Harper Perennial, 1992), 297–99.

33. Annette R. Smith, *The Social World of Alcoholics Anonymous: How It Works* (New
York: iUniverse, 2007), 7, 12, 49, 33, 66. In a 2016 article, David Best et al. developed a social
identity model that defines recovery as "a social process, underpinned by transitions in
social network composition . . . and involves the concurrent emergence of a new recovery-
based social identity." See Katie Witkiewitz et al., "What Is Recovery?," *Alcohol Research* 40,
no. 3 (September 2020): 1–12, here 5.

34. *Alcoholics Anonymous*, 25; *Many Paths to Spirituality* (New York: Alcoholics Anonymous World Services, 2014), 4, 6, 11.

35. Kurtz and White, "Recovery Spirituality," 68–69.

36. Morris Markey, "Alcoholics and God," *Liberty*, September 1939, https://aa-semi
.org/archive/alcoholics-and-god/; *Alcoholics Anonymous*, 42, 52–53; White, *Slaying the
Dragon*, 191, 192.

37. Wendy Kaminer, *I'm Dysfunctional, You're Dysfunctional: The Recovery Movement
and Other Self-Help Fashions* (New York: Vintage, 1992), 46, 49; Travis, *Language of the
Heart*, 62–68, 87.

38. Ernest Kurtz and Katherine Ketchum, *The Spirituality of Imperfection: Storytelling
and the Search for Meaning* (New York: Bantam, 1992), 196, 197.

39. White, *Slaying the Dragon*, 200, 194, 195, 196. For another perspective on AA's religious feel, see Oliver R. Whiteley, "Life with Alcoholics Anonymous: The Methodist Class
Meeting as a Paradigm," *Journal of Studies on Alcohol* 38, no. 5 (1977): 831–48.

40. Travis, *Language of the Heart*, 62; *Alcoholics Anonymous: 2014 Membership Survey* (New York: Alcoholics Anonymous World Services, 2014), https://www.aa.org/assets
/en_US/p-48_membershipsurvey.pdf.

41. *Alcoholics Anonymous*, 15, 58, 81; Kurtz, *Not-God*, 120, 123; White, *Slaying the Dragon*,
106, 200. References to AA as a way of life proliferate in *Twelve Steps and Twelve Traditions*.
See especially pp. 15, 40, 70, 77, 85, 88, 107, 108, 111, 114, 130.

42. Stephen P. Apthorp, *Alcohol and Substance Abuse: A Handbook for Clergy and Congregations*, 2nd ed. (New York: Authors Choice, 2003), 6–7.

43. Eva Bertram and Robin Crawford, "Is the Drug War a Just War? Drug Abuse, Drug
Wars and the Church," *Church and Society*, May/June 1992, 68; *Alcohol Use and Abuse: The*

Social and Health Effects; Reports and Recommendations by the Presbyterian Church (U.S.A.) (Louisville: Presbyterian Church [U.S.A.], 1986), 3, 8, 9, 58, 68, 64.

44. Jane Searjeant Watt, "The Feminine Face of Addiction," *Church and Society*, May/ June 1992, 35–45, 43.

Chapter 5

1. Brian J. Grim and Melissa E. Grim, "Belief, Behavior, and Belonging: How Faith Is Indispensable in Preventing and Recovering from Substance Abuse," *Journal of Religion and Health* 58 (2019): 1713–50, here 1725.

2. "2014 Membership Survey," Alcoholics Anonymous Cleveland, https://www.aacle .org/2014-membership-survey/; Joseph Nowinski, *If You Work It, It Works! The Science behind 12 Step Recovery* (Center City, MN: Hazelden, 2015), 28, 167. See also Stephanie Brown's discussion of "synergistic partnership" between psychotherapeutic professionals and AA in *Treating the Alcoholic: A Developmental Model of Recovery* (New York: John Wiley & Sons, 1985), 23–26, 119–20, 156–65, 197–206, and especially 267–90.

3. Jason Pittman and Scott W. Taylor, "Christianity and the Treatment of Addiction: An Ecological Approach for Social Workers," in *Christianity and Social Work: Readings on the Integration of Christian Faith and Social Work Practice*, ed. Beryl Hugen and T. Laine Scales (Botsford, CT: North American Association of Christians in Social Work, 2002), 193–213, here 197; *Adult Children of Alcoholics/Dysfunctional Families* (Signal Hill, CA: Adult Children of Alcoholics/Dysfunctional Families World Service Organization, 2006), 448, 453.

4. Trysh Travis, *The Language of the Heart: A Cultural History of the Recovery Movement from Alcoholics Anonymous to Oprah Winfrey* (Chapel Hill: University of North Carolina Press, 2009), 54–55.

5. Travis, *Language of the Heart*, 12; William L. White, *Slaying the Dragon: The History of Addiction Treatment and Recovery in America*, 2nd ed. (Bloomington, IL: Chestnut Health Systems, 2014), 191; Kurtz, "Whatever Happened to Twelve-Step Programs?," 11, http://www.williamwhitepapers.com/pr/Dr.%20Ernie%20Kurtz%20on%20Twelve-Step%20 Programs%2C%201996.pdf; Edward J. Medara and Abigail Meese, *The Self-Help Sourcebook: Finding and Forming Mutual Aid Self-Help Groups*, 3rd ed. (Denville, NJ: American Self-Help Clearinghouse, 1990).

6. Sharon Wegscheider-Cruse, *Another Chance: Hope and Help for the Alcoholic Family*, 2nd ed. (Palo Alto, CA: Science and Behavior Books, 1989), 25.

7. William L. White, "Focus on Family Recovery: An Interview with Sharon Wegscheider Cruse," 2016, http://www.williamwhitepapers.com/pr/dlm_uploads/2016 -Sharon-Wegscheider-Cruse.pdf.

8. John Steadman Rice, *A Disease of One's Own: Psychotherapy, Addiction and the Emergence of Co-Dependency* (New Brunswick, NJ: Transaction, 1996), 7, 8, 10, 76, 181.

9. AA historian Ernest Kurtz notes that the task of the Twelve Steps is "description, not ascription" ("Whatever Happened to Twelve-Step Programs?," 7); Rice, *Disease of One's Own*, 53.

10. Rice, *Disease of One's Own*, 59, 61; "Early History," Adult Children of Alcoholics World Service Organization, https://adultchildren.org/literature/early-history/.

11. Travis, *Language of the Heart*, 55; Rice, *Disease of One's Own*, 61, 79, 81, 84, 65.

12. Rice, *Disease of One's Own*, 90, 128.

13. Travis, *Language of the Heart*, 55, 189, 144. Hereafter, page references to this book are given in parentheses in the text; *Alcoholics Anonymous*, 76.

14. William James, *The Varieties of Religious Experience* (n.p.: Renaissance Classics, 2012), 88.

15. Travis, *Language of the Heart*, 197, 198; Wendy Kaminer, *I'm Dysfunctional, You're Dysfunctional: The Recovery Movement and Other Self-Help Fashions* (New York: Vintage, 1992), 156, 161, 162, 163, 164. Significantly, Casey identifies the turning point in her own recovery as her introduction to *The Dynamic Laws of Healing* by New Thought guru Catherine Ponder (Karen Casey, "Codependence, Addiction and Spirituality," Addiction and Faith Conference, Minneapolis, September 21, 2019); Karen Casey, *52 Ways to Live the Course in Miracles: Cultivate a Simpler, Slower, More Love-Filled Life* (Newburyport, MA: Conari, 2016).

16. Travis, *Language of the Heart*, 169, 231, 237, 238, 239, 240, 244. Compare Winfrey's statements with the words of a nineteenth-century New Thought practioner quoted by William James: "I was perfectly well and always had been, for I was Soul, an expression of God's Pefect Thought" (*Varieties of Religious Experience*, 78).

17. Grateful Members, *The Twelve Steps for Everyone Who Really Wants Them* (Minneapolis: CompCare, 1975), 33, 85.

18. Christina Grof, *The Thirst for Wholeness: Attachment, Addiction and the Spiritual Path* (San Francisco: HarperOne, 1993), 6, 223, 24, 28, 223, 221, 222, 224, 225, 196, 93.

19. Charlotte Davis Kasl, *Many Roads, One Journey: Moving beyond the Twelve Steps* (New York: Harper Perennial, 1992), 6, 223, xiv, xv, 18, 152, 87, 222, 311, 319, 308.

20. Leo Booth, *The Happy Heretic: Seven Spiritual Insights for Healing Religious Codependency* (Deerfield Beach, FL: Health Communications, 2012), 15–16, 22, 29, 90–91.

21. Lynn Grabhorn, *Beyond the Twelve Steps: Roadmap to a New Life* (Newburyport, MA: Hampton Roads, 2001); Deepak Chopra and David Simon, *Freedom from Addiction: The Chopra Center Method for Overcoming Destructive Habits* (Deerfield Beach, FL: Health Communications, 2007); Rami Shapiro, *Recovery: The Twelve Steps as Spiritual Practice* (Woodstock, VT: Skylight Paths, 2009), xv, 35, 47.

22. J. R. Richmond and Bette Jean Cundiff, *Side by Side: The Twelve Steps; A Course in Miracles* (BookSurge, 2009). The vapidity of this genre of recovery literature is delightfully parodied by the Deepak Chopra random quote generator (http://www.wisdomofchopra.com/quiz.php).

23. Vernon J. Bittner, *Twelve Steps for Christian Living: Growth in a New Way of Living* (Plymouth, MN: ICL Renewed Life Services, 1987), 42, 90, 82, 92, 28, 66. For other references to "finding the 'Christ' within," see 18, 44, 48, 85, 88, 101.

24. Travis, *Language of the Heart*, 75, 78, 79.

25. Travis, *Language of the Heart*, 77; James, *Varieties of Religious Experience*, 80. Among the doctrinal sources of mind-cure, according to James, are the Gospels, Emersonian transcendentalism, Berkeleyan idealism, Spiritism, "optimistic popular science evolutionism," Hinduism, and "an intuitive belief in the all-saving power of healthy-minded attitudes as such" (71).

26. James, *Varieties of Religious Experience*, 74, 75, 76, 78, 79.

27. *Twelve Steps and Twelve Traditions* (New York: Alcoholics Anonymous World Services, 1952), 72; Ernest Kurtz, *Not-God: A History of Alcoholics Anonymous* (Center City, MN: Hazelden, 1991), 3, 196, 206, 215; Ernest Kurtz and Katherine Ketcham, *The Spirituality of Imperfection: Storytelling and the Search for Meaning* (New York: Bantam, 1992), 140.

28. Ernest Kurtz, "The Spirituality of William James: A Lesson from Alcoholics Anonymous," in *The Collected Ernie Kurtz*, Hindsfoot Foundation Series on Treatment and Recovery (New York: Authors Choice, 2008), 8, 3, 6–7; James, *Varieties of Religious Experience*, 68, 69, 84, 95, 98, 103, 114.

29. James, *Varieties of Religious Experience*, 38, 52, 56, 149, 86, 89, 140.

30. Kurtz, "Whatever Happened to Twelve-Step Programs?," 1, 18, 22, 23; Travis, *Language of the Heart*, 22; Dietrich Bonhoeffer, *Creation and Fall: A Theological Exposition of Genesis 1–3*, Dietrich Bonhoeffer Works, vol. 3, trans. Douglas Stephen Bax, ed. John W. de Gruchy (Minneapolis: Fortress, 1997), 113.

Chapter 6

1. "One Step to Freedom Curriculum," http://www.calvaryccv.org/website_archives /One-Step-To-Freedom-Curriculum.pdf; Chad Prigmore, "Is Alcoholics Anonymous the Devil in Your Church?," The Way Ministry Church, March 26, 2015, http://www .recoveryreformation.org/pastor-chads-blog/is-alcoholics-anonymous-the-devil-in -your-church.

2. Neil T. Anderson and Mike and Julia Quarles, *Freedom from Addiction: Breaking the Bondage of Addiction and Finding Freedom in Christ* (Minneapolis: Bethany House, 2006), 303, 325; Michael Wren, *God's Addiction Recovery Plan: The Biblical Path to Freedom* (Bloomington, IN: WestBow, 2015); Russell Willingham, *Breaking Free: Understanding Sexual Addiction and the Healing Power of Jesus* (Downers Grove, IL: InterVarsity, 1999), 207–8; https://www.facebook.com/pg/sinnersanonymous/about/?ref=page_internal; Pam Morrison, *Jesus and the Addict: Twelve Bible Studies for People Getting Free from Drugs* (n.p.: Living Parables of Central Florida, 2018).

3. Boyd Stevens, "10 Principles for Overcoming Stubborn Habits," Recovery Ministries, http://rurecovery.com/10-principles-overcoming-stubborn-habits/; Edward T. Welch, *Crossroads: A Step-by-Step Guide away from Addiction* (Greensboro, NC: New Growth, 2008), 8–9.

4. Nate Larkin, *Samson and the Pirate Monks: Calling Men to Authentic Brotherhood* (Nashville: Thomas Nelson, 2006), 108, 109, 125–68.

5. The "7 Principles of Living in Everyday Freedom" are the basis of Mark Laaser's L.I.F.E. recovery guides, which include *L.I.F.E. Guide for Men* (Maitland, FL: Xulon, 2002). Laaser writes, "I continue to believe the Twelve Steps contain a great deal of spiritual wisdom and still encourage people to practice them and attend meetings. However, I have come to believe the Twelve Steps do not emphasize enough the radical spiritual transformation that can only be achieved through a more intimate relationship with Jesus Christ." See Mark R. Laaser, *Healing the Wounds of Sexual Addiction* (Grand Rapids: Zondervan, 2009), 18.

6. "Celebrate Recovery's Eight Recovery Principles," Celebrate Recovery, https://www .celebraterecovery.com/resources/cr-tools/8principles.

7. William L. White, *Slaying the Dragon: The History of Addiction Treatment and Recovery in America*, 2nd ed. (Bloomington, IL: Chestnut Hill Systems, 2014), 204–6.

8. Ernest Kurtz, *Not-God: A History of Alcoholics Anonymous* (Center City, MN: Hazelden, 1991), 22. My characterization of arguments by Peele and Fingarette is based on Jerry Spicer, *The Minnesota Model: The Evolution of the Multidisciplinary Approach to Addiction*

Recovery (Center City, MN: Hazelden, 1993), 79–84; Jack Trimpey, *Rational Recovery: The New Cure for Substance Addiction* (New York: Gallery Books, 1996), 5, 252; Trimpey, "Recoveryism: Life according to Addiction," 2007, https://rational.org/index.php?id=92.

9. Among the leading non-Twelve-Step recovery programs are Moderation Management, Women for Sobriety, Addictive Voice Recognition Technique, Self-Management and Recovery Training (SMART), the Life Process Program, and LifeRing Secular Recovery.

10. Kurtz, *Not-God*, 117–18; Trysh Travis, *The Language of the Heart: A Cultural History of the Recovery Movement from Alcoholics Anonymous to Oprah Winfrey* (Chapel Hill: University of North Carolina Press, 2009), 37–42; Paul C. Conley and Andrew A. Sorensen, *The Staggering Steeple: The Story of Alcoholism and the Churches* (Cleveland: Pilgrim, 1971), 116.

11. *Alcohol Use and Abuse: Social and Health Effects: Reports and Recommendations by the Presbyterian Church (U.S.A.)* (Louisville: Presbyterian Distribution Management Service, 1986), 26; Travis, *Language of the Heart*, 43, 45.

12. Conley and Sorensen, *Staggering Steeple*, 121, 122, 123; Stephen P. Apthorp, "Drug Abuse and the Church: Are the Blind Leading the Blind?," *Christian Century*, November 9, 1988, 1010–13, here 1011.

13. Travis, *Language of the Heart*, 35, 39, 40; Martin Nicolaus, *Empowering Your Sober Self: The LifeRing Approach to Addiction Recovery*, 2nd ed. (Oakland, CA: LifeRing, 2014), 153, 58; Ernest Kurtz, "Alcoholics Anonymous and the Disease Concept of Alcoholism," 2002, 21, http://www.williamwhitepapers.com/pr/Dr.%20Ernie%20Kurtz%20on%20AA%20%26%20the%20Disease%20Concept%2C%202002.pdf.

14. Kurtz, "Alcoholics Anonymous," 1, 2, 6; *Alcoholics Anonymous: The Story of How Many Thousands of Men and Women Have Recovered from Alcoholism*, 4th ed. (New York: Alcoholics Anonymous World Services, 2001), 44. As Kurtz shows, the *A.A. Grapevine*, especially in its early years, "seemed dedicated to spreading the disease concept of alcoholism," partly because some AAs desired to set up or aid hospital programs for alcoholics; Travis, *Language of the Heart*, 35; Kurtz, *Not-God*, 199, 202; Kurtz, "Alcoholics Anonymous," 7, 12, 10, 18.

15. Travis, *Language of the Heart*, 49, 50.

16. Travis, *Language of the Heart*, 22, 23; David F. Wells, *God in the Wasteland: The Reality of Truth in a World of Fading Dreams* (Grand Rapids: Eerdmans, 1994), 77, 81; William L. Playfair with George Bryson, *The Useful Lie: How the Recovery Industry Has Entrapped America in a Disease Model of Addiction* (Wheaton, IL: Crossway, 1991), 68, 100, 24.

17. Playfair, *Useful Lie*, 137. See also Martin Bobgan and Diedre Bobgan, *12 Steps to Destruction: Codependency/Recovery Heresies* (n.p.: Eastgate, 1991).

18. Playfair, *Useful Lie*, 24, 29, 166.

19. K. Karacsony, "Is '12 Steps' Christian?," https://docplayer.net/3192567-Is-12-steps-christian.html; Stevens, "10 Principles for Overcoming Stubborn Habits." Principles 2 ("every sin has its origin in our hearts"), 9 ("we lose our freedom to choose when we give in to temptation"), and 10 ("accept the blame for your actions and God will remove the guilt") further underscore individual responsibility and cast doubt on claims of powerlessness.

20. C. Wayne Marshall, "Addiction Recovery and the Burden of Self," *Christian Research Journal* 31, no. 2 (2008): http://www.equip.org/article/addiction-recovery-and-the-burden-of-self/; Welch, *Crossroads*, 31, 6, 56; Peter Hitchens, "The Fantasy of Addiction," *First Things*, February 2017, https://www.firstthings.com/article/2017/02/the-fantasy-of-addiction.

21. *Alcoholics Anonymous*, 63, 64.

22. *Alcoholics Anonymous*, 65, 66, 67, 83.

23. *Alcoholics Anonymous*, 69, 70, 77.

24. *Twelve Steps and Twelve Traditions* (New York: Alcoholics Anonymous World Services, 1952), 45, 47, 52, 78, 56, 82, 90.

25. Howard J. Clinebell Jr., *Understanding and Counseling the Alcoholic through Religion and Psychology*, 2nd ed. (Nashville: Abingdon, 1968), 141–42.

26. Sister Molly Monahan, *Seeds of Grace: Reflections on the Spirituality of Alcoholics Anonymous* (New York: Riverhead Books, 2001), 48.

27. T. C. Ryan, *Ashamed No More: A Pastor's Journey through Sex Addiction* (Downers Grove, IL: InterVarsity, 2012), 24, 194.

28. *Co-Dependents Anonymous*, 3rd ed. (Phoenix: Co-Dependents Anonymous, 2016), ii, vii.

29. *Co-Dependents Anonymous*, 30–32.

30. *Co-Dependents Anonymous*, 19, 106, 26, 32, 41, 42, 60–61, 123.

31. *Adult Children of Alcoholics/Dysfunctional Families* (Signal Hill, CA: ACoA/DF World Service Organization, 2006), xi, xiii. Hereafter, page references to this book are given in parentheses in the text. Another subtle adjustment to AA practice is ACA's conception of sponsorship as "fellow traveling," based on adult children's "over-reliance on others for direction and approval and our tendency to try to manage someone else's life" (369–70).

32. According to one scheme, Twelve-Step fellowships adhere to a "compensatory model" that considers an individual responsible for solving but not for causing addiction. Alternative views are the "medical model" (individual is responsible neither for causing nor for solving the problem), the "enlightenment model" (individual is responsible for causing but not for solving the problem), and the "moral model" (individual is responsible for both causing and solving the problem). See Tom Horvath et al., "Addiction and Personal Responsibility: A Fundamental Conflict," CenterSite, http://www.centersite.net/poc/view_doc.php?type=doc&id=48356&cn=1408.

33. Playfair, *Useful Lie*, 93, 94; Robert S. McGee, Pat Springle, and Susan Joiner, "Rapha's 12 Steps in the Wrong Direction: A Critique of 'Rapha's 12-Step Program for Overcoming Chemical Dependency,'" Christian Discernment, http://www.christiandiscernment.com/Christian%20Discernment/CD%20PDF/Book%20pdf/25D%20Rapha%2012%20Steps.pdf.

34. Welch, *Crossroads*, 77; Edward T. Welch, *Addictions: A Banquet in the Grave; Finding Hope in the Power of the Gospel* (Phillipsburg, NJ: Presbyterian and Reformed, 2001), 248.

35. Stevens, "10 Principles for Overcoming Stubborn Habits"; Playfair, *Useful Lie*, 81, 85; Welch, *Addictions*, 5, 14, 109, 37.

Chapter 7

1. "Small Group Guidelines," Celebrate Recovery, https://www.celebraterecovery.com/resources/cr-tools/guidelines.

2. Tim Stafford, "The Hidden Gospel of the Twelve Steps," *Christianity Today*, July 22, 1991, https://silkworth.net/alcoholics-anonymous/01-097-the-hidden-gospel-of-the-twelve-steps-by-tim-stafford-christianity-today-july-22-1991/.

3. *Addictive Lifestyles: Breaking Free* (1984), cited in Trish Merrill, *Committed, Caring Communities: A Congregational Resource Guide for Addiction Ministries* (Austin: Texas Council of Churches, 1995), 39.

4. Robert S. McGee, *Rapha's 12-Step Program for Overcoming Chemical Dependency: A New Christ-Centered Adaptation of the Most Successful Approach to Recovery Ever Devised* (n.p.: Robert S. McGee, 1990), 4–5; Milton Knudsen, "Twelve Steps for Clergy Recovering from Codependence," in Merrill, *Committed, Caring Communities*, 95. See also Melinda Fish, "A Christian's Twelve Steps to Recovery from Addiction," in *When Addiction Comes to Church: Helping Yourself and Others Move into Recovery* (Ada, MI: Fleming H. Revell, 1990), 275–76; "The Twelve Steps of Christians in Recovery," Christians in Recovery, http://christians-in-recovery.org/Tools_12Steps_CIR; "Alcoholics for Christ—12 Step Christ Centered Program for Alcoholics and Substance Abusers," Alcoholics for Christ, http://www.alcoholicsforchrist.com/sa.htm; and "Twelve Steps for Christian Growth," in Philip St. Romain, *Becoming a New Person: Twelve Steps to Christian Growth* (n.p.: Lulu, 2010), 3–4.

5. *Manual of Alcoholics Victorious* (n.p.: Alcoholics Victorious and Christians in Recovery, 2014), 15; Friends in Recovery, *Twelve Steps for Christians: Based on Biblical Teachings* (Scotts Valley, CA: RPI, 1988), xiii–xvi; Terry Webb, *Tree of Renewed Life: Spiritual Renewal of the Church through the Twelve-Step Program* (New York: Crossroad, 1992), 153. According to Webb, her list was prepared by the Institute for Christian Living.

6. For other Step-Scripture links, see Jerry Dunn with Bernard Palmer, *God Is for the Alcoholic*, rev. ed. (Chicago: Moody, 1986), 142–43; Claire W., *God, Help Me Stop! Break Free from Addiction and Compulsion* (Grand Rapids: Zondervan, 1993); Ron Keller, *The Twelve Steps and Beyond: A Transforming Journey through the Gospel of John into Life in Christ* (Burnsville, MN: Prince of Peace, 1989); "Twelve Steps of Sinners Anonymous," in Keith Miller, *A Hunger for Healing: The Twelve Steps as a Classic Model for Christian Spiritual Growth* (San Francisco: HarperOne, 1992), 245–46; Mike O'Neill, *The Power to Choose: Twelve Steps to Wholeness* (Nashville: Sonlight, 1991), ix–x; Frances Jay, *Walking with God through the Twelve Steps: What I Learned about Honesty, Healing, Reconciliation and Wholeness* (Chicago: Liturgy Training, 1996); June Hunt, *Alcohol and Drug Abuse: Breaking Free and Staying Free* (Torrance, CA: Aspire, 2013), 53–59; "12 Spiritual Steps to Recovery," in Ronald Simmons, *Understanding Christian Drug and Alcohol Recovery* (Los Angeles: Free N One Books, 2001), 86; and "The Bible and Steps," 12step.org, http://www.12step.org/references/bible/.

7. "Celebrate Recovery's Eight Recovery Principles: The Road to Recovery Based on the Beatitudes," Celebrate Recovery, https://www.celebraterecovery.com/resources/cr-tools/8principles.

8. "What Is Celebrate Recovery?," Celebrate Recovery, https://www.celebraterecovery.com/?id=1:getting-started.

9. Robert Hemfelt and Richard Fowler, eds., *Serenity: A Companion for Twelve Step Recovery; Complete with New Testament, Psalms & Proverbs* (Nashville: Thomas Nelson, 1990). These Bibles appear in translations, like the New International Version, New Living Translation, or New King James Bible, that are favored by evangelical Christians.

10. Verne Becker, ed., *Recovery Devotional Bible* (Grand Rapids: Zondervan, 1993).

11. Becker, *Recovery Devotional Bible*, A12.

12. *The Journey of Recovery New Testament* (Colorado Springs: International Bible Society, 2006), A102, A69.

13. John Baker, ed., *NIV Celebrate Recovery Study Bible* (Grand Rapids: Zondervan, 2007).

14. *Journey to Recovery through Christ: CASA's 12-Step Study Bible* (Dallas: Quarry, 2015), i.

15. Becker, *Recovery Devotional Bible*, 1039; Hemfelt and Fowler, *Serenity*, 6; Becker, *Recovery Devotional Bible*, 1039; David A. Stoop and Stephen F. Arterburn, eds., *The Life Recovery Bible: King James Version* (Carol Stream, IL: Tyndale House, 1998), 1117; *Journey of Recovery New Testament*, 43. Since the numbers in the *Celebrate Recovery Bible's* marginal notations refer to CR's principles, my assignment of the Steps to these verses is based on CR's description of the connections between its principles and the Twelve Steps.

16. *Recovery Devotional Bible*, ix; *Journey of Recovery New Testament*, 7, A70; *Life Recovery Bible*, A9, A12; *Celebrate Recovery Bible*, vii, xiii.

17. *Life Recovery Bible*, A15; *Journey of Recovery New Testament*, 37; *Celebrate Recovery Bible*, 1454.

18. *Journey of Recovery New Testament*, A69.

19. James B. Nelson, *Thirst: God and the Alcoholic Experience* (Louisville: Westminster John Knox, 2004), 72.

20. The website of Alcoholics for Christ, http://www.alcoholicsforchrist.com.

21. *The Twelve Steps: A Spiritual Journey; A Working Guide for Healing Based on Biblical Teachings* (Scotts Valley, CA: RPI, 2012), 1, 2, 7. McGee, *Rapha's 12-Step Program for Overcoming Chemical Dependency*, 6; Keller, *Twelve Steps and Beyond*, 4, 13.

22. Ron Halvorson and Valerie Deilgat, *Living Free: A Guide to Forming and Conducting a Recovery Ministry* (San Diego: Recovery, 1992), 4, 37, 59–60, 16, 7.

23. The website of Overcomers Outreach, http://www.overcomersoutreach.org/.

24. "How CIR Serves," Christians in Recovery, http://christians-in-recovery.org /AboutCIR_WhatWeDo#background/. "The process leading to full-blown addiction starts with the sin of drunkenness," CIR maintains, "which is a moral choice even for those with a family history of alcoholism" (http://christians-in-recovery.org/AboutCIR_WhatWeDo; http://christians-in-recovery.org/Tools_FAQ_ChristianRecovery#always).

25. *Journey to Recovery through Christ*, 7, 247, 8, 15, 9.

26. Richard Peace et al., *12 Steps: The Path to Wholeness*, Serendipity Felt Need Course (Littleton, CO: Serendipity House, 1989), 7; *Serendipity Bible*, 10th anniversary ed. (Grand Rapids: Zondervan; Littleton, CO: Serendipity, 1988), 44–45; *Beginning a Serendipity Group: Six Sessions to Get Acquainted* (Littleton, CO: Serendipity House, 1991), 3, 4. Interestingly, the *Serendipity Bible Study Book*, published in 1986, contained no references to addiction or recovery. See Lyman Coleman et al., eds., *The Serendipity Bible Study Book* (Grand Rapids: Lamplighter Books, 1986).

27. John Baker, *Life's Healing Choices: Freedom from Your Hurts, Hang-Ups, and Habits* (New York: Simon & Schuster, 2007), 2.

28. Baker, *Life's Healing Choices*, 189, 258, 264, 269.

29. Halvorson and Deilgat, *Living Free*, 19.

Chapter 8

1. See "Delray Beach: Recovery Capital of the USA," Wellness Resource Center, https:// www.wellnessresourcecenter.com/about/news-media/articles/florida-recovery/; and Lizette

Alvarez, "Haven for Addicts Now Profits from Their Relapses," *New York Times*, June 20, 2017, https://www.nytimes.com/2017/06/20/us/delray-beach-addiction.html.

2. "We Believe," Overflow Church, https://www.overflowchurchofverobeach.com/we-believe.

3. Liz Swanson and Teresa McBean, *Bridges to Grace: Innovative Approaches to Recovery Ministry* (Grand Rapids: Zondervan, 2011), 175; Michele S. Matto, *The Twelve Steps in the Bible: A Path to Wholeness for Adult Children* (Mahwah, NJ: Paulist, 1991), 2; Ernest Kurtz and Katherine Ketcham, *The Spirituality of Imperfection: Storytelling and the Search for Meaning* (New York: Bantam, 1992), 101.

4. Claire W., *God, Help Me Stop!* (San Diego: Books West, 1988), vii, 27, 18, 96.

5. Dale Ryan and Juanita Ryan, *Recovery from Addictions*, Life Recovery Guides 5 (Downers Grove, IL: InterVarsity, 1990), 5, 6, 12. The Ryans encourage Christians seeking recovery to join Twelve-Step groups.

6. Dale Ryan and Juanita Ryan, *A Spiritual Kindergarten: Christian Perspectives on the Twelve Steps* (Brea, CA: Christian Recovery International, 1999), 1, 3.

7. Ryan and Ryan, *Spiritual Kindergarten*, 24, 90, 106.

8. Robert Hemfelt et al., *The Path to Serenity* (Nashville: Thomas Nelson, 1991), 4, 11, 16, 234.

9. Sam Shoemaker et al., *Steps to a New Beginning: Leading Others to Christ through the Twelve Step Process* (Nashville: Thomas Nelson, 1993), 20, 79, 106, 107, 24, 114.

10. Mike O'Neill, *Power to Choose: Twelve Steps to Wholeness* (Nashville: Sonlight, 1991), vii, vi, vii.

11. Bill Morris, *The Complete Handbook for Recovery Ministry in the Church: A Practical Guide to Establishing Recovery Support Groups within Your Church* (Nashville: Thomas Nelson, 1993), 243.

12. Morris, *Complete Handbook*, 243, 247.

13. J. Keith Miller, *A Hunger for Healing: The Twelve Steps as a Classic Model for Spiritual Growth* (New York: HarperOne, 1991), xii.

14. Miller, *Hunger for Healing*, 32, 4, 33, 132, xiv, 86, 110.

15. Tim Timmons, *Anyone Anonymous* (Old Tappan, NJ: Fleming H. Revell, 1990), 8, 16, 91, 92. Amid rumors of marital infidelity and financial impropriety, Timmons resigned from his pulpit the year the book appeared.

16. Martin M. Davis, *The Gospel and the Twelve Steps: Following Jesus on the Path of Recovery* (n.p.: CreateSpace, 2016), 159, 50, 41, 67, 122, 160. The first edition of *The Gospel and the Twelve Steps* was published by RPI in 1993; a second edition was released in 2005 by Pleasant Word.

17. Alexander C. DeJong, *Help and Hope for the Alcoholic* (Wheaton, IL: Tyndale House, 1982), 25, 28, 29.

18. John Z., *Grace in Addiction: The Good News of Alcoholics Anonymous for Everybody* (Charlottesville, VA: Mockingbird Ministries, 2012), 15.

19. John Z., *Grace in Addiction*, 221, 239, 251, 252, 254, 255.

20. Matto, *Twelve Steps in the Bible*, 1.

21. John C. Mellon, *Mark as Recovery Story: Alcoholism and the Rhetoric of Gospel Mystery* (Chicago: University of Illinois Press, 1995), 4, x, xi, 11, 12.

22. The Twelve Step Review, http://www.12-step-review.org/index.html; Venerable Matt Talbot Resource Center, http://venerablematttalbotresourcecenter.blogspot.com/; "The

Spirituality of Recovery," Ignatian Spirituality Project, https://ispretreats.org/impact/the
-spirituality-of-recovery/. See Jim Harbaugh, SJ, *A Twelve-Step Approach to the Spiritual Exercises of St. Ignatius* (New York: Sheed and Ward, 1997), and Scott Weeman, *The Twelve Steps
and the Sacraments: A Catholic Journey through Recovery* (Notre Dame, IN: Ave Maria, 2017).

23. William L. White, *Slaying the Dragon: The History of Addiction Treatment and Recovery in America*, 2nd ed. (Bloomington, IL: Chestnut Health Systems, 2014), 291; The Calix
Society, http://www.calixsociety.org/.

24. https://cac.org/about/who-we-are/; Richard Rohr, *Breathing under Water: Spirituality and the Twelve Steps* (Cincinnati: Franciscan Media, 2011), xii.

25. Rohr, *Breathing under Water*, xx, xxii, xxiv.

26. Rohr, *Breathing under Water*, xxi, xxiii.

27. Rohr, *Breathing under Water*, 26, 125–26, 52, 76, 87, 111, 108.

28. "Twelve Step," Contemplative Outreach, https://www.contemplativeoutreach
.org/twelve-step/.

29. Thomas Keating with Tom S., *Divine Therapy and Addiction: Centering Prayer and
the Twelve Steps* (New York: Lantern, 2009), 113, 24, 114, 88.

30. Keating, *Divine Therapy*, 15, 12, 9, 58, 79, 66, 159, 36, 19, 123, 95, 40.

31. Keating, *Divine Therapy*, 149, 154, 36, 34.

32. Keating, *Divine Therapy*, 174, 175. An appendix to *Divine Therapy and Addiction* touts
the benefits of centering prayer for those in recovery, which include enhancement of the
ability to "let go and let God," development of a nonjudgmental attitude, self-knowledge,
and the capacities to listen, serve, and live in the present (223).

33. Sister Molly Monahan, *Seeds of Grace: Reflections on the Spirituality of Alcoholics
Anonymous* (New York: Riverhead Books, 2001), 6.

34. Monahan, *Seeds of Grace*, 97, 99.

35. Monahan, *Seeds of Grace*, 43–44, 178, 180.

36. The view that the Twelve Steps are part of a universal wisdom is espoused, for instance, by Ernest Kurtz and Katherine Ketcham, *The Spirituality of Imperfection: Storytelling
and the Search for Meaning* (New York: Bantam, 1993), and Rami Shapiro, *Recovery: The
Twelve Steps as Spiritual Practice* (Woodstock, VT: Skylight Paths, 2009). Both books illu-
mine recovery with insights from a variety of religious and spiritual traditions, including
Greek mythology, rabbinic Judaism, Hasidism, Roman Catholicism, Protestantism, Taoism,
Confucianism, Hinduism, Islam, Sufism, and Buddhism.

Chapter 9

1. Ryan describes the association's origins this way: "The NACR began its life as a ministry of Christian Recovery International. CRI was incorporated in 1989. Late in that same
year the NACR was 'invented' in a series of meetings between myself, Carmen Renee Berry
and Patrick Means. We began with publication of a mini-magazine (STEPS) and held annual
STEPS conferences every year starting in 1991. . . . In April, 2011 the NACR was transferred
from Christian Recovery International to NorthStar Community, Inc where it remains
today" (email to the author, October 23, 2020).

2. "About: Our Story," National Association for Christian Recovery, http://www.nacr
.org/about-our-story.

3. https://www.epicenter.org/recovery-ministries/.

4. Bill Wigmore, "Finding Jesus in the Basement—One Man's Spiritual Odyssey" (unpublished essay, March 3, 2015).

5. Fr. Bill W., "A.A.'s Pioneer Program and Two Way Prayer: Why Early A.A. Recovery Rates Exceeded Those of Today" (document included in the Friends of Dr. Bob newcomer packet); "Finding Jesus in the Basement."

6. This description is based on a document titled "How to Practice Two Way Prayer," distributed as part of the Friends of Dr. Bob newcomer's packet.

7. See also William Wigmore and Matthew Stanford, "Two Way Prayer: A Lost Tool for Practicing the 11th Step," *Alcoholism Treatment Quarterly* 35, no. 1 (2017): 71–82.

8. "About: Our Story," Sam Shoemaker Community, https://www.samshoemaker community.org/our-story.

9. The website of Friends of Dr. Bob, http://www.friendsofdrbob.org/.

10. Among the resources available from the 12SO website are instructions for practicing centering prayer, planning guidelines for an Eleventh-Step workshop or weekend retreat, and resources for starting a Twelve-Step centering prayer group or Eleventh-Step meditation meeting ("Resources," 12 Step Outreach, https://cp12stepoutreach.org/resources/).

11. *Twelve Steps and Twelve Traditions* (New York: Alcoholics Anonymous World Services, 1952), 98.

12. "Who Are We," Thrive, http://www.thriverecovery.com/what-we-do.

13. The website of Thrive, http://www.thriverecovery.com/.

14. "The Principles of the Recovery at Cokesbury Network," Recovery at Cokesbury Network, http://recoveryatcokesbury.com/racn-knoxville/welcome-to-racn-knoxville; the website of Recovery, Powell Church, https://powellchurch.com/recovery/.

15. Emily Belz, "'The Love Is Here': In Brooklyn, a Church without Much Money Gives Addicts a Rare Welcome Mat," *World Magazine*, January 17, 2019, https://world .wng.org/2019/01/the_love_is_here; "'Idol-Killing Machine': Three Questions for Edwin Colon," Redeemer City to City, March 5, 2018, https://medium.com/redeemer-city-to -city/idol-killing-machine-three-questions-with-edwin-colon-48b49f61a299.

16. "Our History," Faith Partners, http://faith-partners.org/about-us/our-history/.

17. Liz Swanson and Teresa McBean, *Bridges to Grace: Innovative Approaches to Recovery Ministry* (Grand Rapids: Zondervan, 2011), 2.

18. Swanson and McBean, *Bridges to Grace*, 181, 183; "Who Benefits?," Faith Partners, http://faith-partners.org/approach/who-benefits/.

19. The website of Recovery Ministries of the Episcopal Church, https://www .episcopalrecovery.org/.

20. "About," A Better Life—Brianna's Hope, https://www.ablbh.org/about; the website of The Recovery Church, https://therecoverychurch.org/.

21. "The Way," Saint John's United Methodist Church, http://www.stjohnsmidtown .org/worship/the-way/; Facebook page for the Open Door Community, https://www .facebook.com/pg/The-Open-Door-Community-156891801001172/about/?ref=page _internal; website of FREE, https://freespiritualcommunity.com/.

22. UU Addictions Ministry, http://uuaddictionsministry.org/; Adventist Recovery Ministries Global, https://adventistrecoveryglobal.org/; Presbyterian Health, Education and Welfare Association, http://www.phewacommunity.org/paaaddictionaction.html; "Celebrating the Miracle," Presbyterians for Addiction Action, https://www.presbyterianmission.org/wp -content/uploads/celebrating-the-miracle.pdf.

23. "About," Fellowship of Recovering Lutheran Clergy, https://frlc.org/about-2/; "About," Clergy Recovery Network, http://www.clergyrecovery.com/?page_id=2.

24. *Twelve Steps and Twelve Traditions*, 181, 187; Trysh Travis, *The Language of the Heart: A Cultural History of the Recovery Movement from Alcoholics Anonymous to Oprah Winfrey* (Chapel Hill: University of North Carolina Press, 2009), 92.

Chapter 10

1. https://www.reiki.org/faqs/what-reiki.

2. Howard J. Clinebell Jr., *Understanding and Counseling the Alcoholic*, 2nd ed. (Nashville: Abingdon, 1968), 168, 167, 145, 168.

3. Joseph H. Fichter, *The Rehabilitation of Clergy Alcoholics* (New York: Human Sciences, 1982), 135; Eleace King and Jim Castelli, *Culture of Recovery, Culture of Denial: Alcoholism among Men and Women Religious* (Washington, DC: Center for Applied Research in the Apostolate, 1995), 115.

4. Jonathan Benz with Kristina Robb-Dover, *The Recovery-Minded Church: Loving and Ministering to People with Addiction* (Downers Grove, IL: InterVarsity, 2016), 66–67.

5. Reinhold Niebuhr, *The Nature and Destiny of Man: A Christian Interpretation*, vol. 1 (New York: Charles Scribner's Sons, 1964), 235; William Lenters, *The Freedom We Crave: Addiction and the Human Condition* (Grand Rapids: Eerdmans, 1985), 4; Patrick McCormick, CM, *Sin as Addiction* (Mahwah, NJ: Paulist, 1989). See also Christopher C. H. Cook, *Alcohol, Addiction and Christian Ethics*, New Studies in Christian Ethics (Cambridge: Cambridge University Press, 2006), 18–19.

6. Cornelius C. Plantinga, *Not the Way It's Supposed to Be: A Breviary of Sin* (Grand Rapids: Eerdmans, 1996), 138, 139, 140, 144, 145, 147.

7. Linda A. Mercadante, *Victims and Sinners: Spiritual Roots of Addiction and Recovery* (Louisville: Westminster John Knox, 1996), 13, 31, 40, 48, 115, 75, 96, 127, 137; Linda Mercadante, "Sin and Addiction: Conceptual Enemies or Fellow Travelers," *Religions* 6 (2015): 614–25, here 620, 621.

8. Kent Dunnington, *Addiction and Virtue: Beyond the Models of Disease and Choice*, Strategic Initiatives in Evangelical Theology (Downers Grove, IL: InterVarsity, 2011), 125, 132, 134, 133, 137, 138, 139, 140.

9. James B. Nelson, *Thirst: God and the Alcoholic Experience* (Louisville: Westminster John Knox, 2004), 59, 67, 69.

10. Nelson, *Thirst*, 73, 75, 76.

11. Jeffrey M. Jones, "Americans with Addiction in Their Family Believe It Is a Disease," *Gallup News Service*, August 11, 2006, http://www.gallup.com/poll/24097/americans-addiction-their-family-believe-disease.aspx; *Alcohol Use and Abuse: The Social and Health Effects, Reports and Recommendations by the Presbyterian Church (U.S.A.)* (Louisville: Presbyterian Church [U.S.A.], 1986), 44–55; "Drug Addiction Seen as 'Moral Failing,' Survey Finds," *Health Day*, October 3, 2014, https://consumer.healthday.com/mental-health-information-25/addiction-news-6/drug-addiction-seen-as-moral-failing-survey-finds-692298.html.

12. Father Ralph Pfau and Al Hirshberg, *Prodigal Shepherd* (New York: J. B. Lippincott, 1958), 219–20.

13. Nelson, *Thirst*, 49.

14. Nelson, *Thirst*, 42. See also Clinebell, *Understanding and Counseling the Alcoholic*, 168–71.

15. Nelson, *Thirst*, 48, 102–3, 104, 106, 56, 106.

16. Niebuhr, *Nature and Destiny of Man*, 234–35.

17. Jason Pittman and Scott W. Taylor, "Christianity and the Treatment of Addiction: An Ecological Approach for Social Workers," in *Christianity and Social Work: Readings on the Integration of Christian Faith and Social Work Practice*, ed. Beryl Hugen and T. Laine Scales (Botsford, CT: North American Association of Christians in Social Work, 2002), 193–213, here 204; Joseph E. Keller, *Ministering to Alcoholics* (Minneapolis: Augsburg, 1966), 11; Wayne Edward Oates, *Alcohol in and out of the Church* (Nashville: Broadman, 1966), 122.

18. John A. Martin, *Blessed Are the Addicts: The Spiritual Side of Alcoholism, Addiction and Recovery* (New York: Villard, 1990), 4; Shais Taub, *God of Our Understanding: Jewish Spirituality and Recovery from Addiction* (Jersey City, NJ: Ktav, 2010), 19.

19. Cited in Melinda Fish, *When Addiction Comes to Church: Helping Yourself and Others Move into Recovery* (New York: Fleming H. Revell, 1990), 208; Gerald G. May, *Addiction and Grace: Love and Spirituality in the Healing of Addictions* (New York: HarperCollins, 1988), 4, 91; Francis F. Seeburger, *Addiction and Responsibility: An Inquiry into the Addictive Mind* (New York: Crossroad, 1993), 57; Wayne E. Oates, "A Biblical Perspective on Addiction," *Review and Expositor* 91 (1994): 71–75, here 73; Plantinga, *Not the Way It's Supposed to Be*, 131, 148, 121; Richard Rohr, *Breathing under Water: Spirituality and the Twelve Steps* (Cincinnati: Franciscan Media, 2011), 116.

20. Sharon Hersh, *The Last Addiction: Own Your Desire, Live beyond Recovery, Find Lasting Freedom* (Colorado Springs: Waterbrook, 2008), 15; Edward T. Welch, *Addictions: A Banquet in the Grave: Finding Hope in the Power of the Gospel* (Phillipsburg, NJ: Presbyterian & Reformed, 2001), xvi; Kent Dunnington, *Addiction and Virtue: Beyond the Models of Disease and Choice*, Strategic Initiatives in Evangelical Theology (Downers Grove, IL: InterVarsity, 2011), 160; David Foster Wallace, "This Is Water: Some Thoughts, Delivered on a Significant Occasion, about Living a Compassionate Life," cited at https://www.goodreads.com/quotes/100888-because-here-s-something-else-that-s-weird-but-true-in-the.

21. Nancy Van Dyke Platt and Chilton R. Knudsen, *So You Think You Don't Know One? Addiction and Recovery in Clergy and Congregations* (New York: Morehouse, 2010), 34; Samuel Perry, *Addicted to Lust: Pornography in the Lives of Conservative Protestants* (New York: Oxford University Press, 2019), 164.

22. See Cook, *Alcohol, Addiction and Christian Ethics*, chapter 6, where the author explores the writings of Paul and Augustine to advocate for a view of addiction as an expression of "divided will" and one manifestation of the human condition.

23. Saint Augustine, *Confessions*, trans. R. S. Pine-Coffin (London: Penguin, 1961), 164; Cook, *Alcohol, Addiction and Christian Ethics*, 146.

24. May, *Addiction and Grace*, 42; Jack Trimpey's "rational recovery" offers a secular version of the divided-self theory of addiction: "There are two of you inside your head, and often you will hear a voice that is not 'I' using the second person 'you'" (*Rational Recovery: The New Cure for Substance Addiction* [New York: Pocket, 1996], 154).

25. Ernest Kurtz, *Not-God: A History of Alcoholics Anonymous* (Center City, MN: Hazelden, 1991), 136–37; in Mercadante, *Victims and Sinners*, 128; William James, *The Varieties*

of Religious Experience (n.p.: Renaissance Classics, 2012), 284; Ernest Kurtz and Katherine Ketchum, *The Spirituality of Imperfection: Storytelling and the Search for Meaning* (New York: Bantam, 1992), 112–13.

26. Clinebell, *Understanding and Counseling the Alcoholic*, 154 (see also 71–73); Oates, *Alcohol in and out of the Church*, 122; Denise McLain Massey, "Addiction and Spirituality," *Review and Expositor* 91 (1994): 9–18, here 10, 13; Nelson, *Thirst*, 23, 30, 136.

27. Dietrich Bonhoeffer, *Creation and Fall: A Theological Exposition of Genesis 1–3*, Dietrich Bonhoeffer Works, vol. 3, trans. Douglas Stephen Bax, ed. John W. de Gruchy (Minneapolis: Fortress, 1997), 143.

28. Seeburger, *Addiction and Responsibility*, 117; Kurtz and Ketcham, *Spirituality of Imperfection*, 120; Rami Shapiro, *Recovery: The Twelve Steps as Spiritual Practice* (Woodstock, VT: Skylight Paths, 2009), xiv.

29. Dunnington, *Addiction and Virtue*, 10, 145; Anderson Spickard Jr., *Dying for a Drink: What You and Your Family Should Know about Alcoholism* (Nashville: Thomas Nelson, 2005), 195; Benz, *Recovery-Minded Church*, 10, 23, 13, 55.

30. May, *Grace and Addiction*, 16, 2, 20, 40, 150, 149, 181.

31. Hersh, *Last Addiction*, 4, 8; Seeburger, *Addiction and Responsibility*, 111–12, 115.

32. For a view of recovery as a process of faith development whose "stages" can be tracked alongside the "phases" of recovery identified by alcohol researchers, see James W. Fowler, "Alcoholics Anonymous and Faith Development," in *Research on Alcoholics Anonymous: Opportunities and Alternatives*, ed. Barbara S. McCrady and William R. Miller (New Brunswick, NJ: Rutgers Center of Alcohol Studies, 1993), 113–35.

33. Thomas H. Cairns, *Preparing Your Church for Ministry to Alcoholics and Their Families* (Springfield, IL: Charles C. Thomas, 1986), 9; Liz Swanson and Teresa McBean, *Bridges to Grace: Innovative Approaches to Recovery Ministry* (Grand Rapids: Zondervan, 2011), 2; see also 14, 15, 148, 183; William Struthers, *Wired for Intimacy: How Pornography Hijacks the Male Brain* (Downers Grove, IL: InterVarsity, 2009), 178, 188, 189.

34. *Alcoholics Anonymous: The Story of How Many Thousands of Men and Women Have Recovered from Alcoholism*, 4th ed. (New York: Alcoholics Anonymous World Services, 2001), 60, 83–84; "S.L.A.A. Signs of Recovery," Sex and Love Addicts Anonymous, https://slaafws.org/download/core-files/Signs-of-Recovery.pdf.

35. Rohr, *Breathing under Water*, xv–xvi, here xx.

36. Kurtz, *Not-God*, 222; Mercadante, *Victims and Sinners*, 147; Swanson and McBean, *Bridges to Grace*, 135; Hersh, *Last Addiction*, 169.

37. Dietrich Bonhoeffer, *Letters and Papers from Prison*, ed. C. Gremmels et al., Dietrich Bonhoeffer Works in English, vol. 8 (Minneapolis: Fortress, 2010), 479; Dietrich Bonhoeffer, *Berlin: 1932–1933*, ed. C. Nicolaisen et al., Dietrich Bonhoeffer Works in English, vol. 12 (Minneapolis: Fortress, 2009), 356.

38. Rohr, *Breathing under Water*, 125.

39. Rohr, *Breathing under Water*, 18, 125, 126.

40. Rohr, *Breathing under Water*, 39.

41. *Alcholics Anonymous*, xix.

42. Dan P. McAdams, *The Redemptive Self: Stories Americans Live By*, rev. ed. (New York: Oxford University Press, 2013), 198, 202; Nelson, *Thirst*, 14, 15.

43. *Alcoholics Anonymous*, 58.

Chapter 11

1. *Alcoholics Anonymous: The Story of How Many Thousands of Men and Women Have Recovered from Alcoholism*, 4th ed. (New York: Alcoholics Anonymous World Services, 2002), 83–84.

2. *Alcoholics Anonymous*, 25.

3. *Twelve Steps and Twelve Traditions* (New York: Alcoholics Anonymous World Services, 1952), 92; on Bateson, see Oliver J. Morgan, "Addiction and Spirituality in Context," in *Addiction and Spirituality: A Multidisciplinary Approach*, ed. Oliver J. Morgan and Merle Jordan (Saint Louis: Chalice Press, 1999), 3–30, here 14; Stephanie Brown, *Treating the Alcoholic: A Developmental Model of Recovery* (New York: John Wiley & Sons, 1985), 210.

4. William R. Miller and Janet C'de Baca, *Quantum Change: When Epiphanies and Sudden Insights Transform Ordinary Lives* (New York: Guilford, 2001), 7, 131, 53, 55.

5. Joseph Nowinski, *If You Work It, It Works! The Science behind Twelve Step Recovery* (Center City, MN: Hazelden, 2015), 140–41, 142–44, 148–49, 150.

6. Marc Galanter, *What Is Alcoholics Anonymous? A Path from Addiction to Recovery* (New York: Oxford University Press, 2016), 117, 123.

7. John A. Martin, *Blessed Are the Peacemakers: The Spiritual Side of Alcoholism, Addiction, and Recovery* (San Francisco: Harper, 1990), 93.

8. Joseph H. Fichter, *The Rehabilitation of Clergy Alcoholics* (New York: Human Sciences, 1982), 114, 116, 128, 152.

9. Eleace King and Jim Castelli, *Culture of Recovery, Culture of Denial: Alcoholism among Men and Women Religious* (Washington, DC: Center for Applied Research in the Apostolate, 1995), 105, 67, 107, 97, 108.

10. *Alcoholics Anonymous*, 102, 14.

11. Dennis Meacham, *The Addiction Ministry Handbook: A Guide for Faith Communities* (Boston: Skinner House, 2004), 40; Christina Grof, *The Thirst for Wholeness: Attachment, Addiction and the Spiritual Path* (San Francisco: HarperOne, 1993), 196; John Z., *Grace in Addiction: What the Church Can Learn from Alcoholics Anonymous* (Charlottesville, VA: Mockingbird Ministries, 2012), 19, 24, 222, 252.

12. Jonathan Benz with Kristina Robb-Dover, *The Recovery-Minded Church: Loving and Ministering to People with Addictions* (Downers Grove, IL: InterVarsity, 2016), 160; Richard Rohr, *Breathing under Water: Spirituality and the Twelve Steps* (Cincinnati: Franciscan Media, 2011), 65; *Alcoholics Anonymous*, 75; Kent Dunnington, "Small Groups Anonymous," *Christianity Today*, April 22, 2019, https://www.christianitytoday.com/ct/2019/may/small-groups-anonymous.html.

13. Robert Wuthnow, *After Heaven: Spirituality in America Since the 1950s* (Berkeley: University of California Press, 1998), 142, 147, chapter 6.

14. Dan P. McAdams, *The Redemptive Self: Stories Americans Live By* (New York: Oxford University Press, 2013), 121, 108, 112, 291.

15. Trysh Travis, *The Language of the Heart: A Cultural History of the Recovery Movement from Alcoholics Anonymous to Oprah Winfrey* (Chapel Hill: University of North Carolina Press, 2009), 158.

16. The website of Women for Sobriety, https://womenforsobriety.org/; https://familydynamix.ca/Downloads/FRC_16.pdf.

17. John Steadman Rice, *A Disease of One's Own: Psychotherapy, Addiction and the Emer-*

gence of Co-Dependency (New Brunswick, NJ: Transaction, 1996), 53, 161, 163, 177. Emotional Health Anonymous is another Twelve-Step group that has adapted Twelve-Step recovery to the cultural narrative of the redemptive self, as can be seen in its focus on the "spiritual Self within us" and coming "ever closer to the Higher Power . . . within" (Grateful Members, *The Twelve Steps for Everyone Who Really Wants Them* [Minneapolis: CompCare, 1975], 6, 12).

18. *Alcoholics Anonymous*, 62, 63, 71, 158; Ernest Kurtz, *Not-God: A History of Alcoholics Anonymous*, 2nd ed. (Center City, MN: Hazelden, 1991), 218; McAdams, *Redemptive Self*, 291.

19. *Twelve Steps and Twelve Traditions*, 27; Kurtz, *Not-God*, 164.

20. *Alcoholics Anonymous*, 9, 10.

21. *Alcoholics Anonymous*, 28, 29, 51, 57; *Twelve Steps and Twelve Traditions*, 11, 97.

22. *Alcoholics Anonymous*, 10, 11, 12, 13, 25, 28, 45, 46, 49, 53, 55, 57.

23. *Twelve Steps and Twelve Traditions*, 27, 31, 32, 33, 42, 59, 60, 63, 75, 92.

24. *Twelve Steps and Twelve Traditions*, 97, 102, 105, 110.

25. Wendy Kaminer, *I'm Dysfunctional, You're Dysfunctional: The Recovery Movement and Other Self-Help Fashions* (New York: Vintage, 1992), 124, 20; Wuthnow, *After Heaven*, 7, 19.

26. Travis, *Language of the Heart*, 163; https://familydynamix.ca/Downloads/FRC_16 .pdf; Grateful Members, *Twelve Steps for Everyone Who Really Wants Them*, 33, 85, 126.

27. Christian Smith with Melinda Lundquist Denton, *Soul Searching: The Religious and Spiritual Lives of American Teenagers* (New York: Oxford University Press, 2005).

28. Tim Stafford, "The Hidden Gospel of the Twelve Steps," *Christianity Today*, July 22, 1991, https://silkworth.net/alcoholics-anonymous/01-097-the-hidden-gospel-of-the-twelve -steps-by-tim-stafford-christianity-today-july-22-1991/; Linda A. Mercadante, *Victims and Sinners: Spiritual Roots of Addiction and Recovery* (Louisville: Westminster John Knox, 1996), 176.

29. *Twelve Steps and Twelve Traditions*, 26; *Alcoholics Anonymous*, 46; *Alcoholics Anonymous Comes of Age: A Brief History of A.A.* (New York: Alcoholics Anonymous World Services, 1967), 167.

30. *Twelve Steps and Twelve Traditions*, 26, 62, 75, 109, 110, 34.

31. *Twelve Steps and Twelve Traditions*, 31–32; Howard J. Clinebell Jr., *Understanding and Counseling the Alcoholic through Religion and Psychology*, 2nd ed. (Nashville: Abingdon, 1968), 137, 146, 142; Joseph E. Keller, *Ministering to Alcoholics* (Minneapolis: Augsburg, 1966), 40, 41.

32. Anderson Spickard and Barbara R. Thompson, *Dying for a Drink: What You and Your Family Should Know about Alcoholism* (Nashville: Thomas Nelson, 2005), 149; Nancy Van Dyke Platt and Chilton R. Knudsen, *So You Think You Don't Know One? Addiction and Recovery in Clergy and Congregations* (New York: Morehouse, 2010), 81; Rohr, *Breathing under Water*, 26.

33. Claire W., *God, Help Me Stop!* (Grand Rapids: Zondervan, 1989), 26, 100; Terry Webb, *Tree of Renewed Life: Spiritual Renewal of the Church through the 12-Step Program* (New York: Crossroad, 1992), 93.

34. David Rieff, "Victims All? Recovery, Co-Dependency, and the Art of Blaming Somebody Else," *Harper's*, October 1991, 49–56, here 53.

35. Kaminer, *I'm Dysfunctional, You're Dysfunctional*, xx, 27, 49, 94.

36. See, for example, Cecil Williams and Rebecca Laird, *No Hiding Place: Empowerment and Recovery for Our Troubled Communities* (San Francisco: HarperCollins, 1992), and

William White, Mark Sanders, and Tanya Sanders, "Addiction in the African American Community: The Recovery Legacies of Frederick Douglass and Malcolm X," *Counselor* 7, no. 5 (2006): 53–58, where the authors argue that the historical traumas experienced by communities of color determine that "recovery is best framed within the larger framework of liberation and personal/cultural survival" (54).

37. *Twelve Steps and Twelve Traditions*, 15–16.

38. Rice, *Disease of One's Own*, 123, 106, 107–8, 135; Joe Klaas, *The Twelve Steps to Happiness: A Handbook for All Twelve Steppers* (New York: Ballantine, 1982), 3, 7, 8, 29, 20.

39. Vernon J. Bittner, *Twelve Steps for Christian Living: Growth in a New Way of Living* (Plymouth, MN: ICL Renewed Life Services, 1987), i, iv.

40. *Alcoholics Anonymous*, 84.

Chapter 12

1. I don't want to get bogged down in the debate over whether sex addiction is real. I will simply point out that some authorities recognize it, while others don't; that there is a class of professionals known as sex therapists or sexologists who object to the idea of describing sexual behavior as addictive and argue that doing so is pathologizing and shaming; that there is another class of professionals known as sex addiction therapists who maintain thriving practices treating people who struggle with sexual compulsivity according to established therapeutic protocols; that researchers in the field of sex addiction have published a peer-reviewed academic journal (*Sexual Addiction and Compulsivity*) since 1994; that the American Society of Addiction Medicine in 2011 included "sex, alcohol and other drugs" in a list of "rewards" that affect brain functioning; that the current edition of *Diagnostic and Statistical Manual of Mental Disorders* (DSM-5, 2013) does not include sex addiction among the mental disorders it catalogs, since when it appeared the authors judged that there was "insufficient peer-reviewed evidence to establish the diagnostic criteria and course descriptions needed to identify these behaviors as mental disorders" (*Diagnostic and Statistical Manual of Mental Disorders*, 5th ed. [Washington, DC: American Psychiatric Publishing, 2013], 515); that clinicians critical of this decision point out that compulsive sex affects the brain much like other addictive processes, that those suffering from sexual compulsion have a high level of cross- and co-occurring addictions, and that the condition typically manifests with features—abuse, dependency, tolerance, and withdrawal—that fit the DSM's diagnostic criteria for substance abuse; and that the current revision of the World Health Organization's *International Classification of Diseases* (ICD-11) recognizes sex addiction in the form of "compulsive sexual behaviour disorder," which is "characterized by a persistent pattern of failure to control intense, repetitive sexual impulses or urges resulting in repetitive sexual behaviour," and whose symptoms may include "repetitive sexual activities becoming a central focus of the person's life to the point of neglecting health and personal care or other interests, activities and responsibilities; numerous unsuccessful efforts to significantly reduce repetitive sexual behaviour; and continued repetitive sexual behaviour despite adverse consequences or deriving little or no satisfaction from it" ("6C72 Compulsive Sexual Behaviour Disorder," *ICD-11 for Mortality and Morbidity Statistics*, https://icd.who.int/browse11/l-m/en#/http:// id.who.int/icd/entity/1630268048).

2. "The Problem and the Solution," Sexaholics Anonymous, https://www.sa.org /solution/.

3. I will use the term *sex addiction* throughout this chapter to refer to compulsive sexual behavior that cannot be controlled despite escalating personal and professional consequences since this the term favored by most people familiar with this experience.

4. Each of these groups hews closely to AA's steps and traditions, their only substantive change to the Steps being the substitution of "lust," "sex and love addiction," "addictive sexual behavior," or "sexual compulsion" for "alcohol" in Step 1, and "sexaholics," "sex and love addicts," "sex addicts," or "sexually compulsive people" for "alcoholics" in Step 12.

5. *Sex and Love Addicts Anonymous* (Boston: The Augustine Fellowship, Sex and Love Addicts Anonymous, Fellowship-Wide Services, 1986), 130; Saint Augustine, *Confessions*, trans. R. S. Pine-Coffin (London: Penguin, 1961), 43, 57.

6. Gillian Reagan, "Tiger Woods Gets Punked by Plane's Banner at the Masters: 'Tiger: Did You Mean Bootyism?,'" *Business Insider*, April 9, 2010, https://www.businessinsider .com/tiger-woods-gets-punked-by-planes-banner-at-the-masters-tiger-did-you-mean -bootyism-2010-4; Rebecca Rosenberg and Daniel Halper, "Anthony Weiner Rides through Sex Addiction Rehab on a Horse," *New York Post*, November 4, 2016, http://nypost .com/2016/11/04/anthony-weiner-rides-through-sex-addiction-rehab-on-a-horse/.

7. Stefanie Carnes, "Addictive Sexuality: Diagnostic Controversies," *Advances in Addiction and Recovery* 4, no. 4 (Winter 2016): 18; William M. Struthers, *Wired for Intimacy: How Pornography Hijacks the Male Brain* (Downers Grove, IL: InterVarsity, 2009), 77–79; Paula Hall, "Let's Talk about Sex Addiction," YouTube video, https://www.youtube.com /watch?v=-Qf2e3XZ8Tw.

8. *Sexaholics Anonymous* (Brentwood, TN: SA Literature, 1989), 36.

9. Patrick J. Carnes, *Out of the Shadows: Understanding Sexual Addiction*, 3rd ed. (Center City, MN: Hazelden, 2001), 34, 119.

10. Carnes, *Out of the Shadows*, 102, 26–27.

11. Carnes, *Out of the Shadows*, 7.

12. Hall, "Let's Talk about Sex Addiction."

13. Al Cooper, ed., *Cybersex: The Dark Side of the Force, a Special Issue of the Journal of Sexual Addiction and Compulsivity* (New York: Taylor & Francis, 2000), 2; David Greenfield, "The Addictive Properties of Internet Usage," in *Internet Addiction: A Handbook and Guide to Evaluation and Treatment*, ed. Kimberly S. Young and Christiano Nabuco de Abreu (Hoboken, NJ: Wiley, 2010), 135–53, here 144, 141.

14. Greenfield, "Addictive Properties of Internet Usage," 145; Carnes, *Out of the Shadows*, 43.

15. Jennifer Markert, "Porn Drives Innovation: How Adult Entertainment Boosts Technology," Curiousmatic, April 6, 2016, https://curiousmatic.com/porn-drives -innovation/; "Pornhub's 2019 Year in Review," Pornhub Insights, December 11, 2019, https:// www.pornhub.com/insights/2019-year-in-review#2019.

16. For early Christian responses to sex addiction, see Harry W. Schaumburg, *False Intimacy: Understanding the Struggle of Sexual Addiction* (Colorado Springs: Navpress, 1997); Russell Willingham, *Breaking Free: Understanding Sexual Addiction and the Healing Power of Jesus* (Downers Grove, IL: InterVarsity, 1999); Mark R. Laaser, *Healing the Wounds of Sexual Addiction* (Grand Rapids: Zondervan, 1992); and "The Leadership Survey on Pastors and Internet Pornography," *Christianity Today*, Winter 2001, http://www .christianitytoday.com/pastors/2001/winter/12.89.html.

17. "Shocker: Study Shows Most Christian Men Are into Porn," *Charisma News*, October 7, 2014, http://www.charismanews.com/us/45671-shocker-study-shows-most -christian-men-are-into-porn.

18. Jonathan Merritt, "Pornography: A Christian Crisis or Overblown Issue?" Religion News Service, January 20, 2016, http://religionnews.com/2016/01/20/christians -pornography-problem/.

19. Merritt, "Pornography." In 2006 a nonscientific survey of visitors to ChristiaNet revealed that 50 percent of Christian men and 30 percent of Christian women were "addicted to porn," although the condition was undefined. "Evangelicals Are Addicted to Porn," ChristiaNet, http://christiannews.christianet.com/1154951956.htm.

20. Samuel L. Perry, *Addicted to Lust: Pornography in the Lives of Conservative Protestants* (New York: Oxford University Press, 2019), 72.

21. Struthers, *Wired for Intimacy*, 55; Gemma Mestre-Bach, Gretchen R. Blycker, and Marc N. Potenza, "Pornography Use in the Setting of the COVID-19 Pandemic," *Journal of Behavioral Addictions* 9, no. 2 (2020): 181–83.

22. Website of Fight the New Drug, http://fightthenewdrug.org/; "Virginia Legislature Plans to Debate If Pornography Is a Public Health Hazard," NPR's *All Things Considered*, January 9, 2017, http://www.npr.org/2017/01/09/509001363/virginia-legislature-plans-to-de bate-if-pornography-is-a-public-health-hazard.

23. Brian McNeill, "An Interview with Jennifer Johnson on How Pornography Influences and Harms Sexual Behavior," *VCU News*, January 25, 2015, https://www.news.vcu .edu/article/An_interview_with_Jennifer_Johnson_on_how_pornography_influences.

24. Website for Gary Wilson's *Your Brain on Porn*, http://yourbrainonporn.com/; Robert Weiss, *Sex Addiction 101: A Guide for Healing from Sex, Porn and Love Addiction* (Deerfield Beach, FL: Health Communications, 2015), 164–65; Perry, *Addicted to Lust*, 134.

25. In addition to the website of Integrity Restored (https://integrityrestored.com), whose mission is "to help restore the integrity of individuals, spouses, and families that have been affected by pornography and pornography addiction," see Peter C. Kleponis, *Integrity Restored: Helping Catholic Families Win the Battle against Pornography* (Steubenville, OH: Emmaus Road, 2014); Woodeene Koenig Bricker, *What the Church Teaches: Pornography* (Huntington, IN: Our Sunday Visitor, 2007); Audrey Assad, Peter Kleponis, and Joe McClain, *Delivered: True Stories of Men and Women Who Turned from Porn to Purity*, ed. Matt Fradd (San Diego: Catholic Answers, 2014); Dan R. Spencer III, *Every Parent's Battle: A Family Guide to Resisting Pornography* (Huntington, IN: Our Sunday Visitor, 2017); Matt Fradd, *The Porn Myth: Exposing the Reality behind the Fantasy of Pornography* (San Francisco: Ignatius, 2017); and J. Brian Bransfield, *Overcoming Pornography Addiction: A Spiritual Solution* (New York: Paulist, 2013).

I searched "pornography" on the websites of Westminster John Knox (Presbyterian), Fortress (Evangelical Lutheran), Abingdon (United Methodist), Morehouse (Episcopal), Chalice (Disciples of Christ), Pilgrim (United Churches of Christ), Judson (American Baptist), Reformed Free (Reformed Church of America), United Church Resource Distribution (United Church of Canada), Nurturing Faith (Cooperative Baptist Fellowship), Brethren Press (Church of the Brethren), Herald Press (Mennonite Church), AMEC Publishing House (African Methodist Episcopal Church), and AME Zion Publishing House (African American Episcopal Zion Church), all religious publishers that serve mainline churches. Of the resources aimed at adults, I found one book on pornography, Robert J. Baird, *Just*

One Click: Christians, Pornography and the Lure of Cyberspace, published in 2010 by Faith Alive, the publishing house of the Christian Reformed Church, a pamphlet titled *Dealing with Pornography* from Herald Press, and a chapter in a collection of essays published by Fortress Press.

26. *Pornography: Far from the Song of Songs* (Louisville: Office of the General Assembly, 1988).

27. *Pornography: Far from the Song of Songs*, 68, 6.

28. *Pornography: Far from the Song of Songs*, 79.

29. Bob Allen, "Nadia Bolz-Weber, No Shame in Consuming 'Ethically Sourced' Porn," *Baptist News Global*, November 8, 2018, https://baptistnews.com/article/nadia-bolz-weber -no-shame-in-consuming-ethically-sourced-porn/#.XSOzZutKjIU. According to this article, "ethical porn" is a term used in the adult entertainment industry to describe content that is "made legally, respects the rights of performers, and treats both performers and consumers as consenting adults." But it is naive to expect ethical behavior from an industry known for financially incentivizing participation in violent and degrading sex. See "Popular Porn Performer Lisa Ann Describes Extreme Abuse New Entertainers Endure," Fight the New Drug, January 2, 2019, https://fightthenewdrug.org/hall-of-fame-ex-porn-star-talks-ex treme-damage-done-to-new-performers/.

30. *Pornography: Far from the Song of Songs*, 73.

31. Nicholas Kristof, "The Children of Pornhub," *New York Times*, December 4, 2020, https://www.nytimes.com/2020/12/04/opinion/sunday/pornhub-rape-trafficking.html ?referringSource=articleShare.

32. Kristof, "Children of Pornhub."

33. Dietrich Bonhoeffer, *Creation and Fall: A Theological Exposition of Genesis 1–3*, Dietrich Bonhoeffer Works, vol. 3, trans. Douglas Stephen Bax, ed. John W. de Gruchy (Minneapolis: Fortress, 1997), 124; Perry, *Addicted to Lust*, 184, 118–20, 123.

34. Weiss, *Sex Addiction 101*, 101, 72.

35. Jeremy Glass, "Eight Ways Porn Influenced Technology," Thrillist, February 14, 2014, https://www.thrillist.com/vice/how-porn-influenced-technology-8-ways-porn-influenced -tech-supercompressor-com; Jamie Feltham, "Pornhub: VR Porn Gets 500,000 Views a Day," VentureBeat, May 13, 2017, https://venturebeat.com/2017/05/13/pornhub-vr-porn-gets -500000-views-a-day/; Ross Benes, "PORN: The Hidden Engine That Drives Innovation in Tech," *Business Insider*, July 5, 2013, http://www.businessinsider.com/how-porn-drives -innovation-in-tech-2013-7; "Interview with Jennifer Johnson."

36. Amanda Fenrich, "Problematic Pornography Use: A Brief Introduction," *Forensic Scholars Today* 5, no. 1 (July 2019), https://online.csp.edu/blog/problematic-pornography -use-a-brief-introduction/; "Interview with Jennifer Johnson."

37. Perry, *Addicted to Lust*, 25–26.

38. "How We Define Sobriety," Sexaholics Anonymous, https://www.sa.org/how-we -define-sobriety/. Among the few books that acknowledge the existence of Twelve-Step S-fellowships are Laaser, *Healing the Wounds*; Michael Leahy, *Porn Nation: Conquering America's #1 Addiction* (Chicago: Northfield, 2008); Craig Gross and Jason Harper, *Eyes of Integrity: The Porn Pandemic and How It Affects You* (Grand Rapids: Baker, 2010); Craig Gross and Steven Luff, *Pure Eyes: A Man's Guide to Sexual Integrity* (Grand Rapids: Baker, 2010); and David Zailer, *When Lost Men Come Home: A Journey to Sexual Integrity* (El Cajon, CA: Christian Services Network, 2006). In *Healing the Wounds*, first published in

1992, Laaser acknowledges that he became sober with the help of Twelve-Step groups, but in the 2004 edition's opening pages he writes that he no longer refers to himself as a sex addict and has come to rely more on "spiritual growth and biblical principles" than the Steps elaborated in AA-inspired S-groups. Laaser now advocates "Christian support groups . . . that draw on the wisdom of the Twelve Steps," including Faithful and True, an evangelical sexual recovery ministry he founded. See *Healing the Wounds*, 131, and Mark Laaser, *The Seven Principles of Highly Accountable Men* (Kansas City: Beacon Hill, 2011).

39. Among those who foreground neuroscience is Struthers, *Wired for Intimacy*, and Tim Clinton and Mark Laaser, *The Fight of Your Life: Manning Up to the Challenge of Sexual Integrity* (Shippensburg, PA: Destiny Image, 2015). In *The Final Freedom*, 4th ed. (Discovery, 2019), Douglas Weiss includes an exposition of the Steps and an endorsement of SA, SAA, and SLAA. Although Weiss calls the Steps "very spiritual and biblical," he makes the confused claim that they "were taken from an Oxford Bible Study" (141); Perry, *Addicted to Lust*, 32, 33, 53, 64, 69.

40. Perry, *Addicted to Lust*, 153, 157, 150–53, 180.

Epilogue

1. *Alcoholics Anonymous: The Story of How Many Thousands of Men and Women Have Recovered from Alcoholism*, 4th ed. (New York: Alcoholics Anonymous World Services, 2002), 60.

Index